D0914055

*Under Storm's Wing*

# UNDER STORM'S WING

## HELEN THOMAS

### WITH MYFANWY THOMAS

CARCANET

PR
6039
H55
Z838
1988

Published in Great Britain 1988 by
Carcanet Press Limited
208-212 Corn Exchange Buildings
Manchester M4 3BQ
Carcanet
198 Sixth Avenue
New York, NY 10013

**British Library Cataloguing in Publication Data**

Thomas, Helen, *1877-1967*
    Under storm's wing.
    1. English literature — 20th century
    I. Title   II. Thomas, Myfanwy
    820.8'00912      PR1148
        ISBN 0-85635-733-2

The publisher acknowledges the financial assistance
of the Arts Council of Great Britain

Typeset in 11pt Bembo by Bryan Williamson, Manchester
Printed in England by SRP Ltd, Exeter

# E.T.

*'He has out-soared the shadow of our night'*

# CONTENTS

# LIST OF ILLUSTRATIONS

## Between pages 174 and 175

The Publishers are grateful to Myfanwy Thomas and the Library
of University College, Cardiff for making these photographs
available, and to Edward Thomas (ET's nephew) for his advice
concerning the landscape photographs.

# A NOTE ON THE TEXT

*As It Was* was first published in 1926 by William Heinemann Ltd, and *World Without End* in 1931; then Heinemann published a combined volume in 1935. Faber and Faber issued their combined edition in 1956, and in the paperback edition of 1972, Myfanwy Thomas added a key to the characters' names. This Carcanet edition is the first to appear with the real names in the text.

The section of Letters and 'A Remembered Harvest' are taken from *Time & Again: memoirs and letters* by Helen Thomas, edited by Myfanwy Thomas, published by Carcanet in 1978. The letter from Helen to Robert Frost is previously unpublished, and is printed here with the kind permission of Myfanwy Thomas and of Dartmouth College Library. One sketch, 'Men and Books' has been omitted, and a memoir of W.H. Hudson has been added: this was inadvertently omitted from *Time & Again*, and was published privately by The Fleece Press in 1984.

The memoir of her childhood by Myfanwy Thomas has been extracted from a longer work, *One of these fine days*, published by Carcanet in 1982 and still in print.

# PREFACE

It is good – as we say in the country – to be 'lived and spared' to see this new edition of the writings of our mother, Helen Thomas, with fresh photographs, under one roof from one publisher.

Strange now to look back on our thoughts and reactions – Merfyn's, Bronwen's and mine – when *As It Was* first appeared. We were proud of our mother, but while my brother and sister were grown-ups, I, still a schoolgirl, became shyer than ever. I think we were abashed at the unaccustomed frankness of the language, while being moved to tears by some of the passages. It was a relief that the names of the characters were disguised and that the author had used only her initials. We rejoiced for our mother that she was invited to literary parties and made a fuss of: she had a beautiful, extravagant evening-dress made, with a necklace of sparkly beads specially dyed to match the flounced material. Perhaps Merfyn and Bronwen discussed the book, up in London, but we did not speak of it together when I went home for the school holidays. I think we felt a little isolated from Mother at that time, though I remember Merfyn, always warm-hearted and generous, shyly telling Mother that he was proud to be the hero of the book.

I hope no one will be distressed to see that the real names, which had to be disguised originally, have now been restored. In 1926 and 1931, when *As It Was* and *World Without End* were first published in separate volumes, most of the people written of were still living.

There was a wonderful tribute to the books on the radio by Vita Sackville-West, when she was reviewing *World Without End* published under Mother's full name. I was in the typing pool of the BBC then, and our chief, Miss Banks, called me

13

to check the script; we were both in tears after reading it. The first book came in for some black marks: banned in Boston, mocked by a famous writer in a literary weekly; and Robert Frost was so outraged by it that he removed the dedication to Helen from a selection of his poems. Later one of his disciples recalled Frost's saying, with waspish scorn, that Edward's wife had insulted her husband's manhood by writing of his inexperience. Fortunately my mother did not hear of the remark. Strange that he should have had such a conventional notion of manliness, which showed even in the early days of their friendship, when Frost and others, led by my father, were turned out of a wood by a gamekeeper. My father, being a true countryman, understood that the gamekeeper was doing his job, albeit in a surly manner, but Frost was near to calling him a coward for not squaring up to the gamekeeper and knocking him down. Referring to the incident in one or two letters to Frost from the Front, my father told his friend he could not make himself climb up the inside of a small factory chimney for reconnaissance purposes, implying wryly that Frost was right to think him a coward.

But all of this, causing hurt and pride by turns, was of no consequence against the growing awareness of the poems, which the books – now under one cover – had certainly stimulated. *As It Was* and *World Without End* had been written as therapy, to try to rouse Helen from the terrible lethargy and desolation which followed Edward's death in 1917, ending in a serious breakdown in the mid-1920s. She had no idea of publishing her memories – 'Write about the happy times with Edward,' friends suggested – but once started, their story in all its heights of joy and depths of despair had to be written. It was Middleton Murry, to whom a friend showed the manuscript, who encouraged her; he published the chapter dealing with the birth of their son in *The Adelphi* quarterly magazine.

And now Helen's writing and her efforts – talks, articles, broadcasts, readings – have gradually led to her dearest wish and object of her life being fulfilled: Edward is firmly established as an English poet. Twenty years after his death the

Memorial Stone was set on the Shoulder of Mutton hill near
Steep, unveiled by the Poet Laureate John Masefield, born in
the same year as my father. Scarcely an anthology has not at
least one Thomas poem; a great many compilers, alas, look
to other anthologies and so 'Adlestrop' is repeated over and
over. Then, since Helen's death almost exactly fifty years after
Edward's, the beautiful windows engraved by Laurence Whis-
tler at Eastbury and at Steep; plays, recitals, documentaries,
even an opera planned, questions on his work in school exami-
nations. Lastly the noble stone in Westminster Abbey's Poets'
Corner, with the names of sixteen poets of the First World
War, and at the unveiling, the moving tributes to and readings
from the poets' works by Sir Michael Howard, Ted Hughes
the Poet Laureate, Jill Balcon – widow of another Poet Laureate,
C. Day-Lewis – and Stephen Lushington, the son of my
father's C.O. in France. Many of Edward's family were there,
nieces, nephews, great-nephews, grandchildren and great-
grandchildren. And those I thought of and missed so keenly
during the proud ceremony were, I am certain, high up in the
dusk amidst the voices and the music surging in the lacy fan
vaulting and the sturdy oaken rafters, along with Chaucer,
Milton, Hardy and a great company.

*Myfanwy Thomas*
Eastbury, 1987

# ONE

## *As It Was*

# 1

I remember so well that very first meeting. We lived then in a little new villa in a row, in a new road quite near Wandsworth Common. The front room was the dining-room, and the piano was there; the back room at the end of the passage looking on to the tiny garden, which was kept full of flowers, was my father's study. This was lined with books, and in the middle of the room was his knee-hole writing-table. On the table were scattered papers, his tin of Three Castles cigarettes, and his small tumbler of weak whisky and water. As a child I used to marvel at the way he puffed the smoke out of his mouth after sipping whisky and water. He smoked and sipped all day, while he wrote with his thin, delicate hand in his small, thick writing, or lay on the sofa by the window reading the three-volume novels which he reviewed for part of his living. My father had a name as an essayist and critic among a small public, but he had to eke out his means with reviewing and journalism, and we had just moved from Liverpool to London so that he could be more in touch with literary affairs.

Our house was comfortable and pleasant and very cosy, with people always coming and going. My mother and father were both very sociable and hospitable, and, though there cannot have been much money, owing to my mother's wonderful management there was always everything we wanted, and the unexpected guests who often turned up were warmly welcomed. My father's study was the general sitting-room, and here all visitors were invited. Nothing disturbed my father at his work so much as to be left alone. Often when my mother thought we were getting too noisy for him, we would creep out unnoticed by him into the dining-room, but in a few minutes we would hear his strange halting step in the passage, and his voice asking why we had left him, and back we would all have to troop, to read aloud, play games, talk and laugh, while he wrote an essay or reviewed a book.

Our life was very happy, very social, very united. We were unconventional, though in no startling way – just informal and unselfconscious. A good deal of freedom of movement was allowed to us children, and freedom of speech and thought; and so far we had all pulled together, interested in new movements – 'well up in things', I think we should have said – mainly artistic and especially of course literary – and with wide views on religious and social questions. We all went to the Unitarian Church on Sunday, though neither of my parents belonged to this denomination, Father having been born and bred a Churchman, while Mother came of stout dissenting stock. But I expect they were drawn to the Unitarians by the semi-literary, semi-philosophical, nature of the sermons. We were poorer than most of the congregation, our income being very irregular our ways were not so bound by the conventions that seem to be set up by a regular flow of money. By the well-to-do of our type we should have been called Bohemians.

I think at this time we were all at home: that is, my eldest sister Irene; myself, seventeen and just left school; and my youngest sister, Mary, still at school. Both my sisters were clever, and had carried everything before them at school. I hated school, where my sisters' brilliance threw into sharp relief my own incapacity, and I had begged to leave and be at home with my father, whom I adored.

I remember that afternoon. We knew the strange boy was coming. Our Unitarian minister had asked my father to look at some of his work and see if it was any good, and Father had thought so highly of it that we had already nicknamed the boy 'The Genius'. Perhaps we had been told he was shy; anyway we left the study and went into the dining-room, and when he came he was shown straight in to Father, who was waiting for him. We girls were playing *The Mikado* on the piano and singing, and between whiles laughing and talking of the boy and wondering what he would be like, and I think

feeling a slight, amused prejudice against him for being shy
and serious and clever. Soon, when we thought Father had
had enough of him to himself, we thought we should like to
see him, but my two sisters drew back at the door; so I went
in alone. I opened the door, feeling silly, and giggling, because
of the rather extravagant things we had been saying about
him; and just inside the door, standing by the bookshelves
with an open book in his hand, he stood, so that I came upon
him sooner than I had expected. This made me laugh the
more, or feel inclined to laugh, had not his face, into which
I looked, immediately changed my mood. My father intro-
duced us and our eyes met – the boy's solemn grey eyes rather
over-shadowed by drooping lids with long lashes. He did not
smile, but looked very steadily at me and I at him as he took
my hand with a very hard and long grip. I remember feeling
pleasure in that first touch and thinking 'I like him; I like the
way he shakes hands and the straight, intense look in his eyes.'
After I came in, the talk lagged, my father doing his best to
keep things going, but Edward was too shy and constrained
by my presence to be able to talk. And soon he went, refusing
to stay to tea to meet my sisters. I can't remember if he dwelt
much in my thoughts after the first meeting, but I do remem-
ber that though I thought him shy and awkward and silent I
liked him and wanted to see him again.

Edward was tall – just six feet – and slim, with a broad chest
and shoulders, which he carried well – loose-limbed and ath-
letic. He had a beautifully shaped head with a fine brow, and
his thick fair hair, worn rather long, curled a little over his
forehead and ears. His nose was long and straight, his mouth
very sensitive, with the upper lip slightly overhanging the
lower. The chin was strong. The eyes were grey and dreamy
and meditative, but fearless and steady, and as if trying to
pierce the truth itself. It was a most striking face, recalling a
portrait of Shelley in its sensitive, melancholy beauty. His
hands were large and powerful, and he could do anything
with them from the roughest work to the most delicate: they
symbolize for me his strength and tenderness. It is his hands

even more than his beautiful face that remain in my vision when I think of him; I shall never forget them.

He came often, and always Father liked to have him alone, but shortly before he went I used to slip in and try to talk to him. I have no recollection of how we got on, but I think not very well, because his shyness made me shy.

My father helped him a great deal with advice about writing and reading, and with Father he got on well and talked well, whose genial kindness and interest slowly broke down Edward's reserve. My father became very fond of him and used to call him Phil, because his first name was Philip, and my parents had had a little boy called Philip who had died as a baby, and by a strange coincidence Edward's features and general colouring were very like this baby boy's, and I believe my father felt that this was his boy – the boy of his heart, loving the things he loved, and seeking self-expression in the same way that my father had sought it. My mother, on the other hand, grew to dislike him. She was jealous. She could find in this quiet, reserved, clever boy no point of contact, though as a rule she got on splendidly with boys, and preferred them to girls, and many came to the house, but none like this one. The boys she liked were jolly, frank, well-mannered, easy creatures, intelligent enough most of them, though hardly ever speaking seriously of things, but genial and cheery, and who found her a very congenial hostess.

At this time Edward talked exclusively of the books he was reading – buying when he could, or borrowing from my father – and my appearance in the study stopped all talk except what could be dragged out of him by questions. I do not want to give the impression that his manners were those of a hobble-dehoy, for though he was very shy and reserved, he had a natural courtesy and distinction of manner, which, though perhaps stiff for a boy of his age, was always dignified.

His writing was devoted almost entirely to descriptions of nature, of clouds, sky, trees and landscapes, and I had read and liked very much some of his essays. My father got several of them accepted by a weekly paper of which he was then co-editor, and the *Globe* printed some, and Father was encouraging him all he could with appreciation and advice and help. This period is a little vague for me, for I was outside it and was conscious of no attraction towards him beyond the impression, still very distinct, made by that first surprisingly firm grip, and that straight look, which made me patient with his silence, his shyness and his awkwardness.

I had always had a strong yearning for the country. Our life had been spent in towns in the north of England, and owing to my father's invalidism we were not, as so many children are, taken out for long walks by our father, and our times in the country had been confined to our summer holidays in north Wales. But I loved the country, and Edward's knowledge of country things gave us a common interest and subject of conversation, so that slowly we got to easier – though even now not very easy – terms until one day my father said to Edward. 'Here's Helen dying for the country, and a good walker; why don't you take her, and show her some of the places you know?'

Before this happened we had moved to a much bigger and nicer house in a better neighbourhood. It had a very pretty garden, which had been part of an orchard, and had several fruit trees in it – one, a very beautiful old cherry tree, always lovely to look at, and full of fruit in the season. A forked branch made a comfortable seat, and I often sat up there reading, and I remember how Edward once found me, with bare feet and legs, eating cherries and reading, and his surprise and pleasure at finding me unembarrassed by his seeing me like that. The study in this house had french windows opening on to the garden, and so in summer time the garden became our general gathering-place, and the cherry tree's branches provided seats for several of the company. It was from this house that we set off for our first walk to Merton.

Merton was then a pretty rural place, with fields and lanes and footpaths and woods. We walked to it through a wilderness of mean streets, and I can't remember that we talked much. Now it was I who was shy, and conscious of my intellectual inferiority, and I tried to talk 'up' to him, and became more self-conscious and said stupid things. But it was on this first walk that I spoke of the picture of a titmouse in a natural history which Edward had showed me some time before. It was a coloured illustration, and I could not believe that the colours were natural, and that such a lovely bright bird was really a common English, even London, bird. My short sight and lack of observation made me ignorant of even the most commonly known facts of natural history, and this picture impressed me very much, and I told Edward as we went along how I had dreamt of a titmouse, only it was gigantic in size, and the colours of its plumage very, very vivid. He was delighted and amused at this, and this simple incident put us quite at ease with each other. We spoke of poetry, too, of Wordsworth particularly. I told him I didn't care for him because he was 'sentimental', which shocked Edward, and made me feel ashamed. Afterwards, when I got home, I read some of the poems he had spoken about, and from that talk my appreciation of poetry began.

I remember in that first walk how we scrambled about in a little roadside copse. It must have been winter or early spring, for the trees were bare, and Edward showed me many old nests, telling me the names of the birds which had made them, and pointing out to me their special characteristics. Later on he brought me as a present a most beautifully compact, moss-covered nest of a chaffinch, which I could hardly believe was the work of a bird, and all my wonder pleased and amused him in his grave way. In that copse were many burdocks, and I remember asking him to throw some of the burrs on to my skirt, so that I could prove to my people I had really been into the country.

I enjoyed that walk. It was an utterly new experience for me. Everything was new – the very exercise which I found so delightful was new; the country so near to home; my companion, the first boy I had ever been on such terms with. And all his knowledge of everything we saw, and all his intimacy – everything lifted me at once into a new world.

I was at this time about eighteen, and he nine months younger.

We came back to tea in the dusk of the evening, very happy together, and with very much of our former constraint worn away. But even now I felt he was 'The Genius' and I a very ordinary girl, as indeed I was.

After that he came and went, talking with my father, and more now with me, and accepted by my mother in a grudging way. In a little while we had arranged to go on another walk, and my father was delighted with the success of his idea.

This time we were to take the train to Barnes, and walk up Priory Lane and over Richmond Park to the heronry where once at night Edward had climbed to get a heron's egg. I remember the place, which was near a big lake, and the tall trees (were they Scotch pines, or elms?) in which the huge, untidy, insecure nests were built, looking more like rafts of twigs than nests. I, with my dizzy head, could not endure it when he – to show me his prowess, I expect – began to climb the straight tall trunk of one of them.

He told me of his fishing exploits, and of the big pike he had caught in the pond near by, for he was always a keen fisherman, and we spoke of Izaak Walton whom I had read. I learnt here the names of several wild flowers, especially the little low-growing kinds – tormentil was one: I have never forgotten it, and its tiny bright flower always brings me back to Richmond Park, and that day. He found me a good walker; I did not get tired, nor lag behind, but we stepped out eagerly and joyfully always.

Of these walks we took many, but only one other is clearly recalled to my memory. We went again to Merton, and talked of Shelley, whom we were both reading and both very full of. His life I knew very well, and he had for long been a hero of mine. It was his love of freedom, his hatred of injustice and tyranny that I chiefly responded to, I think, but also his spiritual beauty caught up my dawning perception of poetry. That day we talked of Shelley, and Edward had in his pocket a pretty little volume of selected lyrics – the flapping of a book in his jacket pocket as he strode along with his long sweeping stride is one of my earliest and latest memories of Edward – and we read 'Adonais' and the 'West Wind' and 'Love's Philosophy' and 'Epipsychidion' together.

Coming home from Merton, not yet having left the country roads, and in the sunset-flushed mist of an autumn afternoon, as we walked side by side, silent for the most part, but deeply conscious of happiness and friendship, he took my hand, and I, full of a new wonder and a new fear, and a new something –I could not tell what, let him walk thus. When we got home he would not come in to tea, but as we said good-bye at the gate he asked me to keep the Shelley for my own, and I took it, but did not want to, and yet could not tell why.

I was a plain girl, morbidly conscious of intellectual and physical deficiencies. I had often cried bitterly in the thought that no man could ever love me, and that my longing for children would never be satisfied. I had so persuaded myself of this that it never entered my mind as a possibility until that moment when Edward took my hand; and even then I did not consciously think of love; all I felt was an unrest, a fear, a thrill, perhaps also a hope.

I was very affectionate, and almost painfully grateful to people who showed me affection, but conscious of my own unworthiness and with a constant distrust of myself. I think this was partly due to the contrast to myself in my two sisters, one older and one younger. Both were clever and self-confident and admired. They both succeeded where I failed, and my mother constantly said to me when she was irritated by her ugly duckling, 'Why can't you be like your sister Mary?' and that remark made it more and more and more difficult for me to attain that ideal, and I shrank further into my shell of self-distrust.

I loved all children passionately, especially young babies. I loved to see a pregnant woman – I almost adored while I envied her. I desired love, but only, at any rate consciously, in an emotional or spiritual form, for I did not comprehend physical love, and the whole thing was very mysterious to me, and my mother had always refused to discuss the subject. I yearned vaguely for freedom, for something more than this quiet home life, where my mother's word was law. I had begun to have different tastes from the others. In dress, for instance, I took to what were then called Liberty dresses, very simple and plain in line, but of beautiful colours and ornamented with embroidery. The fashions then made this style of dress conspicuous, and my sisters laughed at it, but I was getting to the priggish stage, and I am sure I thought myself superior. I wanted less furniture in my bedroom, and more air, and I read Ruskin and Morris and became their disciple. Edward and I read Carlyle's *French Revolution*, and particularly *Wilhelm Meister*, which we loved, and which influenced us very much, me specially perhaps in my natural instinct for unreserve and freedom and frankness of speech.

I was at that age plain, with a round healthy face and small nose; rather serious in expression, but not entirely unattractive. I had a lot of dark brown hair, which I wore parted in the middle with long plaits wound round my head – a simple style suiting my dress and my general seriousness. I was straight and tallish, and my own well-shaped and strong and – as I think now – really lovely body gave me intense delight. I loved being without clothes, and moving about naked, and I took a pride in my health and strength. Edward and I read Richard Jefferies, and with delight I found the joy in one's body spoken of there as if it was right and good. For with my old distrust of myself I had wondered if the joy I felt in my body indicated some moral deficiency in me, as my mother's teaching had been in direct opposition to what I felt so instinctively.

Edward and I were getting much less reserved together, and talked of anything and everything – of poetry a great deal – Keats, Shelley, Coleridge, Wordsworth and Tennyson chiefly, I think – oh, and Byron too: indeed we read all from Chaucer onwards; all was grist to the mills of our devouring minds. Also we began to speak of ourselves, our hopes, our feeling about life, our intimate thoughts and experiences.

It must have been about this time that I introduced myself to Edward's parents and brothers. He was the eldest of six boys. He had no sisters, and except for brief, awkward attractions for one or two girls who lived near, I was the first girl he had ever become friendly with. He knew nothing of girls; less than I of boys, for though I had never been attractive to boys – my sister Mary taking all these honours – I had met many at home, but had never had a friend among them.

Edward's father, Mr Thomas, was a serious-minded Liberal – a self-satisfied, hard-working and conscientious civil servant, who rose in his department quite remarkably. He was the thick-set, short, dark type of Welshman, handsome, but to me unattractive. He was a Nonconformist, and a student, with a very narrow view of life which made him an extremely unsympathetic father. All the boys except Edward were like their father in appearance, but not one of them like him in character. His mother was a very pretty fair-haired woman, with a sweet melancholy face, very retiring and shy and sad. Edward got his looks from his mother and much of his temperament, and so he adored her – if such a word can be used of so reserved, so undemonstrative an affection, which never wavered. A wonderful sympathy existed between these two, both too self-conscious to give it voice, but both sure of it always. The other boys, though, were beyond her understanding, and there was a strange feeling of disharmony in that house, which, after my own united family life, depressed me whenever I went there.

I went to see Mrs Thomas because I thought it only fair that, as my mother knew Edward, she should know me. I introduced myself boldly and impulsively, as I did things then. She was very kind, though shy and reserved with me; and I think liked me, anyway did not dislike me. When I returned home I told my mother about my visit and she to my great surprise and distress was very angry. She said I had behaved in a very improper way, and that I had practically announced myself as engaged to Edward. I thought her attitude and her anger ridiculous, and there began in me that antagonism to

my mother which on my father's death made home life unen-
durable to me.

After this visit I used often to go to Edward's home, and
became well known to his father and brothers. I tried to pierce
Mrs Thomas's deep reserve, and I believe my warm, impulsive
nature did achieve something. I got on very well with both
Mr and Mrs Thomas, and felt easy and confident with them.
I was a new element in the house, being a girl, and as I was
full of interest, and with a good deal of knowledge, though
immature, of artistic things, Mr Thomas liked to talk to me,
and I remember, in spite of my dislike of him, I felt flattered.
Mr Thomas had a great admiration for my father, as one of
the foremost literary critics of the day. Later on Mr Thomas
made the acquaintance of my father, who was a man of great
charm of manner and distinction of appearance, genial and
humorous and sympathetic, and very generous with all he
had, material and spiritual. So under the wing of my father's
reputation and personality I was made welcome at the Thomas's
and blossomed out there – freed from the everlasting compari-
son with my sisters.

The brothers were a strange lot of rather uncouth boys:
their huge appetites and rough ways amazed me. Their parents
provided no social life at home for them, and at a very early
age they sought their amusements elsewhere. Edward was the
only one who had a love of nature and literature. The very
house seemed to me ugly and uninteresting, and there was
only one room which had for me any character or charm, and
this was Edward's own room – study and bedroom in one.
There he kept his collection of birds' eggs and rods and fishing-
tackle, and here he lived most of his indoor life reading or
writing. A few photographs of Titian and Botticelli and Greek
sculpture were pinned on to the walls, and there was a shelf
of books – not many yet, for he had very little pocket money
to spend. Here we were allowed to sit and talk and read,
though his mother often asked if I thought my mother would
like it, and sometimes, because she was so uncertain that she
was doing right for her boys, she would forbid us this room,

and we had to be content to sit in the cold and formal little drawing-room at the back of the house.

At this time my father, who had always been delicate, began to show signs of the tuberculosis in the throat of which he died. He was not able now to see much of Edward, and when Edward came to the house my mother's dislike of him became more and more obvious. About the same time Edward went away for one of his long visits to Wiltshire, where his grandmother lived, and where he could wander all day on the Downs, and tramp about the outlying country with an old vagabond from whom he had learnt much country lore, and who had first taught him how to bait a hook, and skin a mole, and shout the 'view-hallo' when the hunt was out.

My mother, taking advantage of all the circumstances, forbade me to have anything more to do with Edward – to write to him or receive letters from him while he was away, or to see him when he returned. My father was too ill to be appealed to, and for the first time in my life I took the law into my own hands. I wrote to him secretly, and received letters from him through a school friend of his, who was a great favourite with my mother, and who came to inquire after my father and to bring my letters with him.

# 2

Friendship had now become unconscious love. We wrote to each other every day, concealing nothing of our thoughts and ideas and emotions, and relating all that happened to us in our daily life, and the deeper experiences of our growing consciousness. The writing of my letters and the receiving of his were to me the most wonderful experiences I had ever had. I had found the friend of my heart, and my nature, hitherto so repressed, so morbidly self-distrustful, blossomed out, and I was expressing myself easily and well, and was always brimming over with things to tell him of myself and my reading, and I gained my greatest satisfaction in his appreciation and understanding and response. During his absence in Wiltshire Edward sent me boxes of wild flowers, and a thrush's egg – the first he had found. I have it still with the inscription I wrote on the lid of the box: 'From my dearest friend, Edward Thomas, to be kept always in memory of a happy friendship.'

During this time my father's illness got worse and worse, and after an operation in his throat, a few days after Edward's return, he died. I was alone with my mother the night before his death. We had left him for a little while in the care of the nurse, to get a little much-needed sleep, but we simply lay down on the bed in our clothes, expecting to be called at any moment. While we were alone together in the early hours of the morning, my mother, using all the advantage of our relation, and of the emotional crisis through which we were passing, and which for the while brought us together, asked me to promise to give up Edward's friendship. She saw more plainly than we where it was tending, and she so disliked Edward, and felt jealous of my growing affection for him. In the middle of a terrible discussion the nurse came to summon us to my father who was in his last agony, and when we got to his bedside he was dead.

I remember my mother fainting, and my running upstairs to wake my two sisters, and the feeling of loneliness and despair that I had lost such a dear friend and ally. I remember waiting for the morning to come which would bring Edward outside the house to ask for news, and my running out to tell him, but I cannot remember how he took it.

After my father's death life at home became very different. His genial kindness and happiness withdrawn, my mother's harshness became more pronounced. Quite frankly she showed that her daughters were a bother to her. She had to add to her small income by taking in boarders, and these young men – quite decent and nice of their kind – became as her family. All the affection and sympathy she failed to give to her daughters she gave to these strangers, and they and she lived in the happiest relations. My friendship with Edward when it was mentioned was always alluded to with sneers and contempt. The young men took this up, and with my mother's approval did all they could to make things appear ridiculous. Edward never came to the house now, but though my mother had forbidden it she was powerless to prevent my meeting him and I never hid from her that we did. We met and walked and talked, and love grew.

There was no definite moment when friendship became love, but a natural merging into love as we became closer friends. At this time we both knew that the friendship between us was the happiest thing in our lives, but we did not regard the future. We were content with the present. But I remember one evening very well. It was in the spring and nearing Edward's birthday, March 3rd. We were walking on the Common, very happy, talking of what we had been reading, what doing, what thinking, walking as usual hand in hand. In a space of silence, when thought and emotion went to and fro between us too full even for speech, I felt that wonderful experience of the first stirring of desire, though at this time it seemed half-maternal tenderness for his big, strong body, and his lovely face, and his hand holding mine, which now held his more firmly – mingled with something new and strange that I did not understand. I remember how, with that emotion flooding my being, my heart beat too fast, and my face burned, and I could have fainted with the pain and the joy of it. For it affected me as later I was affected by the first flutter of my baby in my womb.

When we reached the place for good night I could not let him go as he had always done before, but put hands round his head and drew it down to mine and kissed his mouth and looked close into his eyes. And he returned my kiss and my look, and then turned to go. But as I turned to go, too, he caught me in his arms and pressed me to him and kissed my mouth and my eyes and my neck; blindly and fiercely he kissed me, and I abandoned myself to him, not responding but just yielding myself to his kisses. When I was in my bed I could not sleep, but lay trembling half with fear, half with wonder, at what I had awakened in him. I had not known that love could be like that – so fierce, so rough, so greedy.

Quite soon after my father's death my position at home became unbearable, and I left home to earn my living as a nursery governess with relatives of friends living at Broadstairs. I do not remember that this parting from Edward seemed terrible to us at all: we were so happy in our love, and so sure of the future. I do remember that my mother came to see me off, and that she uttered no protest and showed no surprise when Edward came too. So I left home for the first time in my life.

During the time that I was in Broadstairs, we wrote to each other every day. My letters were written last thing at night in the only time of my own that I had. My work filled my day. I had four young children to bathe, dress, teach (including piano and violin), take out for walks, and mend for; and in the evening, when they were in bed, I was expected to play cards with Mr and Mrs Webb on weekdays, and on Sundays listen patiently while Mr Webb read aloud to his patient wife and me Cary's translation of Dante. How I used to long impatiently for ten o'clock to strike, for when the hour came we stopped the game or the reading! They went to bed, and I to my room to read over again the letter I had had in the morning, and to write all that my heart and mind were full of. Long letters they were – poured out of my brimming consciousness. We wrote of our daily lives, our thoughts, the books we were reading, and our emotions. We hid nothing of ourselves from each other, and we now looked forward to a life together, when it would be possible. Marriage did not enter into our plans, but just a passionate desire to be one in body as we were in spirit.

Looking back, it seemed to me unbelievable that we were so ignorant of physical love. But we were very ignorant and very innocent.

During this time at Broadstairs I was very happy teaching and playing with the children, with whom I got on very well. Sometimes it happened that between putting the children to bed and dinner-time I was able to slip out on to the beach just below the house, and then it was my delight to run along the sand with the wind in my hair reciting aloud Shelley's 'Ode to the West Wind' or 'Adonais'. These and most of Shelley's lyrics and many of Keats's I knew by heart. I remember the exhilaration I felt in those few stolen moments as the strong salty wind snatched the words from my lips, and my breath too, and how I delighted in holding my head high and not lowering it against the speed and the strength of the wind, and how the sound of the wind and of the sea drowned the sound of my voice, and how I felt my own strength and my own place in the motion and strength and sound, for love had given me a consciousness of my own part and significance in the universe I had not dreamt I should ever know.

I had been in Broadstairs for many months and I was so inexperienced and I suppose so well, and so happy with my secret, that it never occurred to me to ask for a holiday, and none was ever offered. The servants and the nurse all had their times off, but I never had any. However, one day Edward wrote to me that he was coming into Kent to Horsmonden with a friend to fish together. He had been working hard for

34

a Civil Service Examination, and this was to be a little rest before the examination actually took place. I remember when I asked Mrs Webb for the day, and told her why, she said, as if so surprised to find I had any life more than her children provided for me, 'Oh, I didn't know Phyllis had got a Corydon.' So very early one morning I set off. I had to get up at about five, for the journey was a tiresome cross-country one. The cook, who was very kind to me, had left me breakfast laid in the schoolroom, and I remember stealing downstairs so as not to wake anyone and finding to my great joy that the weather promised to be fine. I was wearing mourning for my father, but I hated it and the idea of it. I was too poor to buy a new frock for this great day; so I had made myself a white blouse to wear with my black coat and skirt; and with a big black hat, from which I had taken the black ribbon, putting instead a coloured scarf, I made the best of myself.

I remember only vaguely the journey. What I chiefly remember is the changing smell of the air from the sharp, salty sea air to the soft earthy smell of the green country. When at last I got to Horsmonden, Edward was there on the platform, and in a moment we were together. We did not speak or kiss, but when we got into the lane and I took in a great deep breath of the delicious air, he said, 'Oh Helen, love me more than anything that you love,' and stopped in the lane, took me in his arms and kissed me, and we leant tremblingly against each other. And I, 'I only love other things so much because I love you, dear.' Then we walked hand in hand silently, till we came to the top of a little hill, when he ran down, pulling me with him till we were both out of breath and laughing, and we sat down by the roadside among cowparsley and speedwell, till we had got our breath again.

I remember every minute of that day – how we talked and talked as we walked, I not noticing where we were going, but deeply conscious of all the beauty, so strange and so especially lovely to me after the sea and the barren country just inland.

We came at last to a mill pond and to a stick planted in the bank. Here Edward leant down and pulled up a bottle of lemonade that he had let down into the cool water, and from under a bush he produced a basket full of sandwiches, eggs, cake and fruit, all wrapped up in cool leaves. Not far from the stream was a little copse, and here in the coolness, within sound of the stream, and on a carpet of dog's mercury we sat and ate and talked. I was very hungry after my early rising, and as I sat with Edward's arm round me, and he was stroking my hair, I soon began to feel sleepy, and when he saw that he made fun of me. It was a hot summer day, and even in the shade of the copse it was hot, and so Edward unfastened the first few buttons of my blouse to let the air in on my throat, and then with dry leaves he made a place for me to lie, and took off my shoes and stockings. And I lay down in the little place he had made for me, and he sat down by me and, kissing my eyes shut, he told me to go to sleep, and soon I was fast asleep. I don't know how long I slept, but I think not long. I was awakened by feeling his face near to mine, and when he saw my eyes opened he kissed my eyes and my mouth and my throat, and took my head between his hands and kissed me again and again, and I, putting my arms round him, drew him to my breast, and so we lay in each other's arms, with our hearts beating wildly together. And yet I can remember no desire for more than this; the new rapture of such an embrace contented us utterly. Then we walked through meadows and woods, and through a beautiful park, where I first learnt to distinguish trees. I remember the lime trees there and the beech, and it seems strange now that there was ever a time when I could not recognize the fine-textured skinlike bark, and the set of the trunk and branches like human limbs, and the beautiful curve that the leafy branches make, like a hand opened for giving.

For tea we made a fire and boiled a kettle. It was the first time we had had a whole day together; the first time we had eaten out of doors together; picnics had been very rare treats in my towny childhood, and this seemed to me the height of happiness. My surprise and joy and excitement in it all were as wonderful to Edward as the whole adventure was to me.

At dusk I went. He saw me off in the train, and that day ended, and we did not see each other again for many months.

During this time Edward was working for his examination, but very half-heartedly, for he hated the idea of an office life. He had very much wanted to go to Oxford, but the idea was not encouraged by his parents, partly on account of the expense and partly because his father thought that university life would encourage Edward in his desire to earn his living by writing, which his father well knew would never lead to a fortune, while fame never entered his mind as a possibility. My father's influence had, of course, been on the side of a literary career, and so Edward's work for the higher branch of the Civil Service was very much against the grain. About this time his first book was published. He had, during his long walks at all times of the year, kept a minute diary of natural events – birds'-nesting, flowers opening, and descriptions of the sky, and clouds and atmosphere, and all sorts of observations made from day to day. This diary he offered on my father's advice to a firm which accepted it. I shall never forget my pride and joy when my copy of the book arrived, and how, in spite of my shyness in speaking to my employers of my own affairs, I rushed up to Mrs Webb to show her the book written by my lover and dedicated to my father. Mrs Webb admired my father's work, and the incident led to my telling her about Edward, and after that I had an interested and sympathetic friend in her.

Soon after this I left Broadstairs. My mother said she wanted me at home, and I did stay at home with her for a little while; but the old antagonism sprang up and I could not endure it for long. I very soon got another post as a governess so that I should not be dependent on her.

She tried again to make me give up Edward, and forbade me to see him; so he could not come to the house. I lived at home, paying Mother for my keep. Each evening Edward and I met, generally on Wandsworth Common, where afar off I would recognize him by his long swinging stride, even though with my short sight I could distinguish nothing else about him. Sometimes on these evenings he would just walk with me as far as my gate, but sometimes we would go to Wimbledon Common. It was on one of these summer evenings we had been talking of Richard Jefferies and his love for the human body. We had just read his essay, 'Nature in the Louvre' and his description of the 'Vénus Accroupie', which he had admired so much. We were sitting in the undergrowth of a little copse in a remote part of the common. Edward had said that he had never seen a woman's body, and I do not remember quite how it came about, but I quite naturally and simply, without any feeling of shyness, knelt up in our secret bower and undid my clothes, and let them fall about my knees so that to the knees I was naked. I knew my body was pretty: my breasts were firm and round and neither too small nor too large, and my neck and shoulders made a pleasant line, and my arms were rounded and white, and though my hips were small, the line of the waist was lovely. I was proud of my body, and took the most innocent pleasure in its lines and health and strength. So we knelt in the grass and dead leaves of the copse opposite to each other, he silent and I laughing with joy to feel the air on my skin, and to see his enraptured gaze. For as he knelt he gazed wonderstruck and almost adoring, quite still, quite silent, looking now and then into my eyes with serious ecstatic look, his eyes full of tenderness and love, searching mine for any sign of regret or shyness. He did not touch me, but just knelt there letting his eyes take their fill of the beauty that was filling his soul with delight. When, without a word, I lifted my clothes about me, he helping me, he only then said, 'Helen, I did not know there was such beauty.'

He told me as we walked home that no statue or picture of a nude woman had ever given him a true idea, and that it was a far more beautiful thing than he had thought. For though he loved the Greek statues, it seemed to him that my body was far lovelier. But that was only because a warm and living thing has beauty which a stone representation of the most perfect body can never have.

38

We were still very ignorant of sex, and only knew in a vague way through the reading of poetry how the human sexual act was performed. I remember very well with what joy I realized that his head would be on my breast, and I would enfold him in my arms.

After that, often when we were in remote places, I undressed and lay in the long grass, often beside the infant Wandle, then still an unpolluted stream. I had always from childhood had a love of feeling the air and sun on my body, and now – to be able often to have that experience and added to it the joy of my lover's delight – my heart was full indeed. He did not undress – at this time being shy – because he said his body would look so ugly beside mine, but he used to lie by me with one arm supporting his head while he read to me, the other over me, his hand wandering over my body as he read till it knew the curves as well as his eyes.

Desire had become more conscious and definite, and often in my breast I would experience a pleasurable pain of longing for I knew not what; I loved to feel his hand caressing me. After such a time he would help me to dress, kissing me as he did so, and I half-ashamed of his too great admiration, and wishing I was indeed all that he thought I was – wishing that I had perfect sight, wishing that my hair was not so straight and my nose was straighter, wishing that I could match his intellect and spirit, wishing that I had more to give him, and longing to give him all. But in spite of all that I knew to be imperfect in me I was utterly happy in his love, and hoped that in his heart he created beauty where none was, out of his love for me.

During these stolen hours we sometimes used to go to his home and read aloud, and sometimes we would go into town to the British Museum or the National Gallery, with Ruskin dictating our taste sometimes, and we finding it for ourselves too. Sometimes we would haunt Booksellers' Row – that queer little back street that used to lie behind the Strand – and spend a shilling or two on a second-hand copy of some book we wanted, or having saved up would buy a new volume of

Ruskin in a good edition, or Shelley or Keats. Often we had no money, and could only turn the books over, and if we saw one we wanted hope that it would be there next time we came. Sometimes we would walk all the way home, along the Embankment and over Battersea Bridge and home through Clapham Junction. Or we would walk to Hampstead and look at Keats's house and walk on the heath where Edward would be sure to find some unexpected wild flower, or hear a bird he did not think to hear there, or notice some beautiful effect of clouds or of smoke against the blue sky. All of this was a new aspect of life to me; for my eye readily caught the beauty of a group of red roofs, and the iron-work of an old entrance gate, or the bend of a street of tall dignified houses, but nature was a sealed book to me until Edward taught me to see with new eyes and hear with new ears. And often I used to escape from home in the evening and go for little walks with him to fields and lanes whose existence so near home I had not dreamed of, and we would talk of life, and books, and love, and nature, and ourselves, and sometimes there was no need for talk – silence satisfied us more.

All this time he was working for his Civil Service Examination, and I was going to and from my work. I liked my work, which was the care of an interesting little boy of four. His parents were foreigners, the father a Russian aristocrat, fierce and cruel and tyrannous, and his mother a most lovable Austrian. She and I became, while I worked for her, great friends. They lived in a luxurious suite of rooms at the Hotel Metropole. Sometimes I would be allowed to bring the little boy home, and then Edward would meet us, and we would go for a walk, he carrying the child on his shoulders, who would delight his mother on his return with the bunches of wild flowers which she and he would arrange in cups and saucers, there being no suitable vases in their grand rooms for such simple nosegays. They left England quite suddenly, making me promise I would return to them when they came back. I promised, for I loved the mother and little boy very much, but the man I hated, and he never paid me about £20 he owed me. So I got another job, this time a resident post in a very pleasant suburb of London. Here I was fairly well paid, and my work was light, still with children. Edward and I wrote to each other every day, and of course on my fixed free times we met. But I felt terribly lonely there, and the week which elapsed between our meetings seemed endless. The child was spoilt and difficult, and the mother an irritable, nervous, highly strung creature, with a cigarette always in her mouth.

I felt a failure here, and that and my loneliness made me very unhappy. Mrs Andrews noticed, I supposed, that I was not happy, and very kindly questioned me about myself. So I told her about Edward, and she at once said that if I liked he could come and spend two evenings a week with me there in the room at the top of the house, which was the nursery during the day and my sitting-room at night. This made all the difference to me, and with increased happiness I could tackle my work better, and very soon the child and I were on the best of terms, and his parents congratulated me on the improvement in him. Affection and praise and encouragement were always to my soul what food is to the body, and in the atmosphere now so happy I know I was at my best, and no employers could have had a more devoted servant. It was my delight to take the child as far out into the country as I could in the time. We went – he in his pram – to Barnes Common and Richmond Park, and there I would tell him all my newly acquired knowledge of birds and trees and flowers. Sometimes we would go in the other direction, along the towpath to Isleworth, and bring home bunches of meadow-sweet and loosestrife. Mrs Andrews was delighted that her child got taken to these places, and the child and I were never so happy as when picking bunches of flowers, or peering into gorse bushes for nests.

Edward used to come at about eight o'clock in the evening and stay till nine-thirty, and once a week I had the afternoon and evening free. Whenever the weather was good enough – and it had to be very bad to stop us – we used to walk on Wimbledon Common and Richmond Park, and go either to his home or mine for tea, for now my mother tolerated his presence. Edward was hating more and more the idea of the Civil Service as a means of earning his living, and at about this time, greatly to his father's anger, he gave up the work, and decided to try and earn his living by writing. Several of the literary weeklies were taking his essays, and his book had had a fair sale. His father, naturally enough, hated the precariousness of this way of living, and after a lot of discussion it was decided that Edward should go to Oxford, which his father thought would be a good start for any career that he took up. He decided to enter for a history scholarship, and as he had now left school some time, this required a good deal of reading. He liked the idea of going to university, but dreaded it too, for he had had so very little social life and was so unused to meeting his fellows; and also the thought of the separation from me was hateful to think of.

We had often spoken of our life together, and had made great plans for the education of our children. We hated the thought of a legal contract. We felt our love was all the bond that there ought to be, and that if that failed it was immoral to be bound together. We wanted our union to be free and spontaneous. We had no idea when it should take place, but the thought of our approaching separation heightened our desire to be united in body as we were in heart and spirit.

My twentieth birthday drew near, and I was to have a whole holiday, which Edward and I were to spend on our favourite Wimbledon Common. We were to picnic there for lunch and tea, and go home to a birthday dinner in the evening. It was July and glorious weather. I had made myself a very pretty white frock, embroidered in flame-coloured silk. I wore a shady hat trimmed with the same colour. it suited me, and I know I looked as pretty as it was possible for me to look. I remember Mr Andrews' saying as I went out, 'Why, Helen, you look like a bride going to meet her bridegroom,' and I remember blushing and feeling a great wave of passionate joy surging up in me, and I could hardly help laughing back at him, 'I am, I am!' I was to bring the lunch, and Edward the tea, and I bought fruit and sandwiches and biscuits and some of our favourite Gruyère cheese and half a bottle of wine.

We met in the horrid, dark tunnel at Clapham Junction Station. He was there waiting for me, so tall, so distinguished from other men, dressed as always with a sort of carelessness that was not at all untidy, but just easy and individual. He was in his person scrupulously careful, and his large hands, which he used so well in all sorts of work, were always well kept. No lover could have pleased the eye more, no girl have been prouder of her man than I of mine and the wonder of his loving me never left me. Our hearts were beating so, and our joy so intense, we could not speak but just in that crowded place pressed each other's hands and walked side by side.

It did not take us long to get to the Common. In the solitude there we walked hand in hand, or Edward with his arm around my waist, and I with my hand over his hand, whose pressure under my breast made my whole body tender with desire. Our souls spreading their wings enfolded us in such dreamlike happiness that nothing disturbed our calm and our utter satisfaction. We talked as we sauntered along of what I should do while he was at Oxford, of our life together when he left, of my longing for children, of his ambitions in literature; and in this talk as in many others there was often hinted that deep spiritual unrest, which as yet we did not recognize, much less realize how it was to overshadow so much of his life and mine. All the beauty of the earth, the grass, the flaming gorse, the lark's song, the high cloudlets, the sweet air laden with the honey smell of gorse, seemed to be a part of our love. We could not speak of it, but as we stood to watch a bumble-bee make the gorse flower deliver its secret to him, he standing a little behind me, with his hands over my breasts, drew me to him and kissed me where my hair grew soft and curly under my ear. So I leaned smiling up at him, and he solemnly looking down at me, his eyes half-closed, his lovely mouth trembling from the kiss. So on, walking with hips moving together, laughing because of my short step and his long one. He picked a little bunch of flowers in the grass, white clover, yellow bedstraw and milkwort, and then remembered he had a birthday present for me. It was a brooch made of gold wire, twisted into a Celtic pattern, and when I had put my arms round his neck and kissed him for it, he pinned the flowers into the opening of my dress, which first he opened a little more to kiss the warm, soft swell of my breast, and while he kissed me I pressed his head yet further down into the warmth and sweetness there.

So we walked on into the remote part of the Common among the trees, until we came to a beautiful little pool, where moorhens and coots lived in the reeds, and where water voles dipped out of their holes in the low bank into the water, making a sound like cream being stirred. Here we sat and paddled our feet in the water and ate our lunch. We were so quiet that the timid water creatures grew bold and birds skimmed over the water, and a flaming dragon-fly darted in the air round and round us, as if weaving us in a web of rainbow colours. As we sat, Edward read to me some of the old ballads, 'Edom O'Gordon' and 'Chevy Chase' and 'Sir Patrick Spens', he leaning against a beech tree and I leaning in the crook of his arm and shoulder, listening to his deep, clear voice, so quiet, so vibrating, so tender. I was caught up into heaven; all beauty, all love, all content was mine. Life gave me all it had to give. As I lay there in the bend of his arm, in the silence that the splash of the voles, and the song of the lark, and the sound of his voice did not disturb, the beating of his heart under my cheek lulled me to sleep, and my eyes were only opened by his kisses. He kissed my eyes, and my funny nose and my mouth and neck and my hands and feet. But I laughed at his serious kisses and pushed him away, and before he knew what I meant to do I had run away and hidden in a thicket of hazel and beech, and crouched down in the dry leaves. I heard his step rustling in the leaves, and I waited, trembling half with fear of his finding me, and half afraid I had hidden myself too well. But he came upon me before I knew he was near, and caught me up in his arms and carried me further and further into the little copse. I lay inert in his arms, conscious of nothing but his beating heart. Soon he came to a little glade in the copse, leafy and mossy and sunny, and putting me down, knelt in front of me and undid my hair, but finding it fell over my face he picked a trail of white bryony and made a fillet of it to keep my hair back. Then, keeping his eyes fixed so tenderly and seriously and passionately on mine, he undid my dress and took my arms out of the sleeves, and unfastened my underclothes, and slipped the shoulder-straps over my arms, so that I was naked to the waist, with my clothes lying round me. Then I held out my hands to him – for he was standing now, and he raised me to my feet, so that my clothes slid down in a ring. I stepped out of them on to the soft moss and dry leaves, and he kneeling kissed my body from my feet up to my knees, and from my knees up to my hips, and when he had kissed me and let his hand wander all over me he laid me down on the moss, and I lay with my eyes closed, just conscious that he was quickly undressing, and hearing his voice speaking some passionate name. And I knowing he was ready, opened my eyes and saw him standing there naked, said 'Come,' and drew him to my breast.

I only remember vaguely that the birthday dinner at home was very jolly and rollicking. My sisters were there, and my youngest sister's sweetheart – a man very much approved of by my mother and full of fun – and well-to-do and practical and a clever engineer. He was for ever scoring off me in some way, and tried to do the same with Edward, but he got as good as he gave, for Edward's wit was quick and penetrating, though he was not often moved to show it. We walked back over Wandsworth Common to Clapham Junction, talking at first happily enough of the books we should buy with the five pounds my mother had given me. I had seen, too, some old brass candleticks, and a nice Morland print I had set my heart on buying him for his Oxford rooms. We kissed our goodnight kiss on the dark Common, and Edward gave me to wear for a wedding ring the beautiful old signet ring which he wore – a red stone set in a very delicately designed gold setting. It had belonged to his great-grandfather, a Spanish sea-captain.

# 3

During August I went away with the Andrews to Sandgate, and I got to know the country about there very well, taking the child for long walks on to the chalk hills behind, and along the coast to Dymchurch, and other villages in the Marsh. I forget when it was that Edward went in for a scholarship at Balliol and did not get it, and went in for one at Lincoln and did. I think it was while I was at Sandgate. However, I know that he was very soon to go to Oxford, when at the end of six weeks at Sandgate without any holiday I was given a few unexpected days' leave. It was too good a chance to be missed, and all in a hurry we decided to go away somewhere together for a tiny honeymoon. For me it was simple, but Edward had to invent some tale of having to go to Oxford or something. He was very eager to show me his beloved Wiltshire Downs, and so we decided to go to a little place he knew very well among the Downs just outside Swindon, and put up in the cottage of his old gamekeeper friend. All this we arranged in the greatest secrecy and joy. We took the train to Swindon and from there walked, with our few belongings in rucksacks, the seven miles to the Downs. I shall never forget the wild excitement we felt at being all alone and free – no one knowing where we were, our time all our own. There was a little risk, too, that added to our enjoyment, for Edward's grandmother and aunt lived at Swindon, and he had often stayed with them, and was well known by quite a number of people. But we risked that, walking quickly through the town until we came to the solitary country road leading through a cleft in the Downs.

I do not remember the hamlet to which our cottage belonged, but of the cottage itself and its immediate surroundings I remember every detail. It stood like a fairy-tale cottage right in a wood, and quite off the road, a track from the lane taking you to it. It had a deep thatched roof almost hiding the little windows of the bedrooms with its deep eaves, and a porch with a little bench on each side covered with traveller's joy and briar roses that filled the air with their musky scent. It belonged to the wood, and the wood to it, as if it had been in reality the brown fur-covered creature that it looked, whose eyes peered out from under its overhanging brows shyly and kindly. All along under the thick untrimmed hedge of the garden was a row of beehives, one or two of the painted wooden new kind, but half a dozen or more of the old-fashioned skeps with earthenware pans inverted over them. The garden was full of bees and of flowers for them, red and blue and yellow. I had never seen anything so lovely, so exactly what I should have chosen for my honeymoon. The old man was full of fun, and he and his old wife, who welcomed us as though we were her children, could not make enough jokes at our expense. They had an enormous tea ready for us, of bacon and eggs and honey and lardy cakes and strong tea with cream in it, in the living-room of the cottage. This room had a flagged floor, with a big open range in it in which burned even at this time of the year a huge wood fire; the walls were covered with pictures and guns and traps. Bunches of herbs in paper bags hung from the raftered ceiling, for the old man was very proud of his herb medicines and ointments for men and beasts, and on a little table in the window, covered with a fox's skin, stood a huge Bible, and on the Bible a book in which he had written down all his prescriptions and remedies. He and Edward talked eagerly over old times of birds' nesting, and fishing in the huge reservoir near by. And there were jokes and nods and winks every now and then which we all laughed at. I was so glad they liked me, for they had known Edward since he was a little boy, and loved him, and I had felt afraid that I might not be the sort of girl they would like. But we got on splendidly. Edward sang some of the old songs in his clear deep voice, and then the old man sang some that he knew, 'The Farmer's Boy' and 'Turmut Hoeing' and 'The

Seeds of Love', and we all joined in at the chorus. Just before bedtime the old woman brought out a bottle of mead, made from their own honey, I do not know how many years ago. It was like cloudy amber to look at, and had the softest, most subtle taste you can imagine. We drank it like a liqueur. It was very strong, and they were delighted that we liked it, and took it as a compliment that we dared not drink much of it – though they tried to make us, telling us it was a right proper drink for lovers. They told me I must call them Dad and Granny as Edward had always done, and they called me Mrs Edwy.

Our bedroom was just as right as all the rest of the cottage was – a small room almost filled by the four-poster, with such a thick mattress, and feather bed on it, covered with a patchwork quilt, that I had to climb on a chair before I could get into bed. The hangings of the bed were chintz in a pattern of the rose, the shamrock, and the thistle, all in bright colours. There was a little dressing-table with a white dimity flounce all round it, and a little corner washstand. The tiny window was draped with dimity curtains, and the window was kept open by a large dried sunflower head. The scent of the briar rose over the porch mingled with the smell of lavender, of which there were two vases full on the dressing-table. Everything was enchanting; I had never been in such a cottage before. Edward was as happy as I, and overjoyed at my delight. It was so lovely, too, to be together like this. So little of our courtship and love-making had been indoors, and it was a delicious experience to be together in this sweet little room, all to ourselves, chatting and laughing together, unpacking our rucksacks, and finding places for our things all so intimate and homely. We washed in rain-water, and even the rough towel smelt sweet. Outside the owls hooted about the cottage, and bats twittered, and starlings stirred in the thatch. No other sound was to be heard, no trams, no people, no traffic, nothing but the sounds that do not spoil silence, but rather deepen it, and a little breeze wandering through the wood, and a leaf flapping against our window.

As we stood together by the window sniffing the sweet air, and looking into the dark wood, Edward took the pins out of my hair, and when I was going to plait it into two plaits he said: 'No, let it be loose.' I got into bed first and sank down into the thick feather bed. All night we were to be together, and all day, and all day and all night again. I sighed a deep sigh of content and happiness. 'Happy?' Edward asked, as he blew out the candle and got in beside me and took me in his arms.

Edward was awake early and, half-dressed, went down to Coate Water to bathe. As soon as he was gone, Granny came up with a huge cup of tea, and a tiny doll's loaf just out of the oven on a plate for me. While I sat up and ate and drank she stood talking to me about Edward, and her sons, and her young days; how Dad was a bit wild when he was young; and how she had had to work hard to keep things going, though many's the time she and the children had sat down to a dish of boiled turnips and bread for their dinner, and not much bread, for flour was dear. But though he had been a bit wild he had never been unkind to her and the boys, and as he got older he settled down, and they had been very happy ever since. She told me they loved Edward as much as their own boys, and showed me letters that they had had from him when he was a little boy, and a handkerchief, bought and chosen by himself, which Edward had sent her one Christmas many years ago. We were gossiping away when we heard Edward's step, and he called to me from the garden to come out. So Granny left me to get dressed saying, with a wink, 'Drat the men, they never leave a poor woman in peace,' and we laughed at the joke. But I knew that all my life my only peace would be to be needed by him. And so it was.

For there were to come dark days when his brooding melancholy shut me out in a lonely exile, and my heart waited too eagerly to be let into the light again. When those days came, with no apparent reason for their coming, bringing to him a deep spiritual unrest and discontent, he would be silent for hours, and perhaps stride out of the house, angry and bitter and cruel, and walk and walk far into the night, and come home, worn out with deadly fatigue. When those days came my heart trembled for what might happen, and I, suffering his terrible spiritual loneliness, had no thought, or seeing, or hearing, for anything but his agony and my own despair. Then my strong body that he loved so came to my rescue, and in hard housework, scrubbing and washing and digging in the garden, I would force myself to *be*, so that when the cloud left him he would find me to welcome him. I did these things mechanically – cooked the food, took the children out for walks, spoke to them, picked flowers with them, but I did not know afterwards what I had done while my spirit waited in the dark.

But this was to come, and it was only now and then that I had hints of this darkness in his soul, this fierce unrest which beyond all found peace in nature, but not in me. Alone he had to be in his agony, but when he emerged from it, exhausted by God knows what bitter contest, he looked for me and needed me, and our love was always the firm ground on which we stood secure and that no storm ever swept away.

But now I washed and dressed and ran down, and as I ran through the kitchen where Granny was cooking the breakfast she shooed me away – 'Get along, you hussy,' she said.

All that day we were out, fishing in the reservoir, and bathing in it and walking in the deep woods, not talking much as I remember. We brought home some perch for supper, which Granny pretended to be cross with Edward for bringing – 'Such trashy fish, all scales and guts,' she said. But she cooked them, and while we ate them Edward read how Izaak Walton would have cooked them, to tease Granny with the white wine and this and that ungettable spice. When Dad came in he brought a dead jay so that I could have the beautiful wing for a hat. I didn't like to think of the lovely bird being killed for such a purpose, but I kept that to myself, knowing it would be incomprehensible to him, and appreciating his kind thought for me. After tea Dad showed me the garden and the beehives, and all the bees swarming over the comb. They filled me with disgust. They are such ugly creatures in a mass like that, and their highly developed social life, so ordered, so cold, so lacking in impulse, repelled me then as it does now. Dad laughed when I tried to tell him how I felt about them. 'Ah, but what about the mead and the honey?' he said, and, of course, I said, 'Yes, I like that,' but I could only regard bees almost as one does machinery. But I loved the hermit, home-making bumble-bees – humble bees of the earth, primitive and indolent and beautiful.

While Dad and I had been flirting over the bees and flowers, and his collection of dried skins of ferret and weasel and rabbit and squirrel, Edward was helping Granny to wash up, much to her amusement and delight, and she had tied her long white apron round him. At the end of our little round he said, 'Now give your old Dad a kiss, but don't tell that boy of yourn, for I be no fighter these days.' So I kissed him and promised I wouldn't tell, and we had our little secret; but Dad, with such winks and significant looks, soon let the cat out of the bag, and all had to be confessed. Then Edward had to kiss Granny to make it quits, and we were very happy together with our jokes and fun. I had never met people like these before, and though the things they said sometimes startled me because they were so new to me, their coarse, simple talk full of proverbs, and shrewd observation and wit did not shock me at all. I felt perfectly at home with them, and knew that they didn't feel they had to make a difference for me, but were with me as they had always been with Edward. He was glad too, I could see. I loved them just as I love the earth, and the rain, and the bumble-bees.

After we had all had some mead, Dad and Granny got very jolly and gay, and Granny rose and began to dance and said, 'I be as young as any, b'aint I, Dad?' and Dad said of course she was, and they danced together hand-in-hand up and down the kitchen, Granny holding up her apron and Dad looking at her with admiration. And as they danced some old dance they had remembered from their courting days, Edward whistled the tune, for he was too shy to dance, and so was I. I wonder when again that lovely old tune was whistled in that cottage, and when again that jig was danced under that roof, for those who danced are dead, and he who whistled the tune is dead, and I think that those who live in that cottage now have forgotten these old things, as soon all will have forgotten them. So we lay another night in the great bed, and slept in each other's arms, slept the sound sleep that lovers sleep so sound and yet so light that like a dream the consciousness of the other is always there – the only dream that enters the deep sleep of lovers.

After breakfast we had to leave, and Dad was all ready to go with us as far as the market-place in the town where he had business. Dear old Granny had already for me a little neatly arranged posy of all the sweet-smelling flowers and herbs from the garden – an outside fringe of 'old man' and for the middle a tight pink rosebud with a circle of mint. She said it was for us to smell in London and be reminded of them and the garden. As if I should ever forget them, though I have never seen them again! They insisted on our taking a pot of honey, and half a dozen of big apples and two great lardy cakes, and Granny gave me a length of fine crochet lace that she had made long ago, with much joking and looking sideways at Edward, and he pretending he didn't know what on earth she meant by all her hints. Dad gave Edward a little old book of receipts he had collected for food, for medicine for beast and man, for curing skins, and all sorts of things. All these with difficulty we packed into our rucksacks, and off we set, with Dad insisting on carrying our traps, and Granny waving to us from the gate.

And soon in the train we left the long line of downs behind us, and were in London.

I have passed those downs since and have seen the places where we walked, and from the train have found, as Edward showed me how, the glint of the sun on the reservoir where we bathed. I have never stayed there again, but I know the place as I know no other. I have my jay's wing still. I never put it in a hat, but the lace I used again and again on my babies' clothes, and it has never worn out.

Then Edward went to Oxford, and I stayed on in my job. We wrote to each other every day, and his letters were full of his new life, and I could tell how he was enjoying the society of his fellows, and also the freedom from home rules which he experienced for the first time in his life. He had always been kept very short of money, and it was quite a new experience to have a small allowance to manage himself. Of course, he thought it would do much more than was possible. He loved beautiful things, and his own home was so devoid of beauty, and he at once went the way of, I suppose, most undergraduates. He spent in his first year much more than he could afford on editions de luxe, pictures, and china. I was always on the look-out for odds and ends for his rooms – brass, and pewter, and bright cushions, and books all the time as I could afford. He now read Pater, and Oscar Wilde, and John Addington Symonds. It was the *Yellow Book* period, and he was very interested in the movement, though never carried away by it. I was rather repelled by it, though as I was young and healthy something in its breaking away from the old conventions appealed to me. I read *The Woman Who Did*, but having done likewise I was not impressed by it – it seemed to me a lot of fuss about nothing. I detested Aubrey Beardsley's drawings and loved Max Beerbohm's essays as they appeared in the *Yellow Book*. It was an interesting time to be growing up in, and Edward and I were both quick to respond to any new ideas in art and literature. But Edward was much more influenced by the old than the new, and I think *The Anatomy of Melancholy* and *Urn Burial*, *Tristram Shandy*, *Lear* and *Macbeth*, and Keats and the Bible, to name a few, were the foundations of his taste. These were the books we read at the same time, and in our letters we wrote about them and about ourselves and our love and our future life together.

At this time I became an intimate of a circle of people living in Hammersmith. The centre of the circle to which I was introduced was Mrs Logan, or Beatrice as we all called her. They were artistic Bohemian people, young mostly, though

Mrs Logan was not. She had three lovely daughters, the eldest
about sixteen or seventeen when I first knew them. This
household and their ways were a revelation to me. I loved
their large spacious rooms with very little furniture in them,
the polished floors bare except for a rug or two, and the almost
bare walls; the absence of stuffy upholstery and curtains, and
the simple beauty and comfort of everything delighted me. I
had, of course, read William Morris and been very attracted
by his ideas, but I had never before seen a house decorated
and furnished with his designs and in the way he advocated.
The beauty of it delighted me, and I thought it the perfect
setting for these people, with their freedom of manner and
thought. The house was always full of men and women living
in delightful freedom of intercourse – all people interested in
some form of art from Church embroidery to acting. There
were a poet, Charles Dalmon, who has since achieved fame,
Franklin Dyall, an actor who is at the top of the tree, a painter
who is now an acknowledged master, and several notable
craftsmen whose work is now known to connoisseurs. Folk
songs were just being collected, and it was here I first heard
these beautiful old songs being sung. They were eager,
enthusiastic people, and I admired them immensely. I look
back upon this household as having been – after Edward – the
strongest influence in my life. It opened new windows for me
on the social and artistic world, a world I was strangely un-
familiar with, and because they liked me I felt at ease with
them and found pleasure in talking to them, and looked for-
ward to the discussions which took place in their beautiful
drawing-room. There were no servants; but everyone, men
and women, helped in the house, and everything ran smoothly.

I introduced Edward to these people, but he didn't get on
with them. He was too reserved, and sat among them like
some judging Sphinx. But I, being so much simpler, and so
frankly admiring, was accepted at once. I was often there when
Edward was at Oxford, a humble disciple of what seemed to
me a higher ideal of freedom than I had ever imagined possible.
Edward used to make fun of their serious cults of purity and

54

freedom and nakedness, but I thought it very fine, and admired and loved them. They regarded no convention, and I did not see till later that their unconvention was almost as intolerant as my parents' convention. But they were kind and gracious people, and proved good friends to me when I needed friends, which I was soon to do.

I cannot quite remember how events hurried on, but I think the estrangement between Mrs Andrews and Beatrice did not happen till Edward had been at Oxford some time, and I cannot remember individual vacations. Mrs Andrews disliked my going to Beatrice, and because I would go she became suspicious, and after a while I found that she had been reading Edward's letters to me. She never confessed that she had done this, and I could never prove it, but I gathered that she had discovered what our relationship was. So I asked the advice of Beatrice, who of course knew that Edward and I were lovers, and she advised me to leave, and offered me a post in her own household, which I gladly accepted. My duties were to do anything that wanted doing, and included cooking and housekeeping, as well as sewing and helping the children with their lessons. Edward did not wholly like this, but it had certain very great advantages. I was with friends, and as long as certain things were done I was free to come and go as I liked. Edward in his vacations spent a good deal of time here, and gradually got on better with the circle, who welcomed him and found him an interesting and stimulating participator in their discussions about art and life. But though he got to know and like them better, and they him, something always kept them from becoming intimate. Here I had a very nice room of my own, half bedroom, half sitting-room, where Edward often spent the night with me. From here, too, we had many lovely days in the country, though we never had another chance to go to our honeymoon cottage, for the old couple had had to leave it, and had moved into the town, near the railway works which employed their son.

So here I lived a jolly Bohemian life, working hard, and liking and being liked by the people I mixed with. I would have done anything for Beatrice, and did, in fact, work very hard at anything that came along to be done. The eldest girl was on the stage – a very beautiful and very selfish girl, and I was the one person she had some consideration for. She knew how I admired her beauty, especially her lovely hair, which I used to brush for her, and my natural good temper somehow softened her hard, spoilt heart. Her beauty was to bring her nothing but unhappiness, and I saw it coming, and so used to mother her, and she who was so imperious to her own mother used to be yielding to me.

All this time Edward was working fairly hard at Oxford, and rowing for his College, and experimenting in all sorts of experiences. He tried alcohol and opium, and used to write to me and tell me everything that he went through in these varied phases. He was influenced by the aesthetic school, and his dress and taste in colour and design were all very much affected by that. He had made a large number of friends, many of whom he kept all his life. He had a wonderful capacity for friendship, and inspired love and admiration wherever he went. He exacted a great deal, and gave a great deal.

He was enjoying it all enormously, and this life helped to overcome his natural shyness and reserve. He never wore his heart on his sleeve, as I did, and people had to meet him more than half-way, but this they always found worth doing. He was earning about £80 a year by writing. He became a more or less regular contributor to *The Speaker*, *The Academy*, and *The Literary World*, so that his life was very full. His style was at this time very much influenced by Pater, and he wrote, besides nature studies, romantic and imaginative essays in an ornate precious style which he afterwards dropped entirely. His writing was always full of a deep melancholy; even in his Oxford days this melancholy and spiritual disquietude was becoming more and more characteristic of his temperament.

He had been at Oxford two years, when, shortly after the end of the spring vacation, I found I was pregnant.

# 4

It was May, and we had been in the country on the outskirts of London; and coming back that evening – by what secret sign I cannot tell – I knew what had happened to me. I did not tell Edward, because it was not by reason that I became aware of this, but by something deeper that my mind had no conscious part in. I realized that a calm, deep, secret joy had entered into my spirit. It was not an excited joy at first – for what had happened seemed to me natural and right – that, just as out of friendship had come love, so from love would come a child. It was as it could not help but be, and I felt content and happy with a sense of fulfilment.

Edward returned to Oxford, and in a week or two I wrote to tell him. He wrote to me anxiously to come to Oxford. My serenity and complete acceptance seemed wonderful to him. He was anxious and troubled, and his letters were full of tender passion. All he wanted was for me to go to him, so that he could see for himself if indeed I was as happy and untroubled as over and over again I told him. So I went.

He met me at Oxford Station. We wanted to talk and be alone; so he did not take me through the city – which I saw for the first time many years afterwards when he was dead – but along by the canal, and on by the river. We walked several miles by the river, until we came to a wide meadow enclosed by thick high hedges now all in their spring green and white, and full of cowslips. Never before had I seen cowslips growing, and as I buried my face in their cool freshness and smelt their honey smell, and heard the bees humming in and out of the flowers, I felt my identification with the earth, which in its spring fulfilled itself with grass and cowslips and bees, as I with my baby fulfilled myself.

We sat in the shade of the hedge and ate our lunch, which

Edward had brought with him, and afterwards Edward picked
bunches of cowslips and spilt them all over me, my hair, my
shoulders, my lap, and pulled more and more to bury me
with. His anxieties had gone, and as I lay in his arms he told
me how he had never loved me so much as now; how he had
feared he might see some tiny shadow of reproach or anxiety
that would be there, however much I tried to conceal it; how,
when with my first kiss and look and word I had dispelled all
his fears, the warmth of love and joy and passion rushed in
where the coldness of fear had been.

We talked happily of what had come to us. We decided to
tell no one but Beatrice. We were jealous of our secret, and I
particularly did not want anyone else to share it just yet. We
did not talk much of the future, or plan anything, except that
Edward would try to increase his earnings by more regular
work for the papers which were taking his things. I was happy
with Beatrice and her household, and did not want to leave
her yet. But now we both felt we must be more together,
though how it was to come about we did not know. But I
was as calm and sure about that as about everything. Care and
fear for the future had no place in my consciousness, and
whenever fear and anxiety came to Edward I was able to soothe
and reassure him. The months of which this was the beginning
were for me especially lovely, because Edward needed and
took from me what I had so much of to give him – a serenity
rich and vital like the serenity of the earth. Very soon there
came to me the full significance of maternity, and when during
these months Edward was troubled, I had the strange experi-
ence which I expect most women have, who are in love, of
an eternal tenderness as old and wise as the earth; almost a
physical sensation of being big and strong to comfort and
protect. He was my child, and I the ancient ageless mother in
whose arms was unfailing comfort, and in her heart the deep
wisdom of the earth.

I left in the early evening. For long, long afterwards, when
I thought of Oxford, that murmuring sea of green meadow
grass with golden froth of cowslips came into my mind, with

the thin strip of the Thames dividing it from the grey mist out of which the spires and towers and domes of the city rose.

Edward and I had not spoken of marriage. Indeed, it had not occurred to us. At about this time I came into possession of £250 – all that remained of a considerable legacy left to each of my sisters and myself, which had been stolen by the trustee. The thing had just come to light, and the sum of £250 each was all that could be recovered. This seemed to me a great deal of money, and coming just then it was like a miracle. It removed any anxiety on that score. Not that I had felt any – nothing could disturb the deep serenity of my being – but I was glad for Edward's peace of mind that this money came then. My calm spirit was only equalled by a wonderful glow of physical well-being, and it was difficult for me to find even the hard work I had to do in Beatrice's house sufficient for my overflowing energy. I noticed with joy my breasts growing larger and my body changing its shape.

During this time Edward came to London once or twice to see me, and now I used to try to imagine him a father – this tall, fair man, so young, so handsome, so grave, so elegant – tasting for the first time the freedom and pleasure of a university. He was going through the phase of being influenced in his tastes by Wilde and Pater, and this appeared in his dress, which was individual and scrupulous without being either freakish or dandified. Now, as always before and always after, his love for, and need of, nature were the same. Whenever he came, we spent the day out of London, he tenderly careful of me now, lifting me over gates we had to climb, and calling at farmhouses for glasses of milk. We talked of our baby and of our future life. He told me what to read – Chaucer and Shakespeare and Wordsworth. More's *Utopia* and Plato's *Republic*, I remember, I now read for the first time. I was to go to the National Gallery, and choose one or two satisfying pictures and fill myself with their beauty. But most of all, I was to go into the country as often as I could, and lie in the grass and look at the clouds, and become familiar with the life in the hedges and trees, and with the solitude and the silence.

I read the books and enjoyed them, but I got tired of the pictures; I had in my heart always the picture of my lover, and I longed passionately for a boy like him. I remember at about this time feeling the first flutter of my baby in my womb. It was as if he spoke to me, and I was thrilled with joy and pleasure, with this intimate and direct communication between us. I loved to feel him striving within me.

On one of Edward's visits we decided to tell Beatrice. To my surprise and disappointment she, now as ever affectionately sympathetic and interested, strongly advised marriage. Perhaps she felt she had unduly influenced me against marriage, and she did not like having that responsibility. She put before us very wisely and carefully the argument for marriage. It was I who most strongly opposed this; so she weighted her argument with reasons which she thought would most easily convince me. They did not convince me, but Edward was sure that Beatrice was right. When we went to bed I cried and cried, and distressed Edward very much, who had never seen such tears. He did all he could to comfort me with wise and tender talk, quietly insisting that our love was our own and that no one could interfere with it or spoil it but we ourselves, and telling me that free love was only another bondage, a new-thought-out idea with no tradition of human wisdom behind it. After a while he kissed my wet eyes shut, and in the morning I woke happy and comforted.

All this time I was keeping in touch with my home, and I went to see my mother fairly often. I had now very little in common with my family, but though my sisters and I were in most things strangers to each other we always felt very strongly the tie of family affection.

There came to stay with Beatrice a great friend of mine named Janet Hooton. She and I had grown up together and had been very intimate. She and her husband and Edward and I got on splendidly together, and they were also intimate with Beatrice. For convenience she and I shared the same room, and when we were undressing at night she noticed my altered

figure, and I told her. To my great grief she was indignant
and angry. And as we lay side by side in bed she said many
hard and bitter things to me. Chiefly she accused me of deceit
in having kept my relationship to Edward so secret even from
her, my oldest friend. I was sorry she felt like that, but I could
not feel I had done wrong in this. Next she drew a picture of
what this would mean to my mother and sisters, and how our
baby would suffer. In excited and angry words she called me
selfish and self-indulgent. I was utterly overwhelmed by the
torrent of her words. She seemed to want to hurt me, and I
shrank from her, sobbing uncontrollably. She, noticing my
movement away from her, said, 'You see, you are ashamed.
You know you have done wrong.' And I, in my violent and
now hysterical sobbing, could only cry, 'No, no, no.' My
body became so convulsed with my crying that she began to
be alarmed and tried to calm me, telling me to think of the
harm I might be doing the baby, and that she was my friend,
and had only been saying what she thought was for my good.
She put her arm round me to comfort me, and whether in
doing so she felt my altered shape I do not know, but suddenly
all was changed: from a scolding teacher she became a sweet
friend again, full of love and sympathy and interest, and I,
who responded so quickly to warmth and affection, pressed
up to her, and soon we were talking of plans and baby clothes
and names.

I can't remember this time very clearly – only that I was
very happy among these kind people. One of the many fre-
quenters of the house, an artist, had a house on Chiswick Mall,
with a lovely old garden behind and a great spreading mul-
berry tree in it. Here a little company of friends used to gather
– a poet, half-gipsy, whom I liked best; a painter; an actor;
and one or two craftsmen; and they would talk, and I would
sit and sew and listen enraptured with their ideas and gaiety
and enthusiasm. Edward came to this garden once or twice,
and was one of the best of the talkers.

This artist had designed for me a beautiful dress, which
Beatrice made for me. It was of my favourite flame colour,

61

and was embroidered in blue, and the coat was lined with blue silk. She was a very clever dressmaker, and I was delighted with it, and kept it to surprise Edward with on our wedding day, which was now very near. We had very little money, for we were carefully hoarding the £250, and so we were glad to find a shop where we could buy a wedding ring for eight shillings.

In June we were married. Janet and her husband and one or two of our Hammersmith friends came to the register office.

Very soon after this things became rather complicated. Beatrice's divorce was coming on, and she was giving up for a time the house in Hammersmith, and Edward and I did not quite know what to do. Janet and her husband invited me to stay with them, and as it was Edward's vacation, during which he was reading hard, he stayed at home. The Hootons lived in a flat near the Crystal Palace, and there I went with my few belongings. I was very sorry indeed to leave Beatrice and the friends I had made there, and I believe they were sorry, too. With some of them I kept in touch for many years, but others I did not see again. In their various ways they became well known, and I was glad when I saw their names in appreciative notices.

This visit to the Hootons was to be only temporary – I had quite other plans. I wanted more than anything to be out in the country, and with my little capital it seemed to be quite easy. Edward also desired this for me and himself for we hoped that we should be able to be together in his vacations.

I had, years ago at Broadstairs, met a nurse who lived, I knew, at Esher. I had made friends with her, and she had said that if ever I had a baby she would be my nurse. So to her I went. My idea was to take rooms in a cottage in Esher – which was then a pretty little village – and so be near her when my time came. Here Edward could come, and here when he was at Oxford I could occupy my time in reading and sewing and walking, and writing my daily letter to him. Edward and I went there one afternoon and met the nurse, who recommended us to just the rooms we wanted. The cottage had a clear view of the downs, and the two rooms were neat and clean and simple. The front door opened into the sitting-room, and the bedroom was above it. The rooms were real cottage rooms, not of the furnished lodging type, and the woman was a nice motherly creature of about thirty-five, with one little boy. We took an instant liking to each other, and she was interested in our affairs, and quite willing for my baby to be born there.

Edward, though so reserved and quiet, always got on well with simple, natural people. I don't quite know what it was that attracted them to him: whether it was his looks, or the quiet humour that these people always brought out in him – or whether it was the instinctive knowledge of his love for the earth, and those racy, natural qualities which are so near the earth – that made them feel at home with him at once. But there it was – we were soon chatting together in her kitchen, hung round with coloured prints of famous race-horses, for her husband was a stableman in the racing stables near by, and her little boy was destined to be a jockey. So we left mightily pleased with our day's work, and I all agog to move into my new home.

As yet neither Edward's people nor mine had any knowledge of our union, and I wished very much that they need not know till my baby was born. I knew that directly our secret was out all sorts of things would rush in and disturb the wonderful and happy calm, and this I dreaded. So far Edward and I had never had to explain or justify ourselves to anyone, and to each other there had been no thought of such a thing. What would be thought queer by others was just natural and right for us. Our cottage woman took it all without comment or question; but I knew it would not be so with others. Edward would be blamed for my sake, I for his, and both for the baby's. Our affairs would all be put under the microscope and distorted, and all would at the best be 'queer', and the worst wicked. I thought if we could only wait until my baby was born there would be nothing to discuss. Our parents would accept a living baby in a way they could not

63

accept my being pregnant, and Edward a married under-
graduate. They would fall into my living alone at Esher till
Edward left Oxford the easier when I was firmly established
there. A hint of all this had been given us by the Hootons,
who thought the Esher scheme quite mad.

I had no reasons to bring to people in support of my desire
for the country and the continuation of our blessed isolation
from the jangle and confusion of family discussion, and so I
was soon argued into acceptance. Edward who did not, could
not, share my calm happiness, was eager to listen to the advice
of our friends as to what was best, the more so because dimly
he perceived that I had withdrawn into an inner room of my
spirit, into which no one, not even he, could enter. A cocoon
had, as it were, spun itself about me, and secretly inside I
waited. So all the more he felt things must be arranged for
me and action taken. His parents were told, and his mother
at once came over to see me, and could not have been kinder.
She at once accepted me as her daughter, and though she
regarded it all as a disaster she uttered no blame or reproach.
I was very touched by her sad acceptance of it all, and her
concern for me. As I had feared, she would not hear of my
being alone at Esher, but insisted that I should come to live
with them. I appreciated the kind consideration of this, but I
was terribly disappointed that the Esher plan had to be aban-
doned. However, so it was, and it did not seem to matter.
My sanctuary was still inviolate.

My own mother behaved very differently. We had always
been antagonistic, and all I could feel during the scenes which
took place was sorrow that she should have had such an uncon-
genial daughter, and a certain relief that at last we knew with-
out any reserves at all that we were strangers speaking different
tongues. I wrote to my sisters. From the youngest I got a very
sweet letter saying she had always hoped to be an aunt, and
though disapproving, still warm and affectionate. This letter
touched and pleased me very much.

So I again moved my home and went to live with the
Thomases, in conditions the exact opposite to anything I had

wanted. Only Mrs Thomas's generous kindness, which even her deep reserve and sadness could not hide, made the prospect tolerable. I was reintroduced to Edward's brothers as their new sister. I helped in the house, though a big strong Welsh woman did not leave much to be done. The huge batches of bread and cakes that she baked every Friday amazed me, as did the huge joints of meat that were carved by their mother for the boys. I got on very well with them all, though the atmosphere was very uncongenial to me – Mr Thomas, when not at his office, wrapt up in his studies, and quite unsympathetic towards his boys, who openly despised him; Mrs Thomas, reserved and sad, suffering for lack of any social life, devoted to her boys, who were strangers to her. How different it was from my own home life before my father's death, so united, so jolly, so varied; or from Beatrice's household, where freedom and tolerance and sympathy overwhelmed the fierce Bohemianism. But I was well and happy. The chilling atmosphere of the house, created, I suppose, by the strange disharmony of everyone in it, could not chill me, though it was entirely foreign to me, and would have been painful to me had I not been irradiated by my love and my secret joy. The boys, after the first surprise and curiosity, accepted me, and were in their way fond of me, and I of them. They, with their rough ways, their comings and goings, no one knew where, their seeming indifference to their parents, the entire absence of communion even with each other, surprised and puzzled me. I helped with huge piles of mending, and in the evening after the last meal, if Mr Thomas was not going to a political meeting or a lecture, he and Mrs Thomas and I would sit in the little sitting-room, and I would sew my baby clothes, and Mr Thomas would read aloud. If he went out, Mrs Thomas and I did not read, but talked together as intimately as it was possible with so shy and reserved a woman. I never really penetrated that reserve of hers; sometimes I thought I had, when my happiness overflowed and gave me courage to take her by storm, and kiss her and tease her, and tell her how pretty she was, for she still bore traces of having been a lovely girl. So I would, perhaps, be able to coax her out of her shell for a little while, but soon she would turn away with a sigh and shut me out again.

The day which she and I in our different ways looked forward to was the day Edward came back from Oxford. Edward and his mother understood and loved each other. He of all her sons was like her. He was like her in looks and temperament; for though he needed and loved my impulsive and demonstrative nature, these qualities were foreign to him as they were to her. This reserve and melancholy grew as he grew. Now, overwhelmed by the high hopes and the passion of youth, I had no more than caught glimpses of it, but in after years it became at times a darkness about his soul which I could not enter, nor my love light.

While I was with the Thomases he came home for his vacation twice, but it is the December one that I particularly remember. Ann made a great doughy cake, I helping to knead the currants and sugar and butter into the dough; and I cleaned and polished our room at the top of the house. As the time got near for his arrival I sat down by the fire in the little old rocking-chair, with the kettle on the hob and the tea-things ready, and even the slices of bread cut ready for the hot buttered toast. At last I heard his cab drive up, and the bang of the street door, and the murmur of voices for what seemed a long time, and then his step on the staircase – great steps taking two stairs each time. For one panic-stricken moment I wondered would he realize that by now I was very big, and then he was in the room and I in his arms. Then with his old, lovely gesture he pushed the hair from my forehead and looked into my eyes and said, 'Happy?' and I nodded, no words coming for my great happiness. Then we had tea, at which his mother joined us, afraid she was intruding though we insisted she was not. She did not know what to make of it when I told Edward I knew my baby was a boy – he kicked so – and Edward put his hand where he could feel him moving so strongly. I asked him if he had expected to see me so big, and he said, 'No, not quite so large and proud – but it suits her, doesn't it, Mother? and her face is still round and pink. I've got a present for you

66

– I don't know what you'll do with it, but it has such a beautiful name, and looked so lovely in the shop, it reminded me of those cowslips – do you remember? I thought you could make something out of it – a little jacket for when you are in bed perhaps.'

Then he showed me a length of crêpe-de-Chine. It was quite a new material then, and I had never handled it before. It was heavy and soft and rich, and in the folds it glowed deep golden. He held it against my face, and said it suited my dark brown hair and eyes. Mrs Thomas was pleased and shocked at his extravagance, and sighed because life would not always be like that for us. I was delighted with the beautiful stuff, and thought I could never bear to cut it. But most of all I loved to think of Edward's going into the shop and buying this costly silk for me because it reminded him of those cowslips.

Our life was very quiet and uneventful. We walked on the Common every day, and sometimes got as far as our beloved Wimbledon Common, for I still felt very well and active, and walking with him was my greatest pleasure. Indoors he had a good deal of reading and writing to do, for he had a certain amount of regular reviewing. While he worked, I sat in the little chair and sewed or read. But when I think of this time it is chiefly those teas by the fire that I remember, and later, when Edward turned out the lamp, and the fire still glowed red, we lay in bed talking of our life together, and our baby, and Edward's work, until with his arm round me, and me holding his thumb tight in my fist, we fell asleep.

During this vacation I met one of Edward's Oxford friends, E.S.P. Haynes. He was a Balliol Scholar, and though very different, Edward and he became very friendly, and Edward wanted me to meet him. So we met in Hyde Park. He was a brilliant talker and experienced in things of which I had no knowledge. But I got on quite well with him, and he liked me, and we were all easy together. His cynicism disturbed me. Still I was so interested in people that I did not dislike him for it. I thought it strange for him to say things which I felt sure he did not feel. I had not heard this kind of talk before, and I was puzzled by it, taking it seriously, as I did everything. Humour I was familiar with, and could understand and enjoy, but this sharp, cold wit was different, and I had to learn to appreciate that. To me he was kind and courteous, though I expect he was amused by my grave talk; and his evident affection and admiration of Edward quite won my heart, and Edward was well pleased with this, my first introduction to his Oxford friends.

Christmas passed and January came. I had nothing left to do. All my baby clothes were made and arranged neatly in the drawer, the cradle was covered with white muslin and made ready for its occupant, with frilled pillow and fleecy blankets and blue eiderdown. I could only wait, and began to wonder anxiously if my baby would be born before Edward had to return to Oxford. The serenity that nothing had been able to disturb during these nine months began to give way to impatience and a sort of excited activity. We still went for our daily walks, but indoors I could not now sit and read, but for ever had to be arranging and rearranging the room and the baby's things in the drawer. My baby lay quiet, and I felt lonely. As before I had felt alone with my joy, so now I felt alone with this strange excitement; but whereas before I had been content in my solitude, now my spirit as it were paced backwards and forwards, impatiently resentful of this loneliness which shut it in like a cage.

# 5

But I had not long to wait. The New Year was still quite new when one night I woke up and knew that at last my baby was making ready for his mysterious entrance into life. I held my breath and waited, for I was not quite sure what it was that had wakened me, and conveyed to me so surely that my time was come.

It came again – a small, sharp pain. For a little while I lay quite still, too moved by its significance to turn and speak to Edward by my side. I must be quiet while with my baby – he in the dark mystery of my body, and I in the dark mystery of my soul – our bond, and the breaking of that bond made manifest by the small, sharp pain that came again.

I felt his shape in my great belly, and closed my eyes in the darkness, that in such double dark I might see him as I had so often seen him thus, turning and trying his strength, and beating against the tender wall of his prison. He did not strive now, but lay quiet and expectant under my wildly beating heart.

My breasts for days had been big with milk, which, running out and trickling over my body, made me laugh to think of his greediness. For by all that waste of milk I knew he would be a boy and greedy, and I was glad.

Again the sign.

My thoughts wandered happily to the night he was conceived. I remembered it was a warm, still evening in May, and the stars were very high and very small, and there was no moon. The air was full of the smell of spring, the rich, cool, fresh spring-earth and young foliage and flowers giving up their essence into the air. The birch trees and young oaks and hazel of the copse were full of birds, which woke and fluttered a bit and then slept again. We lay upon dog's mercury and last year's beech leaves just shed. I remembered the walk back by the river to Hammersmith, and my secret that I could not speak of. In my mind I went over all the months of pregnancy that were now at an end. I had had nothing to disturb the tranquillity of my soul – no bodily distress, no fear, no weariness – happy in a strange solitude that I could share with no one, and was content not to share. I was so glad of my strong, proud body. My pretty breasts and my slim hips I saw losing their shapeliness, but the emotion I felt was one of joy, not fear.

I knew I must keep my body strong and healthy, so that it should not fail my baby in any way. This was the final consummation of my bridal.

I remembered all the sweet times during those months – my walks with Edward – the sewing times in the evening when he had read to me. I remembered that moment when I had felt first my baby's life stirring within me. Like a bird caught in the hand, he fluttered in my womb, and my heart, filled with joy and wonder and love beating so near him, spoke to him secretly unutterable things. I remembered the times when I had arranged and refolded and busied myself needlessly with my baby's clothes. The cradle was ready, the basket, too, and the pile of white napkins. I wondered if I had everything he would need.

The sign again.

I woke Edward and told him. He kissed me sleepily, and drew me into the hollow of his arm, and we fell asleep till morning.

The morning came, a cold winter morning. I woke feeling as I used to when a child on my birthday morning, or on the morning when we were going away to the seaside. Something was going to happen that I had been counting up the days for. What was it? I had forgotten. But my baby had not slept: he was impatient to be out, and the sign was so sharp this time that it made me catch my breath. Edward was in his bath – I got hurried and flustered and called him to be quick and let me have mine, for the pain now was so sharp, and seemed so impatient that it excited and unnerved me. Everything before had been so slow, so calm; this was a new and unexpected note; I could not at once attune myself to it.

I bathed and dressed as quickly as I could, the pain speeding me with its insistence. My baby called me and I must hurry to him, but how? when? Edward, tying his tie at the mirror, saw my face reflected in it, and came and held me against him, and when I felt his body tremble my panic fled and I was calm again.

I ran downstairs to tell Mrs Thomas, and met Ann, who disapproved of the bother of a confinement in the house; so all she said was, 'Ye'll be worse afore ye be better.' But I was not to be frightened out of my calm any more.

Edward had arranged that day – it was Sunday – to go for a long country walk with the Oxford friend I had met, and when he came I insisted that they should keep to their plan. So they went, sending a telegram to my nurse on the way. In a few hours she arrived, greatly to the surprise of Edward's youngest brother, Julian, to whom his mother refused to tell the reason of the capped and aproned stranger who took no notice of him.

I remember standing at the door of our room and seeing it with a new vision – this attic reaching over the whole house, with a large old-fashioned fireplace with hobs at each side, on which a copper kettle always stood. It had a sloping roof, and a dormer window at each end. Half of it was Edward's study, and our sitting-room, where his books, his fishing rods, his clay pipes and walking-sticks were kept, and where he wrote and read, and I had spent such happy hours sewing and reading and dreaming. The other half was our bedroom, with the big bed, the bow-fronted chest of drawers, the low rocking-chair, and the large semi-circular dressing-table with a muslin petticoat round it. On the floor was an old faded carpet that had once been gay with bunches of impossible flowers. In the study part was a huge arm-chair that we had bought for the Esher rooms, a replica of one that Edward had at Oxford. On the mantelpiece were the brass candlesticks I had given him for his birthday, his tobacco jar, and a miniature of his mother as a young and beautiful girl. The pictures in the study were two old silhouettes of Welsh ancestors above the plain oak table, which served as a desk; a large photograph of the Vénus Accroupie, which Richard Jefferies so much admired; an old rather ribald ballad, with a coloured picture at the top, which we used to sing to a jolly tune; and a funny old painting on glass of Tintern Abbey. In the bedroom part was a large coloured reproduction of Botticelli's Primavera, and his round Virgin and Child, and a water-colour drawing of my father.

I had always loved this room, and on that day every detail of it imprinted itself on my mind for ever. I was content that it should be the birth-room of my first-born.

On an oak chest which Edward had made, near to the fireplace, stood the cradle. Round the huge fire on a fireguard I hung a complete set of baby clothes to air. If I had been laying an offering on the altar of my God, I could not have felt a deeper ecstasy than in that simple act. It was humbleness, pride, joy, wonder, tenderness and seriousness, combined into an overwhelming emotion, lifting my soul nearer truth than it had ever been before, or ever will be again. I cannot recall what I thought, but I believe in that moment I took on my motherhood.

The pain came fiercer and more often now, but I was full of restless energy. I went up and down stairs, and went down to lunch, and read aloud to Julian, who begged me to finish the chapter in *Treasure Island* I had begun the day before. Mrs Thomas brought tea up to our room, and we had a sort of picnic round the fire, she and nurse talking of practical matters, but I was lost to all but my own excitement, which not even the pain could subdue. I must be doing, my soul was singing and free, my body must respond however foolishly. The fierceness of the pain stopped me in all I began; I had to hold on to anything stable, and when I looked at Mrs Thomas's face I saw pity there. But she could not speak of her feeling to me, and I was glad she could not.

I wanted to be alone with this fierce exultation of pain. My spirit sang in triumph after each paroxysm, but my body was like a dead weight on it. I only knew that my baby and I were struggling for him to be born. He could not go back to his quiet darkness. All was changed. He had begun his perilous journey to life – I must speed him and help him; keep him with all the strength of my body and all the strength of my desire for him, pressed forwards towards the light where his soul waited for him. I did not think this, but dimly perceived it was so.

I cling to the bed, and feel that the pain is overwhelming me. I must not let it. Nurse comes to hold me. 'No, don't touch me; go to the fire; I can smell the baby things scorching.' So by trivial ways I try to keep in touch with reality. My few garments are unbearable. I try to undress, but become confused as the waves of pain break over me, making consciousness more and more difficult to retain. But I will not let my spirit be drowned. I will not lose touch with my baby. I have a feeling that if I let go my hold on consciousness I shall be leaving him alone.

Nurse says a word of praise and encouragement, which gives me confidence in myself again. I shiver as I lie on the bed, but I use every ounce of effort and strength when the paroxysm comes, and feel again the triumphant exultation. My body labours, but my spirit is free. My baby and I are struggling to be rid of each other. That strange, secret link must be broken. He must be himself apart from me, and I must give him to mankind.

My body is seized by a new strangely expelling pain. I am again terribly alone – a primitive creature, without thought, without desire, without anything but this instinct to rid my womb of what encumbers it. I hear voices far away; I feel hands about me, but I am not I; I am only an elemental instinctive force bringing forth after its kind.

A pain more rending than all bears me on its crest into utter darkness. A cry, a strange unearthly cry strikes piteously at my heart, and pierces my darkness. My consciousness strives towards that cry, my soul recognizes it. It is my baby's cry, and it leads my spirit away from the dark back to the light.

Someone says 'A fine boy,' and I, wearily, 'Is he all right?' They say 'A perfect child.' Then blessed rest and content – not unconsciousness, but just a sense of fulfilment, with no remembrance of pain, nor even of the baby, who is silent.

They say 'Here is your husband,' and I hear them tell him I have been brave, and I hear his voice low and tender speaking to them or me – I do not know whom – I am too tired to listen, and when he bends over me to kiss me I cannot open my lips or my eyes for weariness. But I can smell the violets he puts on my pillow.

I don't know how long I lie like that, but after a while they give me my boy. I see he has Edward's fair hair and blue eyes, and I am glad; but his nose is small like mine; his ears are like his father's, and covered with soft, fine down. His tiny fingers clasp my finger. His eyes are wide open: what does he see as he moves his head from side to side? The light of the winter dawn fills the room; his eyes unblinkingly seek the window, not with wonder as one coming from darkness, but as if in this strangeness the light alone is not strange.

Suddenly the realization of life and of all that may separate us comes to me, and I hold him close. I want him still to be all my own. His eyes close, and he nuzzles against my breast, and with his groping mouth finds my nipple. He is soft and warm and sweet. As he draws the warm milk from me, and I feel that mysterious pleasure half spiritual, half physical, I realize that the link between us is imperishable. I am for ever his mother and he my son.

# TWO

## *World Without End*

# 1

Two days after our baby was born Edward had to return to Oxford for his last term. My memory of this period is not very vivid but on looking at letters that I wrote to Edward I see that they are full of unalloyed happiness. They are full of the baby's ways and development and of my joy in him; but fuller still of my passionate love for Edward and of the longing to be together continually when he should leave Oxford. Interwoven with this and occurring again and again in these letters is the longing for the country.

When I was strong enough I would often take the child in his pram to our beloved Wimbledon Common – a very long way to push a heavy infant – and if I could not get so far I had to be content with Clapham Common. In those days there were still large old-fashioned houses standing in acres of gardens – the country houses of bygone city merchants – falling into decay. These gardens were a source of great pleasure to me, and looking over the broken palings I sought eagerly for signs of spring flowers. I remember, on seeing the first snowdrops under the bushes of a wild over-grown garden, I held the baby up to see them, and picked sprays of young leaves and perhaps an isolated celandine for him to hold, so ardently did I feel the need for him to come into contact with the earth, and even in the hideous suburb in which he was born, to become aware of beauty.

But sometimes when the weather was good we would venture as far as Wimbledon. This meant a long and tiring hill walk; so I would take some food and sewing with me and make a day of it. I was not content until we had reached the remoter parts of the common, where no one ever came, where the grass was untrodden and from where the wilder and more timid birds had not been driven away. Here he – with his

77

napkins unloosed – could lie on the grass and stretch his limbs in the sun. I could not read or sew for watching his eyes as they opened wide with wonder to see the chequered pattern of the sky through the leaves, and his hands held up to catch the far-off fluttering things. I made him pick flowers before his baby fingers could do anything but feebly grasp, and in this way he picked a little bunch of flowers for his father: and finding a trail of bryony, I made him pick a leaf of what had been my bridal wreath. I talked to him, before words meant anything to him but the sound of a familiar voice, of flowers and birds and of spring; or sitting by his side while he cooed or slept I wrote my letter to Edward, sending the flowers we had picked. Sometimes I would take him to the pond and dabble his toes in the water, and this he liked so much that he cried when I took him out. But his griefs were easily soothed by my suckling or singing to him, and as he drew the milk from me while he spread his little fingers over my breast I experienced that wonderful pleasure half-physical, half-spiritual which makes it an ecstasy.

On these days when I could get so far I was especially happy, for I felt that I was giving him something that it was urgently important he should have, and his obvious pleasure in his surroundings – the moving trees, the bright flowers and the touch of the cool grass and the sweet untainted air – gave me a deep content. And these little excursions away from streets and houses, noise and ugliness renewed and refreshed me too. Edward especially welcomed the letters written under these conditions, for my happiness reacted on him, and the blessing of the place fell on us all.

# 2

Edward's letters to me during this period show how often a terrible cloud of melancholy brooded over his spirit, and how at these times he depended wholly on me and on my joy, to be a perpetual spring to stimulate and gladden him. When now I read his letters to me and mine to him side by side, I wonder that I could have kept that joyous happiness flowing from my heart; for over and over again his letters were full of the deepest dejection. But only very, very rarely did I let anything dam what for him was this necessary life-giving stream, and over and over again my heart must have been overwhelmed with delight because of the passionate words of love and gratitude which were my reward.

What a strange dissimilarity there was in our lives then! Edward at Oxford, one of a set of brilliant young intellectuals, entertaining, debating, drinking, rowing for his college, working for his degree. All this was a new experience to him, though he never forsook his love of nature which took him long walks in the Oxford country, and in which he found the content and satisfaction that nothing else gave him, and I, an unsophisticated girl, knowing nothing of such a life except what Edward's letters told me, cut off from any social inter-course, living in that hateful suburb, but because of my lover and my child and all that life seemed to hold for me feeling the joy and ecstasy of life to the uttermost. Nothing clouded my happiness. I felt strong enough to overcome all difficulties, and with my eagle wings of love to bear my lover into my own heights.

About this time Edward had a party in his rooms to celebrate the birth of his son. He bought a pewter drinking cup, and each member of the party engraved on it some motto appro-priate to drinking and to life, and also his name. Some of the party wrote to me congratulating me, and the friend I had met before Merfyn's birth undertook the duties of a godfather, and presented the baby with a Bible inscribed with flippant verses. The occasion was unique, I suppose, and a good opportunity for the display of wit and philosophy, and I enjoyed reading about it in Edward's letters after the event. As was natural, his work suffered a good deal during this last term, and it was no surprise to Edward, though a bitter disappointment to his father, when he got only a second-class degree. This, and the natural antagonism of their natures, made life at his home – when he returned from Oxford – no longer possible. Even I, to whom outside circumstances mattered so little, had begun to feel the strain of living in that uncongenial atmosphere. It was not long before an open break occurred between Edward and his father, and we looked about for somewhere else to live.

We were very poor. The £250 which we had been depending on was almost gone, and the essays Edward contributed to one or two literary weeklies had earned only about £80 during the year. But Edward with his tall graceful figure and handsome sensitive face, wearing the elegantly negligent and for him very becoming style of dress of the young aesthete of the day, did not at all look the part of the impecunious husband and father, and Mr Thomas's puritanism rose almost in hatred against his son. Edward on his side did nothing to placate his father's anger and intolerance, and refused to consider going into the Civil Service, and only answered his father's bitter anger with sneers at those very qualities which Mr Thomas most prided himself upon. With Mrs Thomas it was different. She was no doubt troubled by this new phase in her son, and his circumstances must have been a continual source of anxiety to her, but she had always a far wider outlook on life than her husband, and a generous tolerance and sympathy for the young, which she now extended during this difficult time to Edward. Indeed there was a spiritual understanding between these two which though never expressed, and by his mother hardly recognized, was never violated, but was sustained in growing intensity to the end of Edward's life.

As I could not go house-hunting it fell to Edward to find a new home for us. He found, in a new street in what was obviously doomed to become a slum, a half-house of which the rent was seven and sixpence a week, and to this we moved. It had a good sitting-room which, very much to the builder's surprise, we chose to have distempered a warm grey; a bedroom which just held our bed, the child's cot and a chest of drawers; and a little kitchen with steps leading from it to a tiny squalid back-yard, used by the downstairs people for keeping ramshackle rabbit hutches and hanging out washing which was always wet and never clean. There was a notice printed in the rent book which at first puzzled me – 'Broken windows must be repaired by the tenant,' but we had not been there a week before we understood the significance of this regulation. The downstairs people frightened me rather because of their way of moving out in the middle of the night. Very seldom did the downstairs tenants stay longer than a fortnight, because, as I heard later, they could not be sued for rent under a fortnight's tenancy. Sometimes they were quiet, but more often noisy, quarrelsome, rough men and women and pale dirty children, often with a poor frightened dog tied up to a barrel in the back yard. All were terribly poor and degraded.

Here we lived for a few months. During that time Edward was out a great deal looking for work, going from one editor's office to another, sending in his card; sometimes being received courteously and sometimes not; sometimes given a book to review or the half-promise to accept an article. He returned from these dreadful expeditions tired and depressed and angry, hating himself for his failure, hating the polite indifference of some of the people, hating more the sympathetic interest which others, who refused him work, put into their voices. But a few there were who were not indifferent to the reserved, shy, sensitive young man, who looked so proudly careless of their favour, and who refused to ingratiate himself, but whose heart was full of angry humiliation and despair. One stands out among the rest as coming out to meet Edward with friendly understanding from which the hint of patronage was entirely absent. He was the literary editor of a great daily newspaper whose literary page was written by men of distinction, and earned for its editor a great name in journalism. This man was attracted to Edward by the very qualities which others had found so disconcerting, and divined by his sympathetic understanding of Edward's austere sincerity the intellectual power in him. He became our friend and benefactor. The work which he gave Edward was the mainstay of our life for many years, and Edward made, on that page, a name for himself as a critic of belles lettres, and particularly of contemporary verse. His name was H.W. Nevinson.

How anxiously I waited for Edward's homecoming on these days, and how with the first glance at his face I knew what the day had been. If it had been a bad one there was no need of words, and none were uttered. I could do nothing, for if I said one word which would betray that I knew what he had endured and was enduring, his anger and despair and weariness would break out in angry bitter words which would freeze my heart and afterwards freeze his for having uttered them. So as he ate the evening meal in silence, I talked quietly about the doings of the day, of the baby, of the walk we had been; and soon in our pretty room he would lie back in his big Oxford chair by the fire, smoking his pipe, while I sat on a stool near and sewed; and gradually the weariness would go out of his face, and the hard thin line of his mouth would relax to its lovely curve, and he would speak of an essay that had been suggested to him by something he had seen in London, or of a notable volume of poems that Nevinson had promised he should review for the *Daily Chronicle*. Then I would slip from my stool to the floor between his knees, and he would put out his hand and rest it on my neck, and I would know that the cloud had passed.

But sometimes when his spirit had been more than usually affected by the too great strain that his circumstances put upon it, the cloud did not pass, and my chatter ran dry in the arid silence. After a ghastly hour or two with the supper still uneaten on the kitchen table he would say: 'Go to bed, I'm not coming,' and I would know that he would sit up all night, and in the morning would be deeper in despair than ever – or he would go out and walk till morning, and perhaps from the silence of night and from the natural sounds of early dawn, and from the peace of solitude and the beauty of intangible things he would find healing and calm. I did not sleep on these nights but took my baby into bed with me, and in suckling him and holding him close, hope and comfort came to me again.

Some days Edward would be at home all day writing and reading, happy and eager with the impulse for creative work which gave him greater satisfaction that anything else. If the weather was fine he would break off his work in the afternoon and putting Merfyn in his pram we would set out for Wimbledon or Richmond Park, somewhere where we could sit on grass and look at trees and clouds and hear birds. There the baby would play himself to sleep while Edward read a book for review, or aloud to me, and we would return in the evening laden with flowers and branches of leaves or berries for our room. Some of the days at home were idle and hopeless – no commissioned work to do, and no impulse for original work – and on these days the squalid surroundings obtruded upon our spirits, and the harsh voices of the other tenants and the crying of children sounded inhuman like the sounds of hell. One of these days I remember very well. I had not got into the routine of housework and looking after the baby, and I asked Edward to peel the potatoes for the mid-day meal. This he angrily refused to do. But at dinner he praised my cooking, and I, still hurt by his unkindness, could not restrain a few tears at the welcome change of mood. Seeing my distress he jumped up from his chair, ran down the stairs into the street, and returned in two minutes with a bottle of cheap wine. Never was so homely a meal turned into such a joyous banquet. Even the baby sitting in his high chair joined in, for Edward dipping his finger in the wine let Merfyn suck it, and though he looked more surprised than pleased at the taste, he grinned at the joke when he saw us laughing.

Often we were quite reckless with money. Once when a cheque was bigger than we had expected we bought a beautiful and costly brass lamp made in the William Morris workshops. At other times we were so poor that when Edward was out for several successive days I lived on the remains of a Christmas pudding Mrs Thomas had given us. But I was strong and healthy, and both my baby whom I was nursing and I flourished.

It was a queer hand-to-mouth way of living, but when we had enough money we entertained our friends and had many evenings of lively talk with beer and pipes as the inevitable accompaniment. In this way I met some of the Oxford friends who had written to me, especially three or four whose friendship for Edward lasted all his life, and was extended to me after his death. These young men brought others with them, and I looked forward to these evenings when our room was full of eager talkers and lively wits who were all about our own age, and all enthusiastic adventurers into life.

When we had not enough money for anything else we lived on bread and cheese and tea. I remember having only ninepence one Saturday to buy provisions for the weekend. It is the only time in my life I have bought a pennyworth of butter.

Yet little by little Edward's work was increasing, and before we left London he had published his first volume of essays for which he got a small sum on account of royalties. This volume still sells a few copies a year.

# 3

The squalid surroundings affected Edward much more than me, though I, who had spent my life in towns, had always dreamed of life in the country, and longed to be in the country in spring. My happiness depended much more on people than on circumstances, and when Edward was free from care, and he and Merfyn and I were together, I wanted nothing more. But now my longing for a country life was intensified by the feeling which Edward and I had that the child must grow up in the freedom and beauty of the English countryside, and we made up our minds to move as soon as we could find somewhere to go.

The irksome task of house hunting devolved upon Edward, and he and one of his brothers set off on bicycles into Kent. They spent several days away, but wrote that they could find nothing that we could afford in a neighbourhood that satisfied Edward. He returned tired and dispirited, so that I was surprised when he told me he had found a house that would do. It was in a lovely part of Kent and was called Rose Acre, and in spite of Edward's denial of any sort of beauty in the house I pictured a sort of replica of our honeymoon cottage. Edward kept saying as I grew excited in talking of it:

'I know you'll be disappointed, it's not a bit what you imagine it.'

But I said: 'It's got such a lovely name, I know just what it is like.'

So packing up our belongings, which were mostly books, we left London for ever.

I shall never forget my first sight of Rose Acre. I could not at first believe that this was indeed the house that I must exchange for my dream cottage. It was a square box built of bright red brick, with slate roof and four uninteresting windows and a cheap stained-glass door in the middle. It stood nakedly on the top of a little hill in a railed-off piece of rough ground, untidy and bare and uncultivated, full of couch-grass and the ranker kinds of weeds. Inside there was a narrow passage with a room on each side papered with hideous red paper. Nothing could have been more unlike what I had imagined; my spirits sank at the sight of it, and I had difficulty in keeping tears out of my eyes. Edward, too, knowing what I was feeling was depressed and angry, angry with himself for having taken such an uncongenial house, and angry with me for having had such romantic ideas of it. He at once began putting up his book-shelves and unpacking the books, and after I had lighted fires and put Merfyn to bed, and we had boiled the kettle, and discussed the planning of the rooms, my spirits rose.

The house faced south, and in front was a little copse of hazels on the other side of the lane. At the back the land sloped down to the village and the railway, and then rose again in the steep dark yew-clad sides of the North Downs whose ridge, west and east, ran as far as we could see. On the left of the house was a large cherry orchard, in which a little later on the cuckoos were to call to each other in different keys all day long, and the foam of the cherry blossom to be blown into drifts, and where later still, in spite of the boy with a rattle walking from dawn to sunset under the laden trees, the blackbirds would sing and scream and eat the forbidden fruit. But of all this I as yet knew nothing, and I could only try to bury my dream cottage away, and accept this so different reality.

Edward was busy in the room that was to be his study, and Merfyn was asleep in the new bare room upstairs, while I washed up the supper things and arranged the cups and plates on the dresser. The kitchen led out directly into the garden, and when I had done my work I stood in the doorway emptying my heart of disappointment and sadness. The dusk was falling, and the dew-wet earth and all the newly born green of spring filled the air with scent, and as I leaned against the door I took in a deep breath. The sweet freshness of it filled

me with joy, and again and again I breathed deeply to experi-
ence an elation, as from a magic draught, that I had never felt
before. I stooped down and took up a handful of earth and
crumbling it let it fall through my fingers. Its harsh touch and
its pungent clean smell thrilled me with a new awareness. My
eyes were opened to the beauty of the night, to the dark ridge
of the downs against the cloudless blue sky, where now stars
appeared like pebbles dropped from above. Away to the east
was a radiance where soon the moon would rise, and a soft
wind as of ushering voices stirred on the hill side. A white
owl flew past me silently like a ghost, and like the cry of a
ghost sounded its quavering note from the elm tree at the end
of the garden. The cherry trees thick with pendulous buds
breathed – as it were – softly in sleep. The slender moon rising
timidly above the trees laid her spell on the earth, and all was
silence and darkness and sleep. On me too she laid her spell.
I turned to go to Edward, and met him coming towards me.

'There's a new moon,' he said; 'you must wish.'

'There's nothing left to wish for,' I said; 'we are in the
country and it is spring.'

We were about a mile from the village of Bearsted which
lay at the foot of the North Downs. It is a most attractive little
place built round a large green. The church with its strangely
gargoyled tower is at one corner with the vicarage, and a
beautiful manor house encloses the south side. At another
corner is the pond where the cows, grazing on the green, drink
or stand on hot summer days, ruminating and looking at the
ducks who swim about among them. On the north side with
their back gardens running down to the railway are the smithy
and the wheelwright and the baker all occupying lovely old
workshops and houses. There are two inns – 'The Black Swan'
and 'The Lion'. 'The Black Swan' is the only new building
near the green and is ugly and incongruous among a thicket
of yews and beeches where often I was to hear the nightingale
sing. Near this inn was the station on the main road mounting
up to join the important Maidstone and Ashford road. The
road up our hill took us past the pond and the grounds of the

manor house. The Lion Inn at the other side of the green was an old half-timbered house with uneven roof ridge, and windows in unexpected places, and low, dim, panelled rooms inside, where beer was served in pewter pots, and where in winter the bar parlour, with its brick floor, and great oak settles each side of the fireplace, was bright and cosy with a huge fire of logs. Mr Tompsett the innkeeper became a friend of ours. He was a splendid gardener as well as host, and helped us with advice and presents of cuttings for our garden.

We made the house as pretty as we could, though I never liked it. Edward's study, which was also the sitting-room, became homely and comfortable with the books and our more precious possessions, and for the kitchen I had an affection, chiefly because of the view of the downs and the yews which marked the Pilgrims' Way. I spent many hours at the table under the window ironing or sewing or cooking, and Merfyn sitting in his high chair near me would amuse himself by banging on its deal top with a wooden spoon, or turning over the pages of a linen scrap-book I had made for him, and pointing with his fat finger at the picture for me to name, for he was very late in learning to talk, and his double Dutch became so expressive and I understood it so well that I began to be afraid he would never learn proper speech. He was at this time a splendidly healthy boy, with a mop of loose golden curls, and blue eyes, lively and intelligent and a great joy to us.

The friends who had so often spent evenings with us in our London slum soon found their way here, and the house was often full at the weekends. Edward would go to the station to meet them, and I would stay behind to finish a batch of cakes. Merfyn and I would hear the train run in and in a few minutes we would see Edward and our friends coming up the lane that was a short cut to the station. Then I would whip off my apron and Merfyn's overall, take the cakes out of the oven, put on the kettle and spread the cloth on the kitchen table – for we had meals there – and be just in time to meet them at the gate. I looked forward to these times, and the extra work they made was richly rewarded by the talks and walks and the friendly way in which everyone accepted our simple way of living. I had felt very timid at first on meeting these clever young men, but after a while I got more confident, finding that when I was natural and myself I was able to contribute something to the general atmosphere which was welcomed and expected. These were great days, and other days too there were when Edward was happy and eager and would take Merfyn on his shoulders, and I carrying the lunch, we would go to Thurnam Castle on top of the Downs, or to some lovely spot along the Pilgrims' Way. There we would spend the day, Merfyn playing in the grass and sleeping when he was tired; Edward reading to me, or going off for a little walk by himself – while I sewed – returning with something for Merfyn – a rare orchid, or a large striped Roman snail shell, or a piece of strangely shaped flint. Then down again in the evening and back to Rose Acre which after such a day of sweet content would look welcoming and homely.

But many of the days were saddened for us by Edward's anxiety, and by that melancholy which had its roots in no material circumstances, but came to cloud his spirit and our life, unbidden and uncontrollable.

The work that we chiefly depended on came from Mr Nevinson of the famous London daily of which I have spoken. The advent of books to review, or suggestions for articles for the paper were always heralded by a letter from our friend the editor. His neat clear handwriting became as familiar to me as Edward's, and it was these letters that we looked for each day. It had become my habit to take Merfyn for his morning walk down to the village, and call for the letters which we would thus get several hours earlier than if we had waited for delivery by the postman. So I became the daily bearer of good or bad news. Merfyn was now a sturdy boy of two and a half years; he loved this walk, for we generally timed ourselves when the school children were having their morning's interval of play on the green, and sometimes the children would beg that Merfyn might join them in 'Poor Mary sits a-weeping' which he was eager to do. But on this morning of which I speak I was in no mood for games because Edward had been for days wrestling with his demon of melancholy, and as was his way when like this he had been going long walks, getting from the solitary places and the sky and the hills the spiritual comfort that he could get from no other source, but often wearing out his body with hunger and fatigue, so that he came home as on this morning haggard and weary and silent. I took my way to the village heavy at heart, and at the post office there were no letters. This filled me with dread and dismay. I had hoped that news of work would have helped him to emerge from this destroying gloom, and I well knew that my empty hands would deepen and prolong it. I remember toiling up the hill noticing nothing, not even that Merfyn had lagged behind to peep through cottage gates at the flowers and bee-hives, and to look at little things in the hedges that interest children. I called him but he would not come. I called him again, but he was too much engrossed in watching a snail to take any notice of me, and I was in feverish haste to get my dreaded mission over. I ran to him and taking him angrily by the arm dragged him along roughly and unkindly, speaking in a voice he had never heard before. He screamed with fear and bewilderment, and I looking down and seeing his distorted face realized what I had done. I sat down on the hedge bank, and taking him in my arms mixed my tears with his and bending over him tried to sing his favourite good-night songs to comfort him and stop his sobs. A little bunch of flowers grow-ing within reach and a feather found on the thorn soon com-forted him, and he forgot as I shall never forget that dreadful morning.

I put Merfyn to bed before going to the study where I found Edward sitting as I had left him, not reading, not smoking, with his head in his hands, staring with eyes that saw nothing.

'There are no letters.'

'Why tell me what is written on your pale wretched face? I am cursed, and you are cursed because of me. I hate the tears I see you've been crying. Your sympathy and your love are both hateful to me. Hate me, but for God's sake don't stand there, pale and suffering. Leave me, I tell you; get out and leave me.'

# 4

The gentry of the village were nearly all people much older than ourselves, and openly, but in quite a friendly way, showed their curiosity about the young couple whose sitting-room – they could see from the lane – was lined with books. They could not help noticing Edward as he went with his swinging stride along the lanes, and when we were out together and Merfyn was mounted on his father's shoulder they certainly were a striking couple. Soon the vicar and his wife called. They were charming people – he a scholarly old man who was writing a learned book on some aspect of Hebrew history; and delighted to find someone with whom he could talk of Oxford and books. A curious interest of his was ghosts. He told us of a ghostly horse and rider he had seen on the Pilgrim's Way, and of other curious experiences of his. Later on he got Edward a job in connection with the organ of the Psychical Research Society. I liked his wife, a childless woman who became very fond of Merfyn and me, and we spent many afternoons in the beautiful garden of the vicarage, and came home laden with fruit and flowers. The vicar on these afternoons would drive us back in the pony-cart, and make this the excuse for having, before he went back, a little chat with Edward as he dug in the garden or smoked in the study.

The people with whom we became more intimate lived just across the lane in a big ugly house standing among trees. Their name was Crossman. Mr Crossman was a retired wine merchant, and a man of wide culture, but whose particular passion was maps of which he had a magnificent collection. He was of the country-squire type to look at, being red-faced and jolly and rather a heavy drinker of the choice wines for which his cellar was famous. He had a genuine love of good literature, and Edward and he had much in common. He was not a great walker, but he loved tracing on his maps the forgotten ways so many of which Edward had explored, and determining boundaries and estates; finding out from his maps the dates of new roads, and reinstating houses or buildings long since demolished. Hillsides now bare rose on his maps dark with their ancient timber, and streams long since degraded into sewers flowed clear and sweet through meadows, turning mill wheels by villages and widening into great lakes in stately parks. Great towns became for him again wayside hamlets, and where reeking chimneys and clattering machinery now stand he saw broad fields furrowed for the corn.

Mrs Crossman was a gentle delicate woman with a keen Jane Austenish kind of humour. She was a wonderful gardener, and the ugly dinginess of their house was forgotten in the wide herbaceous border never bare of flowers, and the rock garden for which she had collected plants from all over the world. All the work of the border and rock garden she did herself, and it became the custom for me to go at least once a week and spend the day with her, taking Merfyn, and help her weed and tidy up her precious flowers. On those days Edward would come over to lunch, and Mrs Crossman brought out of him that quiet dry wit which he did not often exhibit. He and this gentle shrewd woman got on very well. They played off their wit on each other until Mr Crossman would interrupt and drag Edward off to the smoking-room, to a glass of port and the maps.

So in a small way we lived quite a social life, and both of these elderly couples took us under their wings, and accepted us with our poverty and unconventionality in the friendliest manner. They became used to Edward's changes of mood, and desire for solitude, without any explanation. The old vicar was especially kind in unostentatiously putting little literary jobs in Edward's way.

But we were at this time still very poor, and the coming of a second child added a fresh anxiety. So Edward decided to go to London and, staying with his mother, try to get more regular work. The Crossmans promised that they would keep an eye on Merfyn and me.

I remember the day before Edward was to leave us was a perfect spring day. The cherry orchard was foaming with blossom, and all day long the cuckoos called there. But we were to go further afield, by ways which Edward had discovered, along forgotten lanes and green tracks. I carried the basket of food, and Edward carried Merfyn, who with his fist gripping a lock of his father's hair sat easily and securely on his shoulders. Sometimes he would walk if we each held a hand, and we would give him 'flying angels' over tall thistles and hummocks of grass, and his laugh was louder than the woodpecker's. He was a most merry child, though still not able to talk in any but his own language.

When Edward and his son were happy together I was filled with that deep content which I think only women experience. It comes out of such little things. I have felt it surge into my heart when I have been sitting by the fire sewing, and Edward has been writing or reading near me. I have looked up from my work to his beautiful face, the eyes with their heavy lids, the sensitive mouth, the noble shape of the head, and the fair loose falling hair; then at the large powerful but tenderly expressive hand that held the pen or the pipe; and my heart has suddenly been flooded with deep joy, and wonderful content as if life had given all. Sometimes I would get up quietly, kiss the unoccupied hand, slip back to my chair, and go on with my sewing, knowing only by a movement of his finger that he had felt my kiss; but sometimes if he were reading in the big chair, he would draw me on to his knees, and I would lie in the crook of his arm, and he would read on, putting his hand inside my dress over my breast. Then did content become enriched with desire that had no urgency, but flowed like a sweet river watering my being.

So as we walked with the laughing child between us I felt that this day of all days epitomized for me the spring. Going through a little copse where primroses and dog's mercury and anemones patterned the earth, and filled the air with dewy scent, Edward, whose eyes missed nothing of all the life around

94

us, bent down, and almost at our feet in the stump of a hazel tree was a nestful of blackbird's eggs, the first that Merfyn had ever seen. And after that he found (though how I do not know – it was so much a part of the tree) a wren's nest, the first *I* had ever seen; and to this day I have never been able to find one without help, so wonderfully is the entrance made to look like the natural growth of lichen on the tree. The path through the wood led up to a rising meadow surrounded by a hedge of great may-trees, with here and there a holly, and over all honeysuckle, bramble and traveller's joy. Then over a stile to find ourselves on the top of a hill with a wide view of Kent towards Canterbury. Under our feet were grass and daisies and cowslips.

'Oh, cowslips,' I said, 'oh, Edward, cowslips!'

I had not seen cowslips since that day at Oxford three years ago. I knelt down, putting my face among their cool blossoms, and tasting and smelling the sweetness. All over the field the pale gold glimmered – tall, strong many-keyed cowslips. I knew why Edward had brought us here. Three years ago! and now here was our child, too, among cowslips. We made a ball for him of the fragrant flowers, and he trotted about in the grass, tumbling over and clutching at the tall stems to help himself up. After lunch when Merfyn slept under the hedge, Edward read to me the *Prologue to the Canterbury Tales*, and one or two of the essays of a little volume he was preparing, and some of Blake's *Songs of Innocence*. Then we lay down with our eyes shut, near Merfyn, who soon woke up and climbing over us tried to open our eyes with his fat little finger. As we went home in the dark Merfyn saw the moon which was large and clear, and holding on to his father's hair with one hand he pointed with the other to the moon and uttered his first sentence – 'Ont it, ont it.'

So for the first time in my life I saw and felt and knew the coming of spring. Every day some new flower was found of which I did not know the name, and which Edward had to tell me a dozen times before I was sure of it. I became familiar with trees, and began to recognize their bark and shape and slowly unfolding leaves, and each took its place in my heart for ever – the oak flinging its limbs about in the ecstasy of its strength; the tall guardian elms, so strong and tender; the witchy ash with beckoning claw-like twigs, who puts out her leaves so grudgingly and lets them fall so soon; the feminine beeches whose new-born leaves are downy like a baby; the old mysterious yews, whose wood when it is cleft is red like blood, and which in the spring give up their pollen in clouds of golden incense. All these I became familiar with – and the hedges too, with their hollies the hedger always spares, though he trims the elder and dogwood and flaming maple. I became aware in reality, as in imagination I had known, of the living earth out of which all comes, and to which all goes. My spirit was filled and satisfied as never before by a bare field of red earth, over which the teams of plough-horses toiled, or the glow of a corn field, or the smell of hay, or wet woodland, or by the beauty of a tree or by the variety of the tiny details of a hedge bank. I was aware of a deep joy and excitement as if I was a part of the stirring vital earth. Each season became dear to me, and their slow inevitable cycle – the fecundity of spring, the heavy fulfilment of summer, the grateful sacrifice of autumn, and the lovely secret withdrawing of winter. With what eager love we searched for the first violet and were waylaid by primroses! How our hearts stood still when the first cuckoo called, and the coming of the first swallow made the day holy!

# 5

The next day Edward went to London, and Merfyn and I were left, for we did not know how long. But there was plenty to occupy me with the garden and the child, and the preparations for the new baby. I had need of all my courage and natural happiness, for Edward's letters were full of wretchedness and despair. Work was not to be had, at least nothing substantial, and his father raked up the old grievance about the Civil Service, pointing out that his first duty was to provide a proper income for his wife and child, and all the old sensible arguments. But I knew that that sort of security would be too dearly bought, and that Edward must work out his own salvation in his own way. And his way was my way. Life for him would always be painful, but at least he had the country which meant so much to him, and the freedom within the limits his poverty imposed – and with his simple tastes and needs this was not too obvious. The circumstances of his life were what he had chosen, and I would not encourage him to consider changing them. All I could do now was to try to convey my own faith in him and in his work, and my own freedom from sadness and anxiety.

But in the evening when Merfyn was in bed and I was tired with my day's work and the burden of the coming baby, I found it hard not to let my thoughts dwell on our immediate cares – money and the birth of the child and Edward's self-distrust and cruel sneers at himself because of his failure. His reliance on me to encourage and cheer him was the stimulant for my pen, and so I wrote of the things that were permanent, not of those that would pass.

He had been away some weeks, when one evening sitting in such a mood a telegram was brought to me. I read 'Commission for book on Oxford £100. Returning tomorrow.

97

Edward.' I read it over and over again: a hundred pounds was a fortune for us. What a congenial subject too, what encouragement for him! How wonderfully, I thought, was my faith fulfilled! I was so excited that I felt I must tell someone. So without waiting to put on a hat I ran over to the Crossmans. Mrs Crossman had gone to bed, and Mr Crossman was alone in the dining-room sipping the port of which he was too fond.

'What do you think?' I said, having no time for greeting. 'Edward is to write a book on Oxford, and get £100 for it'; and I tried to get round the table to where he sat to show him the telegram. But forgetting how big I was I found I could not squeeze between the wall and the huge table. This made us both laugh, and changed my almost tearful excitement and his tearful sympathy into a joke. For to him there must have seemed something pathetic in such excitement over £100. However, he made me drink a glass of port to celebrate the occasion, and called Mrs Crossman, who came down in her dressing-gown to hear all about it by the drawing-room fire. I grew calmer, and remembering that I had left Merfyn all alone said good night. Mr Crossman saw me to my gate, and leaning over it as I turned to the house he said:

'And I'll tell Edward he's got a good wench.' He always called me 'wench', and as it was his way of showing his fondness for me I liked it from him.

Shortly after this our baby was born, and was much to our joy a girl, and we called her Bronwen Rachel Mary, Mary after her grandmother, to whom the advent of a granddaughter was a particular joy. Her hair was dark and her skin dark with glowing red under the russet. She was like a gipsy. Mr Crossman declared that Edward could not be her father, but that in the wood one day I'd met Pan, and Bronwen was Pan's child, 'a wicked wench you've got, Edward, a wicked wench of the woods, and the girl is her mother over again'. And a child of the woods and fields she certainly grew up to be, though her hair soon changed from black to fair.

With the Oxford book Edward's luck took a turn, and I do not remember at this time another period of acute anxiety about money, and indeed we felt we might adventure a little, and when an old cottage in the village which we had looked at enviously many times became vacant we decided to move. Our baby was about a year old when we made this change.

During our married life we moved house many times, and always I had the feeling that somehow Edward would be better for the change. It marked a sort of beginning again. And so now with my hopeful and romantic nature I hoped, because at first we were so busy and so happy settling down in our new house – and this time one which we both loved – that the cloud that I dreaded so much would dissolve, and we should be free of it for ever. And always for a time it seemed as if it might be so. Then unannounced it would return. I should have to face it, and resolve once more not to let it affect me, and once more fail. I used to wish and pray to be different. If only I could be angry at his unkindness instead of hurt, I thought it might be better for him. If only I could really take no notice, instead of pretending not to do so! How I longed to be able to alter my nature. In these times I used to wish I was beautiful, or that he would find another woman who would keep him always happy. These doubts tormented my mind when I let them, but deep in my heart I knew that he depended on me, and would need me when his horrible suffering was over. No one could save him from his demon except himself.

The house stood facing the green. It was a tall, narrow, half-timbered cottage, with a square paned window on each side of the door, three above those, and a little dormer-window high up in the tiled roof. The front garden was long and narrow with a lime tree in the middle of each plot of grass each side of the path. A thick holly hedge surrounded the garden, which on one side was bent inwards by the constant pressure of wheels and timber and tools which the wheelwright in his workshop next door leant against it. The room on each side of the door was tiny but the beauty of the carving on the great oak beams that supported the floor of the room above compensated, we thought, for this. This upper room which ran the

99

whole width of the house and was of beautiful proportions, with an old-fashioned hobbed fireplace at one end, and three windows, was Edward's study and in it our books and few possessions looked better than they had ever done. Its ceiling was low and beamed, and the light that came in through the lime branches was dim. It had great charm and individuality, and was a room for repose and meditation, the peace of which was not disturbed by the ceaseless chatter of birds in the thick ivy with which the house was covered, and whose tendrils of pallid green had pushed their way between the walls and the woodwork of the windows.

The tiny back garden ran down to the railway, and was quite neglected, but charming too, for I have never seen such profusion of white violets. They covered almost the whole space, and we had difficulty in finding where the path had been under their matted growth.

The house was called Ivy Cottage, but it came to be known by the villagers and especially by the children as 'the house with the baby in the garden', for Bronwen used to spend all her time out there in the grass, and the children would gather round the gate to talk to her, and sometimes venture in to play with her toys. Merfyn was big enough now to wander on to the green or to the wheelwright's shop.

I loved the village life, and so did Edward. We used to go and gossip at the 'Lion', and the innkeeper became one of our friends. Our neighbour the wheelwright was an interesting old man, his family had been wheelwrights for generations, and the shop was one of the oldest buildings in the village. He knew the history of the neighbourhood and of the great families who owned it, and as he fitted a tyre or worked with his spokeshave he would tell us of local customs and the traditional tales of the place. He had a wonderful memory, and remembered details of gossip and scandal that had been current when he was a boy. But he was a kindly old man and there was no sting in his gossip, and he would scold us for encouraging him to talk instead of getting on with his work. He taught Edward – who had always loved good tools, and making things with wood – how to use an axe and different kinds of planes, and how to make the simpler sorts of things such as a new handle of ash for a spade. The talks always ended by Edward's suggesting to old Gray that they should go across to the inn and have a drink; so off they'd go with Merfyn between them – Merfyn with his wheelbarrow which Gray had made for him, and in which he'd be sure to bring me back some apples or onions or a great cabbage.

Things went rather better for us during the short time we spent in this house. The village life was a source of constant interest to Edward, and work came in fairly steadily. The work on the Oxford book took Edward away a good deal, and kept him busy, and all this helped him to ward off the dreadful attacks of melancholy.

# 6

Our life in this village was brought to a close by the illness of our baby girl. She developed pneumonia when she was eighteen months old. She was an adorably happy baby, plump and rosy and laughing, and when this illness came she was just learning to say a few words. It was March, and the ground was covered with snow. She lay for days burning with fever, quite unconscious, panting for breath. Edward and I took it in turns to watch by her, and hold the strangely unlifelike child in our arms, trying with whispered baby tunes and words to pierce that dreadful unconsciousness. As I sat by the window over the snow-covered green to the churchyard, an icy fear invaded my heart sometimes, but I shut it out as if it was the devil trying to tempt me to lose hope.

Mrs Thomas came to help me nurse, and one day persuaded me to let her watch while I rested. In a little while she ran in to call me. I hurried to the room where the child lay dead – I thought. The scarlet flush had turned to paleness, the breathing was silent, the eyes closed. I stood shivering and dazed looking at her, but as I looked her eyes slowly opened. I had been told what to do if she got through the crisis, and now realizing that it had happened I followed my instructions, and soon the child was sleeping peacefully. We picked some daffodils out of the garden to put by her bed, and when she woke we saw with joy that her gaze rested consciously on the bright colour. She recovered very quickly, but had forgotten all her baby words, nor could she walk, but had to learn the difficult lessons all over again. With the melting of the snow and the coming of the white violets she was soon running about under the budding limes, and once more gave her name to the garden.

Then I got ill, and we discovered that the house was hopelessly insanitary. We decided sadly that we must leave, but where to go we had no idea, for there was not a house to be had in the village. Merfyn, however, solved the problem for us unwittingly. Running one day into the village shop he brought back with him the local paper. In it we saw an advertisement of a farmhouse to be let in the Weald of Kent near Sevenoaks. It sounded just what we should like. So it was arranged that I should go and see it. I saw and fell in love with Elses Farm, and in a week we left our beloved village with all its friends.

The new house was a large square farmhouse standing away from the road in the midst of its own fields. Oast houses, cow sheds, stables, hayricks and a huge barn were grouped about it on two sides. On the other side was a large garden and orchard, and in the front was a little garden opening into a field in which stood great oak trees, and in whose coppice-like hedges sang innumerable nightingales.

The house had big rooms, and long flagged passages leading to dairies, storerooms and an immense kitchen and scullery. In the scullery was a huge brick oven, and two large coppers, one for brewing beer, one for washing clothes. The outside door opened into a brick-paved shed where there was a pump and another big copper, and here all day the farm boys washed milk cans and churns, and here the milk-cooler was set up. Everything in this shed shone with brightness and here it was always cool.

The cows of which there were about fifty were turned out into the meadow in front of the house, and the children became quite used to these gentle creatures staring and sniffing at them, and soon learned to know them by name. Here on this farm we became familiar with the cycle of work on the land from early spring till Christmas. The bush harrow, plough, sickle and the team of horses became familiar objects to us all, and we saw and took part in many of the operations on the farm. We came to know the whole process of the cultivation of hops from the ploughing between the 'hills', and the stringing and 'twiddling', to the picking and drying, and the feasting on payday. The charcoal burner carried on his ancient trade at our very door. He lived in a tent in the farmyard near his cone, a solitary being, avoided by the village people who looked down on him and his traditional calling. Of course we tried to talk to him and find out about his work, but he was a taciturn fellow, and even over a mug of beer at the inn near-by Edward could not get a word out of him. Once I remember when he was at the inn I saw what I thought were flames coming out of the cone, and thinking that his charcoal would be spoilt I ran as fast as I could to the inn to tell him of the disaster. He shook his head, but nevertheless came with me to reassure me that what I saw was not flame but luminous gas, and that all was well. After that he tried to ingratiate himself with the children, but they were frightened of his black face, and so he withdrew into himself again.

This inn was called 'The Shant', and was indeed nothing more than a sort of rough shed. It was kept by an old couple who lived in a neat little cottage adjoining the inn. Mrs Turner worked for me, and it was she who taught me how to make and bake bread in the brick oven. How I loved this work – getting the oven white-hot with burning faggots, and raking the hot ash in a circle, sweeping the floor clean with a wet besom, then with a long iron spade-shaped implement whose name I forget, putting the loaves in the clean hot bricks, and seeing them begin to rise before I had time to shut the iron door, and banking up the hot ashes against it to keep out the draught. All this had to be done very quickly, so that the oven should not get cool before every loaf was in. She taught me how to make the dough, set it, and shape it into loaves.

All this work I loved, as I did the housework, the gardening or any work which gave my strong body exercise, and which satisfied my spirit with its human necessity. Edward too was glad for me to do these things, and I tried my hand at brewing, wine-making, hop-picking and even reaping. Of course hay-making on the lovely slope of Blooming meadow was a fes-tival for us all at the farm, and we learnt how the ricks that rose like a town in the rickyard were shaped so symmetrically, and thatched as carefully as a house. It is this full life of homely

doings that I remember chiefly at the farm – the early morning
expeditions with Edward to a large pond about three miles
away to fish for perch and roach and even pike; the walks to
Penshurst and Leigh and Ightham Moat; the picking and storing
of apples; the making of quince jam; the finding of an owl's
or a nightingale's nest; the woodpecker which cut the air in
scallops as it flew from oak to oak; the white owl which brought
its young to the roof ridge to be fed; the beautiful plough-
horses with their shining brass ornaments; the cows going
into their stalls like people going into their pews in church;
the building and thatching of the ricks; the hedging and ditch-
ing; the wood-cutting and faggot-binding by men whose
fathers had done the same work and whose fathers' fathers
too; the work of the farm, leisured as the coming and going
of the seasons; the lovely cycle of ploughing, sowing and reap-
ing; the slow experienced labourers, whose knowledge had
come to them as the acorns come to the oaks, whose skill had
come as the swallows' skill, who are satisfied in their hard life
as are the oaks and the swallows in theirs. How I loved it all,
and with what joy and strength it filled my being, so that
when I needed joy and strength they did not fail me. And
often and often I did need them. There were many dark periods
while we were here, many days of silence and wretchedness
and separation, for sometimes in these moods Edward would
stride away, perhaps for days, wrestling with the devil that
tormented his spirit.

In an unconscious way as I grew older I came to realize that
everything that is a part of life is inevitable to it, and must
therefore be good. I could not be borne high upon the crest of
ecstasy and joy unless I also knew the dreadful depths of the
trough of the great waves of life. I could not be irradiated by
such love without being swept by the shadow of despair. The
rich teeming earth from which all beauty comes is fed with
decay; out of the sweat and labour of men grows the corn.
We are born to die; if death were not, life would not be either.
Pain and weakness and evil, as well as strength and passion
and health, are part of the beautiful pattern of life, and as I grew

up I learned that life is richer and fuller and finer the more you can understand, not only in your brain and intellect but in your very being, that you must accept it all; without bitterness the agony, without complacency the joy. Dimly I perceived that it was because I was I that life came to me like this. My strong instinctive body, my too sensitive awareness of Edward's suffering, my utter lack of resignation, my eager passionate exaction from life all it had to give, the romantic ideals in which I so deeply believed, all those qualities which gave life for me its colour and intensity made me also vulnerable to its weapons.

Edward had a fair amount of work, but never enough to keep him from anxiety, and never enough to free him from the hateful hack-work books written to the order of publishers, which though he did them well did not at all satisfy his own creative impulse, the damming up of which contributed largely to his melancholy. Yet against this has to be put that he was untrammelled by routine. He loved the life he lived away from towns, his own master, though in a freedom that perhaps gave him too much opportunity for brooding and for introspective doubts and hatreds of himself. He went to London fairly often, and kept in touch with a large circle of friends, most of them writers and poets, but others whom he had known at Oxford in different professions. And these friends kept up the custom of our lively week-ends, and some became very intimate with the different phases of our domestic life, and helped both Edward and me over difficult periods.

At this time Edward worked at a tiny cottage about a mile away from the farm, which he rented for half-a-crown a week from a neighbouring farmer. We wore a footpath to this cottage – first through a copse, then past a pond, and then over a fence into a rough meadow. It has now been obliterated, and no one would know that the cottage and the big farmhouse had ever had any connection with each other. There was always something to be seen on this path – a shrew mouse running up a corn stalk, a heron flying overhead, a hedgehog nosing about in the dead leaves, or a fox the same colour as the clay of the Weald trotting along by the side of the copse.

Because of Edward's frequent absences I was very much alone here. Apart from the week-ends in the fine weather, I led a very unsocial life, and I missed the friends we had left at Bearsted. For this village, which was itself ugly and repellent though in such beautiful country, did not yield a single congenial friend, and often weeks went by when I spoke to no one except the Turners at 'The Shant' and my own household.

At these times my daily letters to Edward were my great delight, and all day I thought of what I should say and talk about in them. As the evening drew near I longed for the time to come when I could be alone and quiet to write all that my heart and mind were full of. My whole life was expressed in these letters. It was in a state of joyful excitement that I wrote page after page so quickly that only Edward, familiar with my awful writing, could have read them. To these letters I got long replies every day, for always, when he was away, to write and receive these letters was our great need. It was Edward's constant fear that some day I should be infected with his melancholy, and that my naturally happy nature would be changed. But something – a kind of certainty that, in spite of the turgid flood which often seemed to sweep away and destroy everything, there was something which it could not destroy, something which our love had created, and which like a rock supporting us would endure – kept my nature intense and sensitive, so that when happiness came there was not a moment whose preciousness I did not realize and appreciate, whose beauty and fullness even now I remember in every detail. When it seemed that happiness had gone for ever it was into the treasury of memories that I dipped if Edward needed to be reassured that all was well with me.

Edward was so self-critical and uncompromising in his demand for sincerity and truth, and hatred of hypocrisy or flattery, that a little appreciation and success would have been a very valuable stimulant to him. It would not have spoilt him, but would have brought out the best in him, and have given him that faith in himself which would have been a strong weapon with which to fight that other side of his nature, which was so destructive. I used to wish that he had just the little money that would relieve him from the necessity of pot-boiling work, and give him more freedom to do his best work in his own time. But this he never had.

He had many friends who admired his work and loved him. He drew people to him by his exacting need of them. They had to come more than half-way to meet his reserved and shy nature, but their effort was well repaid, for with his personal charm, his talk, his dry humour, his clear intellect, his sincerity, his generous appreciation of his contemporaries, and his ungrudging efforts on their behalf, his never failing loyalty – and added to these qualities his striking appearance and a beautiful voice – it is not to be wondered at that he created in the hearts of the people with whom he came into contact a more than ordinary friendship. He made the same impression on many different kinds of people, and indeed I should think that there are few men who have been loved by his fellows with such a rare and deep affection as was Edward throughout his life. My love for him never lost its passionate intensity. My letters to him were love-letters, and his homecoming meant for me to be lifted into Heaven.

We cannot say why we love people. There is no reason for passionate love. But the quality in him that I most admired was his sincerity. There was never any pretence between us. All was open and true. Often he was bitter and cruel, but I could bear it because I knew all. There was nothing left for me to guess at, no lies, no falsity. All was known, all was suffered and endured; and afterwards there was no reserve in our joy. If we love deeply we must also suffer deeply; the price for the capacity for ecstatic joy is anguish. And so it was with us to the end.

## 7

We lived at this farm for three years. Here Bronwen had learned to walk, and Merfyn had grown from a baby to a little boy. Here things had gone fairly well with us materially, and here more than anywhere else I had become familiar with farm life. I no longer looked at it eagerly and curiously, but lived it, not unconsciously as the labourers did, but aware all the time of its richness and variety, its crudeness and its beauty, its hardness and its happiness, its cruelty and its innocence, so that when we heard we must leave the farm we could not at first believe that this life had come to an end. The farmer was retiring and had let the farm. As the new man wanted the house, we had to go.

Merfyn was now six years old and we felt we had better move to a place where there was a school. We remembered Bedales, the co-educational school in Hampshire I had heard of years ago. So I went to see the school and the country, and, if I liked both, to make inquiries about a house.

I spent a day looking over the school and talking to the headmaster – or rather trying to, but he being very reserved and silent, and I very timid of this austere-looking man, we did not talk nearly as much as I had hoped. However, being prejudiced in favour of the school and liking all I saw, I stayed to see if I could find a house. The country all round was particularly beautiful, being hilly and wooded and untouched by the jerry-builder. I found a house that would suit us perfectly. Edward approved of the house, but the school he left to me. The country satisfied him completely. So we decided without hesitation to move to Berryfield Cottage and send our children to the famous school.

The house was originally a small farmhouse. It was about a hundred years old and built of flint and brick, with tiny flints let into the pointing. It was a saying that the flint and brick houses were held together by tenpenny nails, because of the likeness of these little round stones to the heads of large nails. It stood on a little rise of a winding lane which ran at the foot of the steep sides of a vast raised plateau. The irregular sloping edge was in some parts bare like the downs; in other parts covered in a thick growth of trees – beech and yew for the most part – called hangers. Our cottage lay at the foot of one of the bare slopes – a steep hill dotted here and there with juniper bushes, but crowned with a group of fir trees. To reach this hillside you crossed a rough field sometimes crimson with sainfoin, or orange with dandelions, or silver with dandelion clocks according to the time of the year. A large old-fashioned garden stretched in front of the house running parallel to the lane – and above it, for you entered the garden up half a dozen steps from the lane. Every sort of flower and bush flourished in this garden. Its ancient hedges harboured many kinds of birds, and the yew tree by the gate was the home of a gold-crested wren.

We were very isolated here, for though it was not much more than a mile from the village and the school, we were tucked away among trees and hills, and the winding lane which led to the outer world was the darkest lane I have ever known; so deep and dark it was that the entrance to it on the main road looked like the entrance to a tunnel. On the other side of the house the land sloped down to a stream which flowed through a wild water-meadow full of forget-me-nots, meadowsweet, mare's tails and loosestrife. At night all we could hear was the wind in the hanger, the barking of foxes who lived there, and the hooting of owls. It was a romantic and beautiful spot, and the house belonged to it and we loved it from the first. Edward of course began exploring the country round, and soon became familiar with the footpaths and byways. We found we were a few miles from Selborne and the place where Cobbett was born, and within a day's walk of Winchester.

I was determined to get to know the school and the people connected with it, and this was my greatest interest to begin with. I was whole-heartedly enthusiastic about its ideals, for I was still a rather serious-minded girl, eager for my children's sake to know and understand the school and all it stood for. Its co-education was its chief attraction for me, but I liked too its love of the open air, its unscholastic freedom of discipline, its freedom from monied snobbishness and its social life, simple and free and happy. I found the staff difficult to get to know. They seemed unfriendly and suspicious, but my admiration gave me courage to persevere, and little by little I thawed the ice of their cultured reserve. I attended parents' meetings and the Sunday service. As time went on the married staff called, and I became on neighbourly terms with them.

Edward with his quick eye for superficiality was never taken in by them as I was; though perhaps 'taken in' is too harsh an expression, for they were kind, serious, intellectual people believing in co-education, temperance, votes for women, and hygiene and liberalism. I liked them very much, and the social life they offered me was a new and delightful experience. I soon made friends among them, and became enrolled as one of the fraternity – though always with this modification: first that Edward did not share these interests and activities; secondly that we were poor, and none gave the impression of ever having been less well off than they were. They all – so it seemed to me – had led and would always lead the same quiet comfortable lives, rational, well balanced. Their politics inclined to Socialism and they were on more than usual friendly terms with the villagers, though owing to their temperance they could not hob-nob with them at the inn. They sided with the village against the gentry in discussions concerning rights of way, etc. They were moderate in all things; they read the best books and the *Manchester Guardian*, and loved the best music, and had replicas of the best pictures on their walls. Their houses were in faultless taste outside and in. Their simple oak furniture was made by skilled craftsmen, and their curtains were hand-woven. Their meals were lavish and good, inclining to brown bread and vegetarianism, and of course non-alcoholic. They were hospitable and kind, and yet later they

111

all became for me 'stale and unprofitable'. They were so pleased with each other, so comfortable, so wrapped up in their theories and principles. They had no bigness, no unevenness, no spontaneity, no savour of the earth. Certain things were absolutely taboo among them such as corsets, face powder, beer, coarseness of any kind, free love and any kind of untidiness. Happy-go-lucky poverty and untimetabled lives such as ours they could neither understand nor tolerate. Edward frankly did not like them, and to them he was an enigma – a solitary wandering creature who worked irregularly, who drank and smoked in village inns, who had no political beliefs or social theories, and who was not impressed by the school or its ideals – no, they could not like him or rope him in at all.

With me it was different. My admiration for them, my eagerness to learn from them, and my unreserved enthusiasm amused and a little flattered them, and finding me intelligent and talkative they admitted me into their circle. I spoke at 'votes for women' meetings – though owing to a tendency for the speakers to assume an anti-man attitude I found myself standing up for women's work in the home, and hating very much a lot of the clap-trap of feminism. My romanticism caught on to the idea that a happier and kinder world would ensue when women had more obvious power. I did not realize that politicians would be politicians whether male or female. I read papers at informal drawing-room meetings on various points in the education of children. The women at these meetings were all supported by their husbands, and it was thought strange and a little sad that my husband was not also voicing his belief in the efficacy of the Vote.

We spent three years in this house, during which time our material affairs gradually became better, though Edward's earnings were still in a large part dependent on commissioned books and hack work. He had produced two volumes of essays which had been received quite well, and he reviewed for a number of literary papers which also took an article now and then. In spite of the lifting of financial cares the attacks of gloom and wretchedness had become of late more frequent and more lasting, and there were terrible days when I did not know where he was; or, if he was at home, days of silence and brooding despair. Often during this period while I was doing my housework or playing with the children or working in the garden I was straining to hear his coo-ee from the hillside, or his foot on the steps up to the gate. And often when he came I was terrified by the haggard greyness of his face, and the weary droop of his body, as he flung himself into his study chair, not speaking or looking at me. Once in one of these fits, after being needlessly angry with one of the children who cried and ran away from him, he rummaged in a drawer where he kept all sorts of things like fishing tackle and tools, and where I knew there was also a revolver. This he put into his pocket, and with dull eyes and ashen cheeks strode out of the house up the bare hill. I watched him go until he was lost among the trees at the top. I thought 'perhaps I shall never see him again', but I knew he would not leave me like this; it would not be like this that he would save himself. Nevertheless my limbs went weak and slack, my tongue was dry in my mouth, the questions and chatter of the children were an agony to me. I wanted to be alone and listen. But I could not. I took the children down to the stream in the hollow where they could paddle and sail their boats without wanting me to join in their play. There I sat with my hands in my lap unable to sew or read or think, and while the children played I listened. I prayed too that he might be released from his agony and I from mine. When the sun set and the children got tired of their game I took them home and put them to bed. I changed my dress, made up the study fire, drew the curtains, and got the tea things ready on a little table. I was in the kitchen, ironing, when he came in.

'Hello,' I called, though the word came out like a croak. He was safe. When I could control my voice and face I went to the study. He was taking off his shoes by the fire, and I saw they were coated with mud and leaves. He did not look up.

'Shall I make the tea?' I said.

'Please,' he answered, and in his voice I was aware of all he had suffered and overcome, and all that he asked of me.

# 8

There were other periods of deep calm happiness. Sometimes we would work all day in the garden, Edward sowing or planting the vegetable plot, I weeding and rearranging the flower border. We would not talk much, but just throw a remark now and then from one to the other about our work, and compare what each had done.

'The broad beans are coming up well, and we'll have a good crop if old Ede is right about winter sowing keeping away the black fly.'

'What about this lavender bush? Do you think it is too high?'

'No, you can't have too much lavender; and mind you dry the flowers this year.'

'Look at that flycatcher. Can you hear him snap his beak as he catches a fly? His nest is in the jasmine.'

I loved too the long winter evenings by the fire in the study. Edward would generally be reading lying back in his big chair with one hand holding his book and the other over the bowl of his pipe, and I would sit facing him in my favourite low nursery-chair sewing or reading or knitting, and sometimes writing on a pad on my lap. Edward encouraged me to write. He said to me, 'Always write of things that you know. Don't write out of your head, but about something you have experienced, and if you write simply and truthfully it is bound to be interesting. If you write as you write your letters, it's sure to be all right, except for the spelling which I suppose you'll never learn.' So I wrote stories for the children about things that had really happened, and an essay now and then, though I hadn't much impulse for writing except in letters. But best of all I loved the evenings when we talked. Then Edward explained to me the nature of poetry, or we discussed some book we were both reading. Sometimes he would ask me to

look through and read the innumerable volumes of minor
verse that he had to review, and weed them out for him, and
I remember pouncing on *Poems of Childhood* by de la Mare
amid a welter of worthless stuff. On these evenings I'd bring
the supper on a tray, and with it on a stool between us we'd
continue the talk as we ate the bread and cheese and drank the
beer. Often we would talk until late; then before going to bed
we would walk down to the stream or up on to the hillside,
and Edward would tell me the names of the stars and try to
impress upon me the shape of the constellations. But I was
no good at astronomy, and had no desire to call the stars by
name as I had to name flowers. Nevertheless I loved these
midnight lessons and from my lover and from the night learnt
something which was nameless and unforgettable.

Often I would be busy about the house when Edward would
come out of his study and call me:

'Helen, where are you? I've got stuck with this damned
review. Come on, and let's go to Selborne. You've never been
there. We needn't touch roads at all, you'll love it, and I know
a woodpecker's nest.'

'But, Edward, I'm all untidy, and in the middle of turning
out the children's toy cupboard.'

'Never mind, leave it. Tomorrow I've got to finish this
work, and we'll not have another chance for ages.'

So I whip off my apron and put on thick shoes, and away
we go all day long, tramping by footpaths through woods
and fields, happy to be free of the house and the study and
the children, running hand in hand down bare hillsides, or
walking single file along the narrow paths the dog's mercury
has left in the woods. Walking along hedges Edward would
mark some particularly straight stem of holly or hazel which
later he would cut for a stick, digging down to get a nice crook
of root for the handle. He had a large and varied collection of
such sticks, which it was his pride to season and polish and
fit with ferrules. I had a blackthorn with a knuckle-shaped
knob which I always used. Edward hated any paraphernalia
in walking, and we never carried rucksacks or mackintoshes.

116

He had specially large pockets made in his coats, in which he
carried a book to read or a notebook, and our lunch, and for
the children we filled them with sweet chestnuts or hazel nuts,
or any treasures we found. I hated walking over swampy
places, and he taught me to walk slowly and evenly 'as if in
a dream' so that I should not sink in. He taught me to walk
with my body, not only with my legs, and though I never
achieved his slow graceful stride, for my walk was with quick
short steps, I could go mile after mile without fatigue.

These were my red-letter days when my spirit rose in thank-
fulness for the richness of life. Sometimes when he saw how
happy I was he would say:

'Helen, you ought to have a different sort of husband, one
who would always be happy and careless and never cruel; who
would always love your untidiness as I love it now, and not
mind your short sight as I don't mind it now, and kiss you
much oftener as I kiss you now.'

'Well then' I would say, 'perhaps if you were such a hus-
band, I should be somebody different too, and perhaps not so
happy as I certainly am now. So that's that.'

The lark rising with quivering wings into the blue seemed
to carry my heart with it, and my heart became the source of
that cascade of song.

We could now afford a servant and had a nice country girl
who lived in with us, so that when Edward was away I was
not alone in the solitary house. The children, who were about
seven and four, were strong and healthy, and Merfyn had just
begun to go to school. I had quite successfully taught him to
read and write, and on account of this I was asked to fill a
temporary gap in the staff, which enabled us to help pay the
heavy fees.

Merfyn had inherited some of his father's moodiness which
had become more apparent as he grew up. This quality in the
child, and also the fact that he did not take to the things which
had so filled his own boyhood, exasperated Edward, and I
often found myself in the unenviable position of peace-keeper

117

between the two. Bronwen, however, was very different. She was a regular woodland child. She wandered about the fields by herself, singing and picking flowers, or else played happily with her dolls in the outbuildings at the back of the house. With her sharp eyes and her passion for flowers she always found the first white violet, and her placid happy nature, unperturbed by her father's moods, made her a source of constant delight to him. The children loved their father, and admired him for his skill in making things for them and his knowledge of birds and flowers and the ways of wild creatures. Between both my children and me were profound love and sympathy. I had made up my mind before they were born that at least they should never feel lonely and humiliated as I had so often felt in my childhood, and that I would never tell them lies. So they trusted me, and I them. They were not spoilt, but lived simple free lives, being thrown a good deal on their own resources, having to invent their own interests and pleasures, for we had no money to buy them the toys and expensive destroyers of imagination which make children so discontented. We read a great deal to them; singing also played a part in our family life. Edward's voice was lovely for singing as well as in speaking, and we had a very large repertory of nursery and folk songs. The children especially enjoyed the hour before bedtime spent round the fire singing, each taking it in turn to choose the song. They were with us a great deal and when friends came to stay they would listen to the talk, or else play quietly without disturbing the grown-ups. Edward's word was law, but there were not many rules to break, and therefore few punishments. They had to help in the garden and do small jobs for me in the house, but it was all rather happy-go-lucky. We never ran our house to a timetable; nothing was hard-and-fast. Sunday we always tried to keep for the children. On that day we put on our oldest clothes, and spent the entire day out of doors, taking with us bread and butter, cheese and apples. When the children got tired Edward carried them in turn on his shoulders. I loved those days. Edward was at his happiest and best, looking for nests, seeing who could find the greatest variety of flowers, trying to teach the children and me the songs of birds, exploring new paths and getting the children to understand the map of the district and the use of a compass. We scrambled through hedges, tramped over fields and meadows, sat on gates; and the children and Edward climbed trees; by the time we got home we were a most disreputable-looking crew, but happy and ravenously hungry.

Those were memorable intervals in far different periods and as a friend of ours, a sort of nerve specialist, coming to stay with us about this time, strongly advised us that a complete change from ordinary life would do Edward good, he decided to go away. We had some friends who lived in a coastguard cottage in Suffolk, and it was arranged that Edward should borrow the cottage until – at least – the book on Jefferies on which he was then working was finished. So he left home for an indefinite period.

My daily letters to him were now again my great delight, and eagerly when the last bedtime song had been sung, and the whole ritual of 'good night' and 'tucking up' had been performed, I shut myself in the study and began to write. In the silence and solitude, in this room among the hills and woods, with nothing that jarred or disturbed, but only those lovely sounds that blend into the darkness and become the night – the stream running in the hollow, the murmuring in the trees as of a myriad ghosts wandering among their close-ranked stems, a flock of wild geese high overhead cutting the air with the 'whiss' of a scythe – in the silence and solitude, with pen in hand and a sheet of paper before me, it was as if I came into my natural element. I was alone with my lover, for whom my heart was stored with thoughts and emotions which now could become articulate. Nothing that I had done or seen or thought or experienced was left untold; my pen flew over the pages in happy excitement. All the significance, the richness and beauty of my life were revealed as in a vision while I wrote.

Edward's letters to me were no less full, though only some-

times did his austerity give way to the passion to which I
responded so eagerly. Greatly to my relief and joy he sounded
much happier. The change from home was doing him good,
and after a few weeks he spoke of returning, but I urged him
to stay till the book was finished. His letters at this time spoke
of a girl he had met. She was one of the family with whom I
had lived at Broadstairs, and was now about eighteen. He told
me she was beautiful and timid and unsophisticated; that she
had walked with him on the beach, and had spoken of the
books she was reading, of her love for the open air, the sea
and the flat marshes of Suffolk. He said she was like a wild,
timid seabird, and that only very gradually he had overcome
her shyness. He lent her books and introduced her to poetry.
He told her of me whom she had known as Auntie Helen,
and of the children. He wanted to give her a volume of his
own essays, but she would not accept it, saying that 'Auntie
Helen would not like it'. So I wrote to her and said I did not
mind at all, and we renewed memories of years ago. Then I
got a letter from her which showed me that she was uncon-
sciously falling in love with Edward, and I felt very much
troubled about her. To Edward she was a beautiful creature,
more a dryad or sea-nymph than a human girl, and he did not
and could not understand that their friendship might cause
her pain. She looked up to him as a master, a being of a different
world from any she had ever known, one who could help her
to understand poetry, and who could teach her all she longed
to know about the life of the wild marshes where she loved
to wander. His beautiful face, lovely voice and sympathetic
interest had thrilled her; she innocently exclaimed in one of
her letters to me 'how wonderful it must be to be his wife'. I
wrote to Edward telling him to be very careful with this sen-
sitive girl, as I felt it would be tragic for her first experience
of love to be so unfulfilled; for it to be anything else would
be more tragic still. I knew the nonconformist atmosphere in
which she had been brought up, and the bonds of conventional
religion and behaviour that united this family. She often asked
Edward 'But would it be right?' I gathered that their walks

together were secret, and that once she had cried in telling Edward she had lied to her mother.

Edward did not heed my advice, but was amused and pleased with my attitude to the affair. He wrote to me more light-heartedly than ever before, saying 'I love you for your serious advice, and the artful artlessness of all you say. There never was such an unwifely wife, and I wish you were here to be kissed!' However, it suddenly came to an end. Hope, burdened with emotions of which she was frightened, confided in her elder sister, who revealed all to the parents. Edward was interviewed by the angry father, who told him not to see her or write to her again, and the poor child was sent away.

The termination of the idyll in this rather ridiculous conventional way made Edward very angry; his anger, rather than depression, was, I felt, a good sign. Indeed when he returned he looked splendidly well and was in the best spirits. The children and I had been busy all day preparing for his coming, and we had a festive tea out in the garden. When we were alone I took him round the garden and showed him all I had done since he'd been gone – the peas all neatly sticked, the lettuces planted out, and the young cabbage plants put in for the winter. I tried to get him to talk of Hope, but he only laughed and said, 'All the golden-haired mermaids in the ocean aren't as good as one brown earth-girl,' and swinging me up in his arms ran with me into the house.

# 9

Edward had been commissioned to write a life of Richard Jefferies, and it was well underway when he left Minsmere. It was a book entirely after his own heart, for Jefferies had been one of the earliest and strongest influences in his life, and the years which he had spent in the Jefferies country in Wiltshire were the most treasured memories of his boyhood. There, wandering with an old countryman, he had very early imbibed his minute knowledge of wild life, and learnt to use and develop that power of observation which he had in such a remarkable degree. The downs country about Swindon he knew and loved as no other part of England. We decided to go there to refresh his memory, and to enable him to get some of the facts of Jefferies's life.

The fortnight we spent in Wiltshire was one of the happiest times of my life, and one of the few holidays of any length which Edward and I had alone together. We walked all day long, and Liddington Castle – an old British camp above Swindon – Wayland Smith's Cave, and the White Horse of Uffington became as familiar to me as our bare hillside in Hampshire. We stayed at a farm house some miles from Swindon, but often, when we had wandered too far afield to return the same day, put up for the night at a wayside inn, where once we arrived so soaking wet that we had to go to bed while our clothes were dried.

During this holiday I realized how much the bare downs meant to me; they thrilled me with a patriotism deep and passionate. They had been the home of the earliest human beings of England, and with their relation to the sea they were mysterious and intimate, tender, wild, and sheltering. The west counties of England are her loveliest and most characteristic. Here, still almost untouched by time, is that rural

England where Shakespeare's rustics and Chaucer's yeomen tilled the soil, and in Wiltshire with its stone-built villages, its great barns like temples built to Demeter, its ancient and noble manor houses, with its guardian elms and rich red fallow, its meadows along the banks of the Avon, its flocks and herds feeding as from time immemorial on the downs, its teams of farm horses often silhouetted on the skyline of the hills, its peasants toiling at their ancient craft in ancient traditional ways, I felt that I was at the very heart of England's being. My spirit was filled with content as my feet trod these ancient ways, and my heart with joy to know that this rich country belonged to me and I to it with all its history and tradition, bareness and richness, toil and harvest, simplicity and mystery.

It turned out that I was as good a walker as Edward, for I could go twenty or thirty miles a day without more fatigue than is pleasant to feel when home and rest are reached. But I could not match his stride which was a long slow swing from the hips, while I walked with short quick steps from the knee. I had, too, a bad habit of walking just a step ahead of Edward, of which he tried in vain to cure me. We fared as simply as possible getting two pennyworth of bread and cheese and a mug of beer at an inn. If we passed no inn we ate a handful of raisins which we carried, and for thirst sucked a pebble – poor comfort but effective. I learnt too, with Edward, to be content to walk without talking – hard at first, because with everything so new to me, and myself so excited by it all, I wanted to talk and ask questions. But I got used to long stretches of silence, and to waiting patiently for the opportunity to talk which came when we sat down to eat, or leaned over a gate to rest, or paddled our feet in a dew pond. We bathed too in the dew ponds, and I loved the feel of the water like silk against my skin, and the warm wind drying me. Then in the evening I made notes of anything that had particularly impressed me. Some of these notes Edward made use of, which encouraged me to keep my eyes open and my senses alert. In this way I learnt and saw much more than I should have done had I chattered all the time. Savernake Forest, Marlborough, Malmesbury, Shaftesbury, Amesbury, Devizes, Westbury and Bradford-on-Avon are some of the places I particularly remember we included in the wide area we traversed, and of course the special places connected with Jefferies. Many of the days stand out clear in my mind today – the ways we went, the things we saw, and even the words we spoke, so happy was I during this our longest holiday together.

# 10

I left Edward in Wiltshire and returned home. There sorry news awaited me. The land on which our house stood, and the fields which surrounded it – even the water-hollow and part of the hanger – had been sold to a man who intended to build a large house in the meadow adjoining the garden, and our cottage was to be the lodge to house the gardener. So we were given notice to go, and the problem of finding a new house had to be faced.

Among those whom I had met at the school was a young man who had been a pupil there. He was now settled in the neighbourhood, and occupied himself making furniture. He had means of his own, but being a disciple of Ruskin and Morris he determined to live a simple and useful life, making strong and beautiful things. At the time I met him he was building a workshop at the top of the wooded hill to the left of our cottage, and he intended later to build himself a house there.

This young man, though uncouth and brusque, attracted me by his sincerity, and I expect his good looks, too. He was magnificently built: tall and straight with a large well-shaped head covered with fair hair made fairer by constant exposure to the weather. His eyes were bright blue and very clear, his skin was tanned, and he had a reddish beard. He was like a Viking or a young demi-god.

His name was Geoffrey Lupton. I introduced him to Edward, and they took to each other, though it is difficult to understand why, except that a certain uncompromising sincerity and hatred of affectation and humbug were common to both. I think the genuine simplicity of our life, enforced by our means, and its rather happy-go-lucky ways, contrasted for him favourably with the thought-out simplicity of the school people.

Whatever it was, he became very friendly with us in his queer abrupt way. He was very clever with his hands. He could build a house, fashion a beam out of an oak tree, bake a loaf of bread or darn a stocking as well as it could be done, and he was very critical of similar work by other people. He had some hand-woven sheets which he wanted hemmed, and as he had not time to do it I offered rather timidly, knowing what a high standard he expected. I took great pains to get the stitches small and even, and when they were finished, after examining them most minutely he said 'They'll do,' which was the utmost praise he ever gave.

This incident paved the way for an offer he made to build us a house. He had bought a long strip of land at the edge of the plateau up to which we looked, and here, overlooking a deep and densely wooded combe, our house was to be built. We could reach the site by a path winding up through the hanger by the stream which had its source half way up. This path was an ancient deeply worn track soft with the leaves that for countless years had fallen and rotted between its high banks. It wound steeply up in the angle of the combe among the noble beeches and yews which were characteristic of our hangers. Arrived at the lane on the top you had a wider view of the South Downs from Chanctonbury on the east to Butser on the west. And here on the edge of this great plateau four hundred feet above the sea – which on a clear day you could see like a grey mist below the horizon – our house was built.

It rose slowly, for Lupton himself built it to his own design. In his workshop great oaks – which he himself years ago had chosen as they grew – and which he had seasoned and sawn and planed – were transformed into beams, doors and window frames. Everything for the house that could be made locally was so made: the bricks, the tiles, even the glass were made under Lupton's direction. The great nails that studded the doors, the hinges and the hasps, were forged by our landlord, and he taught us how to make the oaken pegs which held the tiles in their place. The children and I used to go up every day to see the gradual development of the house which was to be our home. We saw the great oak arches to support the roof shaped and hauled into their place, and the children walked on the rising walls which were to keep the fury of those hill-top storms from us.

The house when it was finished was long and low, facing the south towards which most of the windows looked. The east end was taken up by the living-room, which had windows on all sides but the north. The land sloped so steeply away from the house towards the south that from the windows there was no foreground for the eye to rest on – nothing until the downs seven miles away; and when the downs were hidden by the mists that sometimes filled the combe we felt as if we were on a ship at sea.

Just before we moved I found to my great joy that this house would be the birthplace of my third child. The months before the baby's birth were the longest period of unbroken calm that I can remember. I was very well and happy with my new burden, and Edward was glad that the wish of the last seven years was being fulfilled. Both the children were going to school now, and this had made my longing all the greater.

Edward was busy on the Jefferies book for which he had collected all the data, and things were easier financially than they had ever been, or were ever again to be. I had a good maid, and was able to give a lot of time, with Edward, to the garden. It was heartbreaking work, and all the more so for the contrast with the rich, easily worked soil of the garden we had left – for the soil was stiff and stony and full of the most pernicious weeds. However, by dint of hard work we were not long before we had planted fruit trees and prepared a vegetable plot. One of the most enjoyable tasks we set ourselves was the planting of a wild thicket which we hoped would tempt birds to nest in it. For this we collected seedlings and plants of all the wild trees and shrubs and creepers which had sown themselves in the rich leaf mould. Beech, maple, yew, birch, oak and ash trees in miniature we transplanted to our corner, and among the bramble and traveller's joy and ivy, to my great delight a root of white bryony flourished, and soon draped the tiny trees with its vine-shaped leaves. Every Sunday when we went for our picnics the children helped to find these seedlings in the woods and hedges.

My special bit of garden was the built-up terrace running along the whole length of the south wall below the lower windows. This was the only level part of the garden, and the border each side of the wide bricked path I soon had gay with flowers, and dropping over the edge great clusters of aubretia and white and yellow alyssum, and all the things that love a sun-baked aspect. Here Lupton at my special request had built in the wall of the house an alcove with a seat, and here, when I was too big and heavy to be very active, I sat and sewed and looked over to the downs.

Below the terrace at the end of the garden Edward worked in a tiny study which Lupton had built with a thatched roof, a big fireplace and a long window. In the little border by the door he had planted all kinds of sweet and aromatic herbs – thyme, old man, tansy, rosemary, lavender – and from this garden in years to come I took cuttings of them to plant on his grave in France.

The main road to the town and the school ran down the hill on the other side of the deep combe. You passed our house about a mile down the road, but on the other side of the combe, and it was our custom to call to the children as they came from school when they reached this point. We could only see them in winter when the trees were bare, but when a sea of foliage tossed between us their coo-ee rang out loud and clear, and our answering coo-ee cheered them on their uphill walk. If a bridge had spanned the combe they could have been home in five minutes; as it was, it took them half an hour to reach the house which they knew to be so tantalizingly near.

We had plenty of room here for the entertainment of friends, and they liked this unique hill-top house. We had fields and woods all about us, and the lane which went past the house became a rough track whose old untrimmed hedges almost met above it. In the season we could pick as many mushrooms as we wanted, in half an hour. I've never seen bigger blackberries than grew in the hedges here, nor more plentiful wild strawberries than in the stiff clay of those southern slopes. Yet somehow we could not love the house. The heavy oak was raw and new, and seemed to resent its servitude in beam and door, and with loud cracks would try to wrench itself free. There was nothing in that exposed position to protect us from the wind, which roared and shrieked in the wide chimneys, nor have I ever heard such furious rain as dashed vindictively against our windows. The fire of logs burning in the hearth seemed not to respond so much to our fostering care as to the wind which drew it up in great leaping flames and sent sheaves of sparks into the roaring darkness. Often a thick mist enveloped us, and the house seemed to be standing on the edge of the world, with an infinity of white rolling vapour below us. There was no kindness or warmth or welcome about that house.

One felt it would have to win from the reluctant spirit of the place the right to become part of that land, as a house must do, and as this would assuredly do in years to come, for it was a house built for all time.

No solitude could dismay me now after the many nights I spent in that house alone, sitting in the great living-room by the open fireplace. We were not there long enough to conciliate the spirits which for ever moved and complained about the house. Human birth and sweat and tears of joy or grief had not had their way with that house. The stone threshold was still unworn. Doors had not opened to welcome a bride, nor shut on hushed and darkened rooms. The great oak planks of the floor were unmarked by human usage; no swallows had found the eaves nor lichen the roof. These changes would come, but not in our time.

Edward was more affected by this atmosphere than I. I was aware of it, and later when I was anxious it oppressed my spirit heavily. But now other emotions overwhelmed it, and Edward escaped to his study which was cosy and homely and became his refuge.

Our third child was a girl – which was as Edward had hoped – and we called her Helen Elizabeth Myfanwy – Elizabeth after Edward's mother also – and like her brother and sister she was known by her Welsh name. Though I had been so well and strong and happy all the months of my pregnancy, my confinement was long and difficult, and I was many weeks regaining my strength.

This anxiety coinciding with the finishing of the Jefferies book and a renewed period of financial worry had a disastrous effect upon Edward. He was away a great deal either in London, trying to get work, or in some far-away solitude working at an uncongenial task and trying to exorcise that demon which imprisoned and tortured his spirit.

While we were here his father got him recommended for a government post as assistant secretary to a commission sitting to consider the preservation of ancient Welsh monuments. This job brought in for the first time in our lives a regular and adequate income, and for a while it seemed as if material anxiety was a thing of the past. But this security, with its attendant regular hours of work for Edward and the necessity of his being so much in London, was foreign to our ways, and could not last; Edward, too, felt that his father's influence had unfairly secured him this post, and also that the work itself was not worth the money he was getting for it. These circumstances fretted him. It was not life as he understood it, and I utterly sympathized with him. So, enduring another outbreak of anger from his father, he resigned after three months. The argument 'It is your first duty to provide for your wife and children' had not that portentous significance for us which it had for Mr Thomas, and the return to our happy-go-lucky ways was without regrets to either of us.

While we were in this house something happened which more than ever increased our growing dislike of it. Our baby girl, who was a remarkably healthy strong child, fell suddenly dangerously ill of a mysterious disorder.

I had taken her out one morning in her pram to see a meet

of the hounds at an inn half a mile away. It was a lovely clear
fresh morning. Her rosy cheeks bulged out from her woollen
bonnet, and her brown eyes shone with excitement at the sight
of the hounds and horses and people. She moved her hands
in that expressive way that children have before they can talk,
and jumped up and down in her pram and leaned over to
touch the hounds. Then suddenly she fell back as if uncon-
scious, while a strange and dreadful pallor took the place of
her vivid colour. I was terrified, and ran home as fast as I
could, stopping now and then to tuck her in more closely,
thinking she might have got cold. Then just as suddenly she
sat up, her colour and her normal look returning, and her
spirits as gay as before; I thought that what I had seen was a
bad dream, or that my eyes had played me a ghastly trick,
but I nevertheless hurried home. For hours she played happily
in the big living-room, when suddenly she was overcome
again by unconsciousness and that awful pallor. The maid
rushed down to the study for Edward, while I held the child
in my arms thinking she was dead or dying. Edward thought
so too, but while we were looking at her in dazed horror, she
came to, laughing and jolly as before. We sent for the doctor,
who on examination said a serious operation must be per-
formed at once, and he would there and then take us to the
hospital in his car.

The evening had turned wet and stormy, and hardly know-
ing what I did I wrapped the child up, and – forgetting to put
on either hat or coat – got into the car with Edward. We sat
together, with the merry child on Edward's lap. We could
not speak, but only looked in dumb agony into each other's
face. The rain beat against us as the car raced down the steep
hill, and the children who could see the road through the bare
trees shouted coo-ee to us across the combe as we passed the
house. Edward put a rug round me and the child. He was
used to the rain, and did not feel it. At the hospital in the
matron's room where a big fire was burning, Myfanwy ran
about as gay and frisky as a kitten, but when after some time
a nurse came to take her away her look of terror and her

agonized cry of 'Mummy' broke down my courage.

The doctor, understanding all, advised Edward to take me away from the hospital for two hours. We had nowhere to go, even if we had wanted to see anyone, and in the darkness, with nothing but the rug slung round us and pressed close to each other, we walked for two hours over the heath which lay just outside the town. At the end of that time we went back to the hospital not daring to think what we should hear. All was over, but the child was still under the anaesthetic. The operation had not been as severe as they had feared, and there was every hope of a complete recovery. Edward suggested that, as the child had never been in the care of anyone but myself, it might hasten her recovery if I stayed with her and assisted the nurse as well as I could. The doctor and matron readily agreed to this, and Edward returned home to get my things.

I stayed here three weeks, never leaving the building, for the baby was liable to sudden spasms of pain when only I could soothe her and keep her from crying; also she would take from no one else the uninteresting diet which was necessary for her. It was a strange experience living among ill people in such unhomely surroundings. When Myfanwy did not need me I used to help the nurses, particularly with the little children, and was in great demand for my songs. Edward came every day to see us and bring us a drawing or story or painted picture from the two children at home. All was going well with them, but Edward looked ill and haggard. If Myfanwy was asleep when he came, the matron would let us have her cosy little room all to ourselves, and Edward would read to me something he had just written or we'd talk of homely things. If talk failed, he would take me on his knee and I would lie quiet in his arms whose touch round me eased me of all weariness and care.

'Helen, how could you ever suggest I could do without you? I want you, Helen, and no one but you. It's only when I'm unhappy that you think such a thing, isn't it? Don't ever think that again, will you? Open your eyes and promise.'

'Well, you must promise never to be unhappy again.'

'Oh, if only I could, God knows I would.'

The child recovered rapidly as children do, and we were able to leave the hospital and return home. A great welcome awaited us. The children had got presents for Myfanwy: our house was full of wild flowers they had gathered, and looked for once warm and homely. We had a great sing-song in the evening, and the children were brimful of school and home news, and eager to know all about our life in the hospital. It was lovely to slip back into the old ways and duties; the children seemed especially lively and happy after the poor sickly ones I'd been among so long. The baby snuggled down in her cot with a contented sigh, and all was well as before.

But things began to go badly for us. There was no commissioned work to do now that the Jefferies book was finished, and, worst of all, the paper on which our friend was the literary editor, and on which we had so depended, changed hands. The new editor was friendly towards Edward, but naturally he had his own circle of friends to whom he gave work, and little was left for the old contributors. Also the whole character of the paper altered. The literary page, which under its distinguished editor had maintained such a high level of criticism, and won for itself an unchallenged prestige, now under the new management lowered its standards all round, and became a column or two of criticism divided into titled paragraphs out of which everything had been cut that was not strictly popular.

This was a very serious blow to our finances, and though Edward immediately went to London to try to fill up this gap and was partially successful, he gained no work on which we could so depend. I don't know what we should have done if something had not turned up – as it so often did when we seemed to have come to the end of our resources.

The school people asked me if I would take in one or two children who were for various reasons unable to go home for the holidays. This I was very glad to do, and as I often had two or three children at a time for whose care the parents paid me very well, a very substantial sum was added to our dwindling income.

# 11

All this anxiety, following the trying time during the child's illness, and added to the irritation caused by work on a most uncongenial, poorly paid book which Edward dare not refuse to do, reacted badly on his nervous health. We decided it was best that he should again leave home, and with the help of a friend lodgings were found in a farmhouse in a little village not far from Trowbridge in Wiltshire. Here for some weeks Edward worked hard at the book, and when it was nearly finished I went to spend a few days with him. I shall never forget the kindness of those people – the farmer and his two spinster sisters who lodged us in their house and treated us as though we were honoured guests. The farmhouse was tall, and on the top floor Edward had two large rooms with sloping ceilings and wide windows. It was spring, and in both rooms great log fires burned. On the table laid in front of the sitting-room fire was spread a feast of every delicacy these hospitable people could provide us with. A pint jug full of cream and a quart jug full of home-brewed cider were two of the items. Everything came from the farm. I have never tasted such butter and cheese and cream as were made in the huge dairy which the sisters managed, or seen such quantities of food set before two people. It was easy to see how fond they had become of Edward, who looked ever so much better for the change. They treated us like children, and would not believe that we had three children. They loved us to go in the dairy and to dip out little cups of cream to drink, or to draw ourselves a mug of cider from the cask which stood in the corner, or to come into the kitchen when they were baking cakes and beg one hot from the oven. They could not give us enough or do enough for us. They brought us up tea in the morning with a bunch of fresh wild flowers on the tray, and lit our bedroom fire as well as the sitting-room fire before we got up. They treated us as if we were a honeymoon couple, and made us feel that it was not at all inappropriate.

Near the farmhouse ran a stream in which Edward bathed. The brother – who made as much of us as the sisters – got his men to clear away some boulders to make the pool more convenient. Down to this pool we both went each morning. I remember so well the path through the wood which at this time of the year led through a haze of bluebells to the river. I remember as we walked side by side I did indeed feel like a young bride, and Edward said, as he put his arm round my waist and I mine round his, 'I don't believe, Helen, you'll ever grow up, or ever be too old to be made love to.'

'When I am, will you love me as you do now?'

'That's a question I won't answer before breakfast,' he said teasingly, as catching sight of the river through the trees he began to take off his clothes and ran to the bank.

We walked all one day, and in the evening came to the beautiful old manor house where our friends lived – or rather Edward's friends, for I had not met them before. Our hostess when we arrived was gardening, dressed in an oriental costume of diaphanous material, which she declared was much the most convenient dress for the purpose when her husband insincerely chid her for her trousers. They were rich and young and intellectual, and I hated the atmosphere they created in that dignified house. I hated the cold luxury, the polished insincerity, the clever bloodless wit, and the exotic vegetarian food. Their poor wan baby whose nursery was like a princess's out of the Arabian Nights filled me with pity and horror. I felt very conscious when with people of that kind that I fell very far below what they had expected of Edward's wife. Neither beautiful nor brilliant nor original, I was utterly out of my element with those to whom these qualities were paramount. Edward was annoyed with me for feeling like that, for though he saw through their affectations, even openly laughing at them, there was much in them that interested and amused him, and he accepted them as I could not.

135

I was glad to be out in the open air with my blackthorn, walking by Edward's side, back to our farmhouse by way of Bradford-on-Avon.

On my last evening at the farm the sisters asked us if we could spend an hour with them in their sitting-room. So I put on a pretty red dress that I had brought, and after our supper upstairs we came down to the best sitting-room and were received by the two old ladies in state. They both wore black silk dresses with beautiful old lace collars and heavy gold watch chains looped in front of their tightly fitting bodices. The room smelt of roses, from a great bowl of dried leaves which stood on a little table, and on another table were wine glasses, two bottles of home-made wine, and a plate of cakes. A tall old-fashioned piano stood against the wall, with a green silk front behind a fretwork pattern, on which the ladies begged me to play. I was no pianist and felt very shy of being expected to entertain our friends in such a way, but I could not refuse to do something for them in return for all they had done for us. So in order to help out my playing I suggested that I should sing as well, which delighted them. I played and sang as many folk-songs as I could remember. When my repertoire was exhausted Edward was emboldened by my plight to come to my rescue with some Welsh songs. He loved his native songs, and the soft liquid Welsh tongue suited his voice. After we had sung all we knew, our hostesses and host, who had shown their appreciation by their rapt attention, begged us just to play 'God save the King', which we did while all stood up solemnly. Then we had to eat and drink as much as we could, before we were at last thanked by each of them in turn, and told that it had been an evening they would always treasure as a happy memory.

Edward I could see was pleased with the way I had overcome my shyness and done my best for these kind people, and when we were upstairs he said to me – as we stood by the open window sniffing the sweet dew-laden air, listening to the river, and he began taking down my hair –

'I did love you, Helen, when you began so tremblingly to

sing. I felt proud of you, too: your red dress suited you so
well. I know I'll never hear the last of you from the old ladies.
You've quite cut me out.'

I shook my head so vigorously that the last hairpin fell on
to the floor.

'How pretty your hair is, too.' He took my face between
his hands. 'When next I'm unkind to you, Helen, remember
that what I say then is not true. It's a kind of dreadful play-
acting that comes over me. What is true is what I say now –
that I love you.'

In the morning, laden with a basketful of country fare from
the farm, the brother drove me in his gig to Salisbury where
it was market day, and from where I was to take the train
home. He had two calves in the back, so that there was no
room for Edward. He and the two old ladies waved goodbye
to me from the gate and I to them until the windings of the
lane hid us from each other. As I looked back I could see the
roof of the tall farmhouse, over the hedge and the window at
which Edward and I had stood the evening before. When I
think of that time I am still standing there listening to the river
and sniffing the scent of bluebells, and my heart is beating
with my lover's touch as he unloosens my hair.

Only a few weeks later Edward had to leave the farm sud-
denly. The brother had been taken very seriously ill, and died
after an operation, and the sisters gave up the farm.

Edward returned home with his book unfinished and in a
state of depression brought on by the tragic circumstances at
the farm. The book had been an uncongenial task from the
first, but after this interruption it seemed impossible for him
to concentrate on it. Added to this was the difficulty of getting
regular work, for though odd jobs – some pleasant and some
mere tasks – were fairly frequent, it was a regular flow of
money, however small, that we most needed, and which
would more than anything relieve the unceasing pressure of
anxiety. We decided we must reduce our expenses, which
could only be done by living in a smaller house or doing
without a servant.

Some workmen's cottages were being built down in the village quite near the school. The builder was a wealthy socialist and aristocrat. He had bought an ancient half-timbered cottage, which had lately been condemned, and its garden. On the site three couples of semi-detached cottages were to be erected. It was typical of the society which I have described that the cottages were cheaply built and planned, and that, though these people were meticulously hygienic in theory, no bathroom was provided for their tenants. The rents charged were more than the villagers were accustomed to pay, and on that account the houses were mostly occupied by poor gentle-folk like ourselves, or the villagers eked out the rent by surreptitiously taking in a lodger. The scheme in fact differed in no respect from an ordinary commercial investment, and yielded a higher percentage of interest than was compatible with either the socialism or the philanthropy which the owners professed.

There was no difficulty in arranging with our generous land-lord to leave the house. The large oak refectory table and settle he had made for our living-room were too big for the cottage; so we left them there. The books in the house we moved down to the study which Edward was to retain for a nominal rent of a shilling a week, and our landlord said it was to be Edward's for as long as he wanted it. This was an act of con-sideration and friendship that was deeply appreciated by us, for the room had become very congenial to Edward. In it he sought the solitude which was so necessary for his spirit's health, and it had become his refuge where he could best over-come his demon. Besides, the cottage was tiny and cramped, with no place where he could work, and it was, moreover, in the middle of the village.

We did not know when we moved into that cottage that it was to be our last home together. The same hope haunted me as it had always done – that now perhaps Edward would be happier. If ever the old dark yew in the garden that gave its name to the cottage seemed to me symbolic of the dark mys-tery of life which no ray could reveal, it was not then as I stepped across the threshold. The tiny compactness of the house delighted me, and Edward enjoyed, as I did, setting the place to rights, and finding homes for all our things. The living-room and kitchen were one, and the children and Edward gave me a gay cottage tea-set to hang on the dresser. The cottage lent itself to gaiety in a way that our hill-top house had not done. The window sills were wide, and I had a row of scarlet geraniums in pots on them. The curtains were dotted with bunches of blue and red flowers, and to cover the deal table I bought one of those old-fashioned kitchen table-cloths of bright checks.

On three sides of the house was the garden in which the soil was rich, having been cultivated for hundreds of years. Between it and the garden of the big house next door was a hedge of tall wild damson trees, and here one year to our infinite delight a nightingale sang. We soon had the garden in order – vegetables mostly with a border of flowers. By the only door into the house we planted the herbs which Edward so loved. Rosemary, thyme, lavender, bergamot and old man were there, all direct descendants of our first country garden, which we had propagated from cuttings each time we moved. We planted wild climbing plants in the hedge to drape the rather scraggy damson trees. Bryony, traveller's joy and honeysuckle were all successfully transplanted from the lanes, and over the new red brick walls we trained fruit trees. Over the door Edward built a simple porch with a seat each side which was soon covered with jasmine. Everything grew very easily in that kindly soil, and gardening once more became a pleasure.

Edward went every day to the study, coming down for dinner at noon. He walked or gardened till tea time, and went to the study again till supper at about half-past eight. The children were very near school now, and I was only a mile from the town instead of three miles and a half.

Here I came into close contact with the people of the school, and here among them I became aware of their limitations which hitherto my uncritical admiration had not allowed for. I became aware that their conventions were as rigid and intolerant as other people's, and that their calling themselves unconventional was indicative of their whole relation to life. They lived in an unreal world where everyone wore labels – and the label was the man – Socialist, Vegetarian, Humanitarian, or whatever it might be. There was among them a show of robustness and open air jollity, of freedom from the fetters of money and snobbishness, of sensitivity to the less obvious things of life; but all these things had no depth at all, and were like the writing on those magic note tablets when you draw the talc slide over them.

Among the villagers, one of whom was my next door neighbour, I found real people – people whom life had buffeted, to whom it had imparted humour and shrewdness and wide tolerance; people who though poor were incredibly generous when need arose, and incredibly petty sometimes in their social dealings; whose lives were so unordered that there always seemed time in their overworked days, and space in their over-filled houses, for troubles not their own; people who had very little idea of thrift, but who worked cheerfully from morning till night for a wretched wage; women whose only recreation was half an hour's gossip with a neighbour, and men who enjoyed their beer and their wives.

I liked them as they stood in their Sunday black in a ring on the village green watching the gentry who were dancing folk dances in print dresses and sunbonnets. 'Well,' said my neighbour with a shrewd smile, 'I suppose they've got to be up to something.' Many of their habits I didn't like, but in contrast to the school people their genuineness and earthiness shone out as cardinal virtues. They were too busy with their work and keeping their homes going to have formulated theories and principles. They summed up their experience of life in pithy sayings, as, for example, did a woman whom I particularly liked when her daughter was leaving 'good service' to be married – 'I told her,' she said, 'she'd never know the size of her belly till her feet were under her own table.'

# 12

The chequered pattern of our life was still being woven out of the varied elements of Edward's and my temperament and our circumstances. There were days of calm happy ordinariness, and days when on the spur of the moment we would take our sticks and walk along the South Downs to Cocking, or going by train to the nearest point tread once again our beloved Pilgrims' Way. Other days would come in which the preceding happiness was thrown into brilliant contrast by the darkness and despair of what followed. An incident in such a period is still vivid in my memory because of a woman who shared in it, and who became my dearest friend.

Edward had been away for two weeks. I was looking forward to his return, and to the beginning again for me of the routine which made my life and myself, as it were, whole again. He was coming back from a big house-party of men of his own age and interests who met together each year to talk and walk. They met in an old Manor House owned by the host of the party, whom we had visited in Wiltshire, and here with every kind of comfort and luxury, among congenial friends who admired and loved him in a way that very few men are admired and loved by their contemporaries, Edward had spent one of his rare holidays. Two women had been of the party, though in essence it was a man's affair. One was a lovely girl engaged to one of the young men, and the other was a sister of one of the most brilliant of the party.

Of all these people Edward had written to me in his daily letters, but especially of this sister. I knew from him that she was not beautiful, but clever and lively and witty; that she not only equalled the young men in whatever was being discussed, but shone above them all in imagination and humour, and excelled them in the games of mental skill they played. I knew, too, that she had met Edward very much more than half way in their warm friendship which was necessary to win him from sensitive distrust. I knew also from his letters that among this high-spirited, confident, successful crew, in his heart he was bitter and lonely, and that this girl was the only one with whom he had felt easy.

I had merely to give a swift look at his face as he strode in at the gate to see the terrible cloud of melancholy which was hanging low over his spirit, and blotting out like the blackest night all light, all joy, all love. Without a word he flung himself in his armchair in the living-room, staring in front of him or at me, while I spoke to him of everyday affairs.

The elder children were at school; the baby playing with a neighbour's child. I prayed they might not come in just yet, but in a moment I saw them coming down the road. I ran out and told them to do an errand for me and then play in the meadow. 'Daddy has come home, but he's very tired,' I explained, but before they could run off he was there.

'Why are you keeping the children away?' he asked.

'I only thought you were rather tired,' I replied, 'and that I'd get you your tea in peace while they played out of doors.'

'Why should I be tired when I've just had a fortnight of idleness and not a stroke of work done and none to do – not a book from the *Chronicle* – and my article back from the *New Weekly*. Tired! Tired is not what I am. I'm sick of the whole of life – of myself chiefly, of you and the children. You must hate and despise me, but you can't hate me as much as I hate the whole business, and as I despise myself for not putting an end to it.'

Not waiting to have the tea I had been getting ready for him, he strode out, and up the hill through the wood to his study.

After a while the children came in to tea quietly, with questioning looks at me.

'Daddy has gone up to the study,' I said. 'So we'll have tea.'

Bronwen's face fell. 'Oh, and I've picked him such a lovely bunch of primroses. Look, there are 35 flowers, 35 buds, and

35 leaves, because he's 35, and when he comes I'll give him
35 kisses.'

'Not tonight,' I said. 'Tomorrow perhaps. You must go to
bed early.'

He did not return from the study till late. I put the supper
to keep hot, and went to the gate at the end of the garden that
opened on to the meadow from which the wooded hill rose.
I listened with anxiously strained ears in the perfect silence for
the sound of his striding through the dead leaves and cracking
twigs that were ankle deep in the path down the wood. Gen-
erally he coo-eed to me as he neared home, but the squeaking
of the bats and the owls' wild cries were all I heard. Fear was
in my heart, as it always was when this melancholy of Edward's
brooded over him and over us all. Perhaps he would never
come down the hill again. . . . What was he doing? What think-
ing – up there among the trees? How late it was! How hungry
he must be! What agony was he going through? How little,
how terribly little I could do for him. A dead branch snapped
with a loud noise. My heart stood still for a second, and then
hearing his heavy step I turned to go in, feeling slightly faint
now that I became conscious of what I had feared.

Soon he was in the living-room.

'Hello!' I said, 'Supper is all ready, and I should think you
are ready, too.'

His face was pale and haggard, his lips tightly shut together,
his body bent with a fearful weariness.

'Yes, I suppose I must eat. But why have you sat up for
me? I don't want your fussing about me. I know what I am.
I know what I've done to you. Don't stand there looking grey
and worn till I could hate you for it. Go to bed, go to bed.
Take Bronwen with you. I'll sleep in her bed, though why I
eat and sleep God knows. I'm the man who always comes
home to his supper.'

When I lifted the child out of her bed into mine she said,
'Is this a treat, Mummy?'

'Yes, a lovely treat.'

And she curled herself up with a happy sigh.

The starlings were stirring in their nest in the roof just over our bed when I heard him come up, and then I slept.

Another dreadful day. The children avoid him as much as possible, and are afraid to talk at meals. He knows it, and it is fresh torture to this tortured spirit. He tries to make them say they hate him, and they cry and will not. A black gloom is over the house. I dread his going to the study; I dread his coming back. I feel my face stiffen into deep lines. I am possessed with fear. He speaks little, but what he says is said to hurt me and doubly hurt himself. I keep myself hard at work, for if I stopped I should become physically incapable, as spiritually I am paralysed. I should just sit and brood. My soul is in the dark and loneliness and agony with him, but my body has to work, my tongue to make conversation with the children. I drag through it all as if I were weighted with chains.

Of the children, Bronwen is least affected by this gloom. She adores her father and is his favourite, and the next day when he asks her to go with him to the study she joyfully assents, bargaining that he will carry her some of the way on his back. Then I know the worst is over.

By the noon post come two letters, one from his chief editor, and one in unknown writing, but I guess whose it is.

He is still cold and silent to me. I know the strain of these days shows in my face, and I do things clumsily. Tears are very near my eyes, which before were dry and burning. If only I could be alone to cry and cry. But of course I can't.

The letter, as I guessed, is from Eleanor Farjeon, the new friend.

'Eleanor wants to come here for a night. Can we have her? She's walking from Haslemere, and on to Winchester. Shall I say yes or no?'

So this wonder of women is coming, and I am glad.

For somehow, though the thought of meeting strangers, particularly women, fills me with a morbid dread, with her I feel it will be different. But all the same I feel that I shall not be in any way what she will expect Edward's wife to be, and this old fear of letting him down to his friends persists. So

I write to her, telling her what my fear is, and I dare say revealing to her much more about myself than I had an idea of.

I was busy all the morning making the cottage look its best: scrubbing, polishing, and making cakes. The children and I picked flowers for the rooms – for Eleanor's room a shallow bowl of white violets.

Edward was calm now, but I was still shut out from his love and kindness. He had gone to the study to finish some work, and I was to meet Eleanor along the road. I was happily excited, but too conscious of where I fell short of what Edward's wife should be.

Not far from the village we met.

'You are Eleanor!' and 'You are Helen!' was what we said, as we stood for a moment with hands still held. We looked into each other's faces, not inquiringly as if we should say, 'Now what are you like, I wonder,' but as familiar friends we met; and as friends whose hearts are open to each other we turned together towards the village.

I took her up to her little room of which the window opened to the meadow and the wooded hills beyond.

'You are Eleanor!' and 'You are Helen!' we said again, as if Eleanor could be no other, and Helen could be no other, and we kissed. While we were unpacking her rucksack, laughing over the way a pretty frock was stuffed in with books and shoes and sponge bag, Edward's coo-ee came from the wood, and she, leaning out of the window, sent a clear, sweet coo-ee back to him. I hurried her downstairs and showed her the path. 'You go to meet him while I butter the potato cakes; the children are there, too.'

I thought: 'He will be glad to have her. If only I could slip away, so that he would not have the knowledge of my sadness to trouble him; for he punishes himself through me, and all is distorted and wrong.'

Soon they come in, Edward with a child on his shoulders; and all their hands are full of flowers: celandines, catkins, violets, and primroses; and I see that the children have accepted Eleanor as one of the family. Edward still looks pale and weary, but he talks eagerly to Eleanor, and is at his best. The shadow over Edward and me is still there, but if our secret hearts are cold and desolate, the surface life at any rate is irradiated by warmth and laughter and talk. And as he talks and she responds so quickly his face looks less haggard and the eyes less weary, and I want to thank her.

Edward goes to do some gardening, and Eleanor comes to help me in putting the children to bed. They clamour for songs and stories, of which it turns out she knows lots. When I am tucking them up they say:

'Do you like Eleanor, Mummy?'

'Yes, very much.'

And they each say 'So do I.'

And I know by that 'So do I' that the seal of approval has been irrevocably set on her. She is as happy with us as we with her.

'You go and talk to Edward in the garden. I've got several things to do in the house,' I say.

'Let me help you.'

'No, no. He'll like to show you the garden.'

More than all I want to be alone, and I want him to be happy with Eleanor, until I am sure all is well with him again. It is all mysterious to me why this un-love must be. He can comfort me out of any unhappiness with a word or a kiss, just as with a word he can chill me almost to death. But my love seems to mock me with its impotence to help him. And yet I know he is relying on me to wait for him till he can come to me.

At supper Eleanor praises my cooking, and Edward is pleased, and again he is gay and the talk flashes between them. I join in now and then, and the talk takes a turn that reminds me of some little village contretemps that has happened the other day. And Edward says sharply, 'Yes, that is you all over, Helen. You try with your idiotic kindness to please everybody, and succeed in pleasing nobody, me least of all.' Eleanor looks up to see if this is a joke, and she finds Edward's face full of anger and bitterness, and mine unhappily bewildered, trying to smile as if indeed it was a joke.

'Can't you see what a fool you make of yourself?' he adds.

Oh, if only I could slip away to leave him in the peace that I so unwillingly disturb! Eleanor's face is full of astonished trouble. She looks at me, but I can give her no sign.

Soon we are sitting smoking and talking. They do most of the talking. I sit under the lamp sewing, not knowing whether it is best to try to talk, or what. But all seems to be going well when he says:

'Can't you speak, or are you paying me out?'

So I try to join in, though I am sick with misery. The evening is spoilt, and bed is suggested though it is early yet.

'I'm not going to bed yet,' he says. 'I am going out to walk on the hill to leave myself there or find myself, I don't know which.'

'Good night,' Eleanor says to him. 'Good luck to you on the hill.'

When Eleanor and I turn from the gate to the house after Edward has gone, I see that her face is glowing, her eyes are bright, and she is smiling to herself, and is so wrapt in a secret happiness that for a moment she forgets me holding the door open for her. She looks towards the hill sharply black in the moonlight, and waves her hand to it, still smiling, still wrapt, and suddenly I know that she loves him. Then, as I stand gazing at her with a new vision, the lamp from the house illuminating her face, she drops her head on my shoulder, and I put my arms round her.

'You love him,' I whisper, and though she does not reply, her heart beating so near mine tells me again what I know. I feel again that strange sensation of ageless wisdom and tenderness that I have so often felt for Edward.

'Dear, dear Eleanor, we are closer than ever we guessed we could be, aren't we?'

'Oh, Helen, is it like that, can it be like that?' she says, raising her head.

We sit together on the little bench inside the porch looking out to the meadow and the hill where our beloved seeks for what we cannot give him, love him as we do.

'You see how it is with us now,' I say. 'He has shut his heart against me, and love has no place in his heart. He cannot help it. His spirit is too weary for love, his discontent too bitter. I have learnt to accept it – that for a while it must be like that – and to wait for him to come back. The worst to bear is the way he seems driven to hurt himself the more by hurting me. If love could come to him again through you, Eleanor, it would be like a new heaven and a new earth. I should have my own sadness, but I should not grudge you his love, nor him yours, for I know that what is between Edward and me is eternal; nothing can crumble the solid rock of that something which we have made together. So you see, my dear, there is something irrevocable that cannot be changed. If he could love you, Eleanor, I could not help but be the sharer, though how or why I cannot tell you – only I know it would be so. Do you understand a bit what I mean? You ought to be loved, Eleanor, and if I were a man, if I could be Edward, I should love and cherish you. But there! I'm not, and you love Edward, and if on the hill-top he finds you it will be right, and I shall be like the old mother I often feel to you both, who will be like my children.'

So we sit in the porch, drawn into this strange union. She speaks little. Her head is on my breast, but every now and then she presses my hand in understanding of what I try to make plain to her. Then we speak of him, of his beauty and tenderness, of his work and the fastidiousness of his taste, and his hatred of hypocrisy and jargon and cant. The time goes on into hours. It is late but warm, and the night is bright with moonlight.

At last we hear his coo-ee from the wood, and soon he comes walking with his long swinging stride over the meadow, the moon casting his gigantic shadow almost to our feet. Coo-ee we both call, and before we start to meet him we hold each other close, and kiss without a word. Soon we are running through the dew-wet grass.

'Quickly, quickly!' he says. 'I've heard the first nightingale

148

over there in the hazel copse. I've never known one so early. You must come and hear him. He's not in full song, but he's got his best note of all.'

He takes us each by an arm, and we run with the moon full in our faces. I look up at his face all eager excitement and joy. Soon we are at the edge of the copse, dappled with moonlight. The still air is full of the scent of bluebells. We stand arm in arm in tense expectation, not daring to give our breathlessness relief. Then out of the silence, out of the scent-laden, moonlit, dappled copse, comes a long clear, vibrating note of purest tone. Low and tender it is at first, but as it draws out the sweetness becomes strength, the tenderness passion, until in that wild note it is as if God speaks and we understand, but what we understand we do not know. All pain, all ecstasy, all despair, all love are expressed.

For some seconds we stand amazed by what has been revealed to us. Then the scent of the bluebells comes to us again, and at our feet a frog jumps through the grass.

'We are knowing, but the nightingale has wisdom, even more than solemn old Helen,' Edward says, and bends down and, taking my face between his hands, kisses the tip of my nose.

'Kiss Eleanor too,' I say.

And he kisses her, and she him. And we return to the house.

When for a moment we stand saying good night at our bedroom doors, Eleanor whispers as I take her candle in: 'I'm so glad he has found you, dear Helen.'

Edward does not kiss her again, but says, 'It's good to have you here, Eleanor. Sleep well.'

Bronwen is sleeping in our bed, and Edward looks ruefully at her.

'Let's sleep in the copse among the bluebells tonight. There's that roll of camp bedding we can easily carry there.'

But I say, 'No, no, not tonight. Tomorrow night, when we are alone we will.'

'Why, Helen, you're crying. You are not sad any more?'

'No, not really crying. A few tears just came.'

149

We get into bed – the child between us, our hands meeting over her little curled-up body.

'Edward,' I say, 'you'll go a few miles of the way with Eleanor tomorrow, won't you?'

'Yes, of course I will. We'll all go and make it a picnic day for the children.'

'No, you go. I want you to.'

'All right, but you like her, don't you?'

'Yes. I've never met a woman whom I love so much.'

His voice grows sleepy, and soon his hold of my hand slackens, and he is asleep. I lean over the child and kiss him.

I can't sleep, my heart is too full.

I lie thinking of the strange bewilderment of things that is our life. I cannot understand it: birth, love, death, and all the different kinds of suffering; the loneliness of each one in spite of friendship and love and sympathy; Edward, and me, and Eleanor... What can it mean?

My eyes close but sleep will not come, until out of the darkness I hear far away in the copse the trembling note of the nightingale, and peace comes to my troubled heart.

# 13

Then the war came.

Edward and Merfyn had cycled together into Gloucester staying with friends on the way, taking a week or more to reach a little village beyond Ledbury where some Americans Edward had lately met were staying, and where later the two little girls and myself were to join them.

War was declared on the day that I was to start. I shall never forget that journey – the disorganized train service, the crowds at the stations, reservists being seen off by friends, trains full of men going to join the ranks, and complete chaos everywhere. We did not arrive at our destination till the small hours of the following morning, having had to do the last part of the journey by motor car. I remember the drive of about fifteen miles through the Malvern Hills under a large harvest moon. We stopped men to inquire the way, for I had no idea where the house was, and the village constable asked most suspiciously who we were and what was our errand, peering into the car and seeing only an anxious woman and two little girls fast asleep. But such were the times that a few days later, when our adventure had become nothing more than a good story, a policeman called to say that he must make inquiries about us to satisfy people who had suggested that we were spies.

The news of war had of course preceded us, but no excitement disturbed the peace of that beautiful orchard country, with its wealth of choicest apples, pears and plums hanging red and golden and purple from the branches of innumerable fruit trees, which bore in very truth fruit that were jewels of great price.

We living there with the farmer and his wife, and in the constant society of people who became our intimate and beloved friends, did not then realize all that brooded over our lives. We spent those happy weeks in the open air, in the evenings sitting with our friends and talking – talking of people and life and poetry, for our friend was a poet, Robert Frost. Between him and Edward a most wonderful friendship grew up. He believed in Edward and loved him, understanding, as no other man had ever understood, his strange complex temperament. The influence of this man on Edward's intellectual life was profound, and to it alone of outside influences is to be attributed that final and fullest expression of himself which Edward now found in writing poetry. There began during that holiday a kind of spiritual and intellectual fulfilment which was to culminate two years later in his death. In that short time, most of it spent in the army, Edward was to pour out in poetry all the splendid experience of sadness and beauty; and in his poems is expressed for ever the tender loveliness of the English country.

# 14

But now indeed things were bad for us, and after our friends sailed back to America taking Merfyn with them for a year, Edward became torn in his mind as to what he ought to do. There was hardly any literary work to be had, and we were hard put to it to keep going. He got one or two commissions for special articles having an indirect war interest, but naturally the papers did not want his reflective and critical essays, and reviewing had almost ceased. Besides the anxiety of providing for us all, there was the deep conviction that he ought to enlist. He hated the newspaper patriotism. He saw through the lies and deception of the press as he had always seen through untruths. He was not even carried away by the abnormal condition of the national emotion. Indeed his attitude to the war was inexplicable to his father who was roused to fury by what he thought was his son's disloyalty when Edward suggested that the Germans were as brave as the English, and that 'cold steel' would bring fear to the hearts of any man, be he German or English. The old antagonism broke out again and was never healed.

One day when he was in London ostensibly looking for work, he sent me a telegram telling me he had enlisted in the Artists' Rifles. I had known that the struggle going on in his spirit would end like this, and I had tried to prepare myself for it. But when the telegram came I felt suddenly faint and despairing. 'No, no, no,' was all I could say; 'not that.' But I knew it had to be and that it was right. He was – so the telegram said – to come home in a few days a soldier.

During our life there had been many bitter partings and many joyous homecomings. The bitterness of the partings has faded from my consciousness; I know it was so, but I forget how and why. But the memory of the joy and hope and happiness of the reunions has stayed with me, and for ever, so it seems to me, part of me will stand at the gate and listen for his step, watch for his long stride; feel the strong embrace of his arms, and his kiss.

After a terrific furbishing of the house, so that wherever you looked everything – the floors, the crockery on the dresser, the brass candlesticks – shone with cleanliness and neatness, I went to meet him at the station. As I hurried along the country road I caught up village people in twos and threes, all in their best, evidently out on some festive errand; they called to me as I passed, 'Going to welcome the V.C.?' 'No,' I called back gaily. 'My soldier has no medals yet.' As I got nearer the station the road was fringed with people from the villages round, some of whom I knew. 'You'll get a good view of him if you stay here,' said one. 'Oh no, I must be there when the train comes in,' I replied; and flushed and excited I rushed on. The platform was crowded, the town band was there, with the town officials. It seemed right and natural to me that there should be all this fuss, and it accorded with my own joyous excitement, but I stood away from the crowd at the end of the platform. The crowd could have their hero, but I wanted my soldier all to myself. The train came in.

I did not see the official welcome of the V.C., for Edward got out just where I stood. I noticed with a shock that his hair was cut very short, and that the thinness of his face was accentuated, but that he looked trim and soldierly in his uniform.

As he stooped to kiss me I smelt for the first time that queer sour smell of khaki, so different from Edward's usual smell of peaty Harris tweed and tobacco. What a difference the clothes made! The stiffness and tightness too were so strange after his easy loose things. I could not now walk with my hand in his pocket and his hand over mine.

I looked up at his face as we walked along, and in a flash I saw the sensitiveness, the suffering, the strength and the sincerity which had determined for him the rightness of this step. I was proud of him, and my heart silently responded to the cheers with which the crowd welcomed their hero. I passed

154

again the woman who had spoken to me. 'You be luckier than us,' she said, 'with a V.C. all of your own.' Edward saluted her, and I nodded in acknowledgement of the truth of what she said.

The children were excited and eager to hear all about soldiers, and after tea, as we sat round the table polishing his buttons and badges and buckles, he told us about enlisting, and how he was now a soldier for the duration of the war. He had already learned some soldiers' songs which had good choruses in which we all joined.

The three days he had before joining his regiment were busy with gardening, and putting papers and books in order in the hill-top study, and making preparations for a long absence from home. We had one glorious walk together. On that day he discarded his khaki, and but for his short hair, which I could not get used to, was his old self. We talked of ways and means, of the children and the garden, of the men mostly painters and writers like himself who were to be his companions and to learn with him the uncongenial business of warfare. Sometimes, walking through familiar country which we loved, we talked of that, and sometimes in the old way we walked silently. I remember thinking, 'Oh if only we could walk on like this for ever, and for ever it be summer, and for ever we be happy!' And then I remembered that, after all, the war itself was the reason for this very walk, and had its part in the depth of our deep content with the English country and with each other. Because of the war our souls were now drawn into the circle that was our love, and we understood and loved each other completely.

The war ruthlessly made clear the difference between the various people who lived in the village. All the able-bodied village men had enlisted – the young men out for life and adventure, the older because they felt it their duty to do so. Only the old and infirm were left.

The school as a whole stood for pacifism, and though the roll of honour in the school hall lengthened each day as old boys fell, the spirit of the place was anti-war. Young athletic men in sweaters and shorts carried on the great work of co-

155

education, and at the village debating society tried to hold
their own against the onslaughts of the more instinctive villa-
gers and landed proprietors. I could hardly believe in the sin-
cerity of the men who said they would not fight for anything,
and if they were sincere I thought them even more contemp-
tible. When I told a leading member of the staff that Edward
had enlisted, he said disapprovingly, 'That's the last thing I
should have expected him to do.' How I hated him for that
remark, and hated more the schoolmaster smugness from
which it came. So by degrees I became antagonistic towards
the school people and all they stood for. I felt stifled – especially
at that agonizing time – by the self-confident righteousness,
by the principles which proved so irresistible to hypocrisy,
by the theories which remained in the head and never reached
the heart. A meeting was called at the school at which it was
decided that, as the men of the village were all at the war, the
cottagers' gardens should be dug and planted by pacifist mem-
bers of the staff, 'for we realize,' they said to the women who
composed the audience, 'how much you depend on your gar-
dens, and that the soil is too heavy for you to tackle'. The
women clapped for the vote of thanks, but were not much
impressed with the magnanimity of this offer, because being
wiser than their betters they knew that if they did not dig their
gardens themselves no one else would. And so indeed it turned
out.

# 15

Edward had been in the army a year. He hated it all – the stupidity, the injustice, the red tape, and the conditions of camp life. But he worked hard to perfect himself in the job he had undertaken to become a proficient soldier, and it was with real pride that he brought home his first stripe for me to sew on his sleeve. He practised the Guards' smart salute, and was meticulously careful that his uniform was in order, with buttons and buckles polished, and puttees wound in regulation style.

The map reading and the work with the prismatic compass he enjoyed; he also got a certain satisfaction from the route marches in Essex – a county he had not known before, which he found interesting and beautiful. His own inner life was submerged under these strange and difficult conditions, only coming to the surface in the odd moments when he could be alone, when he found infinite comfort and satisfaction in expressing himself in his poems. He offered some of these poems to various editors, but no one had any room for such quiet meditative verse, in which the profound love and knowledge of his country were too subtle in their patriotism for the nation's mood. This failure was a great disappointment to him, and it was difficult for him in the face of it and with his lack of self-confidence to believe the appreciative criticism he obtained from his friends.

The payment for these poems would have been a useful addition to our meagre income, but more valuable than that would have been the encouragement. The public acknowledgement of his worth as a writer of either prose or poetry he was never in his life to have. Death came leading Fame by the hand.

But his old periods of dark agony had gone for ever. The

sensitive introspective quality of his nature remained, but the black despair had given way to calm acceptance. He was not resigned to the army life: he hated it, and saw clearly and without any illusion its cruelty; but having undertaken the job there was nothing that he shirked, and to the end his only fear was of being afraid.

When the time came for him to be drafted from the Artists' Rifles to a unit, he worked so hard at mathematics, which he had no aptitude for and only the most elementary knowledge of, that he passed high in his examination and was given a commission in the Artillery. In this mathematical work he was greatly helped by Merfyn, whose abilities lay in that direction, and a new and lovely relation sprang up between father and son.

When Edward came home on his short leaves he always spent some hours in his study at the top of the hill. He loved the little room looking out to the downs and beyond to the sea, and here he wrote several of his loveliest poems. If he had no special work to do, he browsed among his books, or weeded his herb garden, or made a great fire of shavings from Lupton's workshop to air the place. This room was his special sanctuary, and I only went up there when he was away to open the window and keep it dusted.

One day something happened which precipitated my departure from the village, to whose atmosphere I was becoming more and more antagonistic. I received a letter from Mrs Lupton, whose husband, our friend, was at the Front, saying that she needed an extra room for a woman she was engaging as a companion, and requesting me to remove as soon as possible all Edward's belongings from the study. It would be impossible to express the emotion with which I read those few curt words. I wrote at once saying there was some mistake, pointing out that her husband had granted the study to Edward for as long as he wanted it. I told her, moreover, all that the study meant to Edward, how now that he was living such an unnatural life in the army the little room had become on his leaves a special sanctuary, a blessed spot where he could be quiet among his

books, a place that had become his by every claim of use and
association. In passionate language I begged her to consider
all this. Her reply was, 'The place is mine, and I must have
it; please remove your husband's things as soon as possible.'
I wrote her a letter of furious denunciation. Nothing that I
felt I left unsaid, and my heart was full of bitter anger and
despair.

The following day I was alone in the house. I had just washed
my hair which was hanging in wet strands when a knock came
at the door, and answering it I found a member of the school
staff standing there with my letter to Mrs Lupton in his hand.
He explained that he had come to ask me on Mrs Lupton's
behalf to withdraw what I had said, murmuring some plati-
tudes about brotherly love. I invited him into our living-room.
Sitting before him white and trembling, with my black hair
wet and lank hanging over my shoulders, I must have looked
like a witch; and so in the end I believe he thought me, for I
poured out all the antagonism for the school and its disciples
which had been accumulating since I had come to live among
these people. All my despair on Edward's account I vented in
scornful and contemptuous words. Nothing that my visitor
could interpolate could stop the verbal flood that surged from
my heart, and taking the letter from his hand I told him there
was not one word which I would retract because there was
not one word which I did not feel to be true. Dismayed and
speechless the poor man hurriedly left me still sitting by the
table. When he had gone, burying my face on my arms out-
stretched over the table I cried till my heart was dry of tears.

The next day with the help of an old man and a donkey-cart
I emptied Edward's beloved study of his books, manuscripts,
and pictures. It took me all day, for I had to carry the books
a few at a time the whole up-hill length of the garden to the
lane, the old man being too feeble to do anything but take
them from me and pack them into the cart. Only Mrs Lupton's
face at her window watching me gave me strength for the
tremendous task.

This incident, which at the time assumed such momentous

significance, finally sickened me of the place, and as Merfyn was being apprenticed to an engineer at Walthamstow, I decided to move somewhere within reach of him.

Edward, who had accepted the loss of the study in the same spirit in which he accepted everything which affected himself and for which the war was responsible, was camping in Epping Forest. In this neighbourhood he found us without much difficulty a cottage standing in the grounds of a nursery garden which had run wild owing to the lack of men to keep it in order. It was, Edward warned me, a horrid little place, but it was within cycling distance of Merfyn's works. I could take no interest in a house which Edward was not to share. All I wanted was to leave the village in whose county of hangers and plateaux, downs and deep combes we had spent twelve years. I loved the place. Every hillside, every wood and meadow, every green lane and steep chalk track, almost every tree had its associations. There our baby had been born, there I had grown from a girl to a woman, and learnt much about nature and people and life. It is the country of White and Cobbett, and is even now as it was in their days. The line of its hills, the windings of its lanes, the details of its villages and farms are imprinted on my heart for ever. Walks that Edward and I took there I shall never forget; even our talks as we went are fresh in my memory. The bare juniper-dotted hill with the clumps of pine trees at the top, at whose feet and crest we had lived, whose multitudinous but tiny cowslips, orchids, milkwort and violet we so joyously welcomed when they came and shot the grey turf with various colour; up whose steep side I had watched Edward stride away angry and weary of everything, or down which he had run perilously with a child on his shoulder; this hill which had become almost human for us with its austerity, friendliness and tenderness, is more than any other place in England linked with Edward in my memory and my dreams.

But now my love was overwhelmed by dim forebodings which my natural happiness, hopefulness and vitality were powerless to subdue, and which robbed me of the courage to stay there and make believe to continue a life from which without Edward all significance had gone: forebodings which though vague and unformulated urged me to wrench myself from these associations before they became unbearable to me.

Edward could not get leave from camp to help me with the move, but a week or two before we left he came home to say good-bye to those hangers and our hill; and at this period, so fraught with sad and poignant thoughts and memories, some of his loveliest poems were written. He read them to me in the evening when we were alone. I could not speak about them when he asked me for my criticism, so deeply had their beauty and significance sunk into my heart. The jerry-built cottage is made sacred to me because of those last evenings with Edward there. Only on a few more occasions were we to sit together by our own fireside, and as if I knew it, my heart hurt with unsheddable tears, and, when he had gone, with a bitterness new and dreadful to it.

# 16

The move was a grotesque nightmare of incompetent drunken men and books hurled pell-mell into cases, but somehow or other we and our goods arrived at the cottage in Essex. It was a horrible house on the top of a high hill in Epping Forest, ugly, cold and inconvenient – an impossible place to make either pretty or comfortable. Single-handed it took me a long time to get things ship-shape, and even when all was done there was a makeshift feeling about the place which could not be eradicated, and which I hated it for.

It was October, and already the first snow of what was to be a terrible winter had fallen. Merfyn had to leave the house at six o'clock in the morning, and bicycle some miles to the engineering workshops where he was apprenticed. He and I got up soon after five in the dark, bitterly cold mornings. There was no proper cooking stove; so after lighting a fire in the sitting-room we made porridge and fried bacon on a primus. Then off Merfyn would go in the darkness with the stars still twinkling over the forest as if deriding its stark immobility.

Sometimes I would go back to bed beside Bronwen, but more often as the dawn slowly filtered through the trees I would sit by the fire not thinking, not reading, emptied of all emotion, even loneliness – as if waiting for I knew not what. An unutterable fear, an icy chill had taken possession of my heart. I was not always conscious of it, but it had the effect of making me feel that life had stopped, that it was simply marking time until something should happen that would set it going again. What that something would be I didn't ask, but dimly supposed it would be the end of the war.

When Edward wrote to me that early in the new year he would be going to France, the fear and the icy chill took a closer grip, and the sense of statically existing – not living – grew more intense. Yet on the surface all was as usual – the housework done, the children played with, happy hours spent wooding in the snow-capped forest. My daily letters to Edward were written, and only then as I wrote to him did the chill melt away; thought and feeling returned, and words in which to utter them ran as swiftly as ever from my pen.

His letters were full of his work and of his life in the various camps to which he was sent to complete his artillery training. Often he would enclose one or two poems, and these with their quiet sad beauty, their feeling for the English country, and most of all their intimate revelations of the soul of the man whom I knew so well, and whose love was the core of my being – these poems sank into my heart like prayers.

He wrote that his last leave was imminent, but would not include Christmas, which was now a few weeks distant. We each knew what we felt about this, and neither of us said a word. We had always made so much of festivals, but that we should not be together for this Christmas was all a part of that stoppage of living.

I remember the day this double news came. The children had been invited to a party at the house of a poet – a very dear friend. I had made Myfanwy a pretty dress of some cheap but unusual material, and at the party several of the mothers came up to me and praised the child and the frock. But the sentence 'And Helen, I can't get home for Christmas' thumped out a sort of tune in my head, and though with my ears I heard 'How lovely Myfanwy looks,' 'How cleverly you have made the frock,' I listened with all my being to 'And Helen, I can't get home for Christmas'. Our friends too were affected by the news, and during the gaiety of the party we comforted each other with unexpressed but none the less understood sympathy.

'Christmas must be prepared for, however,' I thought, and I became busy with cakes and puddings and what I could afford of Christmas fare, which was little enough. The children with me planned the box I should pack for Edward, with something of everything, including crackers and sweets, and they began to make their presents for him. Into these preparations which before had always gone with such happy zest the same feeling of unreality entered and my eagerness was assumed for the sake of the children. But they too found it difficult to anticipate with joy a Christmas so strange, and the activities fell flat. Outside circumstances mattered as never before – our poverty, the severity of the weather, the dreariness of the house – and over us all an indefinable shadow fell.

But a miracle happened. Suddenly this Christmas of all Christmasses became the most joyous; the snow-bound forest sparkled like Aladdin's Cave; the house was transformed into a festive bower of holly and ivy and fir boughs, and our listlessness was changed into animated happiness and excitement.

Edward after all *was* coming home for Christmas!

The letter telling me this arrived by the first post along with one in a strange hand which I opened first, little suspecting what news Edward's contained. Inside this letter was a cheque for £20 made out to me and signed by the name of a writer of distinction whom I did not know. I stared and stared, and fumbling in the envelope for some explanation found a note from Eleanor telling me that she had been asked to forward this to me as a gift from a private fund. What could I not do with £20! I had never had so much in my life. But oh, if only Edward had been coming home!

Seeing his letter, which in my bewilderment I had forgotten, I read only the first words: 'My dearest, my draft leave will include Christmas after all!' I raced upstairs to the sleeping children. 'Wake up, wake up! Daddy is coming home for Christmas. He's coming home. He'll be here tomorrow, and I've got £20 to spend, and we'll all have the most wonderful presents; and oh, he's coming home.' Half-crying and half-laughing I lifted the children out of bed, and we danced in a ring and sang 'He's coming home for Christmas' to the tune of 'For he's a jolly good fellow'.

How we worked that day to get all ready! I snatched a couple of hours to go to London and do the shopping. I bought for Edward the best Jaeger sleeping-bag and thick gauntlet gloves and a volume of Shakespeare's sonnets, and for the children a real magic lantern with moving slides, and a special present for each one. I brought fruit and sweets and luxuries we had never tasted before, and wine as well. A frock of Edward's favourite red was my present to myself, and secretly for Myfanwy the children and I dug a little Christmas tree out of the garden and loaded it with toys and trinkets, and candles ready to light.

Life was not paralysed now, but with new-found vigour sped along eager and joyous. Nor did time stand still. I was up half the night arranging the greenery that the children had ransacked the forest for during the day, and the finishing touches to all that was to make this Christmas of all Christmasses shine above its peers.

Never did my strong body serve me better, for after an hour or two's sleep and up again in the starry morning I felt revivified, wishing God-speed to the hour that would bring Edward home. Besides all this, the feast had now to be prepared – the great turkey stuffed, the pastry made, the dessert arranged in dishes. No one was idle. Merfyn brought in a great pile of logs; Bronwen sat busily finishing the story she was writing about a horse, for her father's present; while Myfanwy embroidered with gay-coloured wools a picture of a butterfly outlined on cardboard and pricked beforehand with holes for her blunt-pointed needle. Everybody was talking or singing or teasing me by pretending to look into places where secrets were known to be concealed. I had to stop the chopping of parsley to thread Myfanwy's needle, and Merfyn cleaning the family's shoes kept his eye on the clock for when it should be time for him and Bronwen to go and meet Edward.

'Tomorrow is Christmas Day,' they kept saying. 'Tomorrow is Christmas Day.' In the midst of all this happy activity and looking forward, that word 'tomorrow' struck a note I could not help hearing, but I would not let it mean anything to me then. Tomorrow and tomorrow and tomorrow – the word was trying to shatter the joy of my soul with its knell-like reverberations.

'Today Daddy is coming home. Soon he'll be here, and after you've been to sleep you'll wake up and today will be Christmas Day,' I said. 'Don't talk of tomorrow when today is here and is so lovely.'

'Don't you want Christmas to come then, Mummy?'

'Yes, but I think today is nicer than tomorrow.'

'I see what Mother means,' Merfyn said, 'now that the war's on, some tomorrows are bound to be sad for lots of people, and *she* doesn't want to think of them, do you, Mummy?'

'Yes, it's a bit like that. But look at the clock. If you don't hurry, today will pay you out and vanish before you've met Daddy.'

Merfyn and Bronwen were soon ready to go to the bottom of the hill at the cross-roads about a mile from the house, where they were to meet Edward. Myfanwy and I stayed behind to toast the crumpets and boil the kettle. The last stitches were being put into the butterfly, and I had a piece of blue ribbon ready to thread through the top to hang it up by.

'I'm glad I didn't choose the duck. I think Daddy likes butterflies much better than ducks.'

'I'm sure he does. He showed me once a butterfly called a painted lady, but this one must be an embroidered lady.'

'Oh no, Mummy, this is not a lady butterfly; it's a father one.'

'Hark, what's that! Let's go to the door and listen.'

But no sound came from the windless snow-laden forest.

'I wonder if I ever shall see a real Christmas-tree like the one Bronwen told me about that she had at school with toys and candles,' said Myfanwy with a sigh, reminded of the subject by rows of fir trees still growing in the nursery garden.

'Oh my darling, you shall have everything you ever dreamt of this Christmas.' And I catch her up in my arms, and she throws her arms round my neck. While I stand thus the air is cut with Edward's clear voice calling the old familiar coo-ee; then the sound of voices; then of heavy snow-clogged footsteps; then Edward at the door. He is here. He is home.

# 17

Christmas had come and gone. The snow still lay deep under the forest trees, which tortured by the merciless wind moaned and swayed as if in exhausted agony. The sky, day after day, was grey with snow that fell often enough to keep the surface white, and cover again and again the bits of twigs, and sometimes large branches that broke from the heavily laden trees. We wearied for some colour, some warmth, some sound, but desolation and despair seemed to have taken up her dwelling-place on the earth, as in our hearts she had entered, do what we would to keep her out. I longed with a passionate longing for some sign of life, of hope, of spring, but none came, and I knew at last none would come.

The last two days of Edward's leave had come. Two days and two nights more we were to be together, and I prayed in my heart, 'Oh, let the snow melt and the sky be blue again!' so that the dread which was spoiling these precious hours would lift.

The first days had been busy with friends coming to say good-bye, all bringing presents for Edward to take out to the front – warm lined gloves, a fountain pen, a box of favourite sweets, books.

This was not a time when words of affection were bearable; so they heaped things that they thought he might need or would like. Everyone who came was full of fun and joking about his being an officer after having had, as it were, to go to school again and learn mathematics, which were so uncongenial to him, but which he had stuck to and mastered with that strange pertinacity that had made him stick to all sorts of unlikely and uncongenial things in his life. They joked about his short hair, and the little moustache he had grown, and about the way he had perfected the Guards' salute. We got

167

large jugs of beer from the inn near by to drink his health in, and an end to the War. The hateful cottage became homely and comfortable under the influence of these friends, all so kind and cheerful.

Then in the evenings, when just outside the door the silence of the forest was like a pall covering too heavily the myriads of birds and little beasts that the frost had killed, we would sit by the fire with the children and read aloud to them, and they would sing songs that they had known since their baby-hood, and Edward sang new ones he had learnt in the army – jolly songs with good choruses in which I, too, joined as I busied about getting the supper. Then, when Myfanwy had gone to bed, Bronwen would sit on his lap, content just to be there, while he and Merfyn worked out problems or studied maps. It was lovely to see those two so united over this com-mon interest.

But he and I were separated by our dread, and we could not look each other in the eyes, nor dared we be left alone together.

The days had passed in restless energy for us both. He had sawn up a big tree that had been blown down at our very door, and chopped the branches into logs, the children all helping. The children loved being with him, for though he was stern in making them build up the logs properly, and use the tools in the right way, they were not resentful of this, but tried to win his rare praise and imitate his skill. Indoors he packed his kit and polished his accoutrements. He loved a good piece of leather, and his Sam Browne and high trench-boots shone with a deep clear lustre. The brass, too, reminded him of the brass ornaments we had often admired when years ago we had lived on a farm and knew every detail of a plough-team's harness. We all helped with the buttons and buckles and badges to turn him out the smart officer it was his pride to be. For he entered into this soldiering which he hated in just the same spirit of thoroughness of which I have spoken before. We talked, as we polished, of those past days: 'Do you remember when Jingo, the grey leader of the team, had colic, and Turner the ploughman led her about Blooming Meadow for hours, his eyes streaming with tears because he thought she was going to die? And how she would only eat the hay from Blooming Meadow, and not the coarse hay that was grown in Sixteen Acre Meadow for the cows? And do you remember Turner's whip which he carried over his shoulder when he led Darling and Chestnut and Jingo out to the plough? It had fourteen brass bands on the handle, one for every year of his service on the farm.' So we talked of old times that the children could remember.

And the days went by till only two were left. Edward had been going through drawers full of letters, tearing up dozens and keeping just one here and there, and arranging manuscripts and note-books and newspaper cuttings all neatly in his desk – his face pale and suffering while he whistled. The children helped and collected stamps from the envelopes, and from the drawers all sorts of useless odds and ends that children love. Merfyn knew what it all meant, and looked anxiously and dumbly from his father's face to mine.

And I knew Edward's agony and he knew mine, and all we could do was to speak sharply to each other. 'Now do, for goodness' sake, remember, Helen, that these are the important manuscripts, and that I'm putting them here, and this key is for the box that holds all important papers like our marriage certificate and the children's birth certificates, and my life insurance policy. You may want them at some time; so don't go leaving the key about.' And I, after a while, 'Can't you leave all this unnecessary tidying business, and put up that shelf you promised me? I hate this room, but a few books on a shelf might make it look at bit more human.' 'Nothing will improve this room, so you had better resign yourself to it. Besides, the wall is too rotten for a shelf.' 'Oh, but you promised.' 'Well, it won't be the first time I've broken a promise to you, will it? Nor the last, perhaps.'

Oh, God! melt the snow and let the sky be blue.

The last evening comes. The children have taken down the holly and mistletoe and ivy, and chopped up the little Christmas-

tree to burn. And for a treat Bronwen and Myfanwy are to
have their bath in front of the blazing fire. The big zinc bath
is dragged in, and the children undress in high glee, and skip
about naked in the warm room, which is soon filled with the
sweet smell of the burning greenery. The berries pop, and the
fir-tree makes fairy lace, and the holly crackles and roars. The
two children get into the bath together, and Edward scrubs
them in turn – they laughing, making the fire hiss with their
splashing. The drawn curtains shut out the snow and the star-
less sky, and the deathly silence out there in the biting cold is
forgotten in the noise and warmth of our little room. After
the bath Edward reads to them. First of all he reads Shelley's
*The Question* and *Chevy Chase*, and then for Myfanwy a
favourite Norse tale. They sit in their nightgowns listening
gravely, and then, just before they kiss him good night, while
I stand by with the candle in my hand, he says: 'Remember
while I am away to be kind. Be kind, first of all, to Mummy,
and after that be kind to everyone and everything.' And they
all assent together, and joyfully hug and kiss him, and he
carries the two girls up, and drops each into her bed.

And we are left alone, unable to hide our agony, afraid to
show it. Over supper, we talk of the probable front he'll arrive
at, of his fellow-officers, and of the unfinished portrait-etching
that one of them has done of him and given to me. And we
speak of the garden, and where this year he wants the potatoes
to be, and he reminds me to put in the beans directly the snow
disappears. 'If I'm not back in time, you'd better get someone
to help you with the digging,' he says. He reads me some of
the poems he has written that I have not heard – the last one
of all called *Out in the Dark*. And I venture to question one
line, and he says, 'Oh, no, it's right, Helen, I'm sure it's right.'
And I nod because I can't speak, and I try to smile at his
assurance.

I sit and stare stupidly at his luggage by the wall, and his
roll of bedding, kit-bag, and suitcase. He takes out his prismatic
compass and explains it to me, but I cannot see, and when a
tear drops on to it he just shuts it up and puts it away. Then

170

he says, as he takes a book out of his pocket, 'You see, your Shakespeare's *Sonnets* is already where it will always be. Shall I read you some?' He reads one or two to me. His face is grey and his mouth trembles, but his voice is quiet and steady. And soon I slip to the floor and sit between his knees, and while he reads his hand falls over my shoulder and I hold it with mine.

'Shall I undress you by this lovely fire and carry you upstairs in my khaki greatcoat?' So he undoes my things, and I slip out of them; then he takes the pins out of my hair, and we laugh at ourselves for behaving as we so often do, like young lovers. 'We have never become a proper Darby and Joan, have we?'

'I'll read to you till the fire burns low, and then we'll go to bed.' Holding the book in one hand, and bending over me to get the light of the fire on the book, he puts his other hand over my breast, and I cover his hand with mine, and he reads from *Antony and Cleopatra*. He cannot see my face, nor I his, but his low, tender voice trembles as he speaks the words so full for us of poignant meaning. That tremor is my undoing. 'Don't read any more. I can't bear it.' All my strength gives way. I hide my face on his knee, and all my tears so long kept back come convulsively. He raises my head and wipes my eyes and kisses them, and wrapping his greatcoat round me carries me to our bed in the great, bare ice-cold room. Soon he is with me, and we lie speechless and trembling in each other's arms. I cannot stop crying. My body is torn with terrible sobs. I am engulfed in this despair like a drowning man by the sea. My mind is incapable of thought. Only now and again, as they say drowning people do, I have visions of things that have been – the room where my son was born; a day, years after, when we were together walking before break-fast by a stream with hands full of bluebells; and in the kitchen of our honeymoon cottage, and I happy in his pride of me. Edward did not speak except now and then to say some tender word or name, and hold me tight to him. 'I've always been able to warm you, haven't I?' 'Yes, your lovely body never feels as cold as mine does. How is it that I am so cold when my heart is so full of passion?' 'You must have Bronwen to sleep with you while I am away. But you must not make my heart cold with sadness, but keep it warm, for no one else but you has ever found my heart, and for you it was a poor thing after all.' 'No, no, no, your heart's love is all my life. I was nothing before you came, and would be nothing without your love.'

So we lay, all night, sometimes talking of our love and all that had been, and of the children, and what had been amiss and what right. We knew the best was that there had never been untruth between us. We knew all of each other, and it was right. So talking and crying and loving in each other's arms we fell asleep as the cold reflected light of the snow crept through the frost-covered windows.

Edward got up and made the fire and brought me some tea, and then got back into bed, and the children clambered in, too, and sat in a row sipping our tea. I was not afraid of crying any more. My tears had been shed, my heart was empty, stricken with something that tears would not express or comfort. The gulf had been bridged. Each bore the other's suffering. We concealed nothing, for all was known between us. After breakfast, while he showed me where his account books were and what each was for, I listened calmly, and unbelievingly he kissed me when I said I, too, would keep accounts. 'And here are my poems. I've copied them all out in this book for you, and the last of all is for you. I wrote it last night, but don't read it now. . . . It's still freezing. The ground is like iron, and more snow has fallen. The children will come to the station with me; and now I must be off.'

We were alone in my room. He took me in his arms, holding me tightly to him, his face white, his eyes full of a fear I had never seen before. My arms were around his neck. 'Beloved, I love you,' was all I could say. 'Helen, Helen, Helen,' he said, 'remember that, whatever happens, all is well between us for ever and ever.' And hand in hand we went downstairs and out to the children, who were playing in the snow.

A thick mist hung everywhere, and there was no sound

except, far away in the valley, a train shunting. I stood at the gate watching him go; he turned back to wave until the mist and the hill hid him. I heard his old call coming up to me: 'Coo-ee!' he called. 'Coo-ee!' I answered, keeping my voice strong to call again. Again through the muffled air came his 'Coo-ee'. And again went my answer like an echo. 'Coo-ee' came fainter next time with the hill between us, but my 'Coo-ee' went out of my lungs strong to pierce to him as he strode away from me. 'Coo-ee!' So faint now, it might be only my own call flung back from the thick air and muffling snow. I put my hands up to my mouth to make a trumpet, but no sound came. Panic seized me, and I ran through the mist and the snow to the top of the hill, and stood there a moment dumbly, with straining eyes and ears. There was nothing but the mist and the snow and the silence of death.

Then with leaden feet which stumbled in a sudden darkness that overwhelmed me I groped my way back to the empty house.

I have not 'set the table on a roar', but I have embraced every aspect of life passionately, that is the best you can say of me. My book in a little has helped Edward's reputation, and he is now among the immortals.

Philip Henry Thomas

Mary Elizabeth Thomas

James Ashcroft Noble

Esther Noble

i

*Edward, 1898/9*

*Helen, c.1895*

*Edward, 1899*

*Helen, 1899*

*Helen and Edward, c.1898*

*Four generations of Thomases, late 1902*

*Edward with Merfyn, 1900*

*Helen with Merfyn, early 1904*

*Edward with Merfyn at Rose Acre Cottage, mid-1902*

iv

*Helen with Merfyn and Bronwen, 1907*

*Bronwen and Merfyn at Elses Farm, Kent, c.1905*

*Bronwen aged 8, 1910*

*The house at Wick Green, above Steep*

*Helen and Myfanwy in Chiswick, 1913 (Merfyn in the doorway)*

*Myfanwy aged 2½, 1913*

*Edward, 1913*

*Bradford-on-Avon*

*Farm: this could be the one near Nettlebridge described by ET*

*Crowcombe*

*The Quantocks*

*Turner's Tower, near Faulkland, Somerset*

*Bridgewater; possibly Cable Street*

*Edward with Myfanwy and Tommy Dodd,
December 1914*

*Edward at Steep, midsummer 1914*

*Myfanwy, 1914*

*Edward at High Beech, 1916*

*Myfanwy in Hampstead, 1917*

*Edward at Steep, 1916*

# THREE

*Letters from Helen*
*1896-1917*

*Janet Hooton,* née *Aldis, to whom most of these letters are addressed, was a girlhood friend and confidante of Helen's. Janet and Helen remained friends all their lives. Edward and Janet's husband, Harry Hooton, also became close friends.*


TO JANET ALDIS

2 January 1896                                    6 Patten Road
                                               Wandsworth Common

Dear Pal,

May 1896 be the happiest year you have ever spent, may you succeed in all you do, and may the happy events foretold by the spirits arrive soon. When you next hold converse with the inhabitants of Borderland, you might ask them if any such event is in preparation for me. I already guess their short but decided answer. No! I send you a picture of myself. Did I ever look like that? Heaven forbid! Perhaps I will when I am a full blown old maid, delivering a lecture to an audience like myself, old maids of uncertain ages, on the advisability of remaining single. We had a very quiet, but *very* happy Christmas. I long to see you especially today because I feel rather dumpy, and you who would blow me up to the skies for thus feeling without the least cause, would do me good. I have begun a diary and I can relieve my feelings, by writing down exactly what I want to say to anybody who would be fool enough to listen.

Do you remember Janet?, when I saw you last I told you of a plan I had made regarding the boy who father is taking up, and who writes Nature sketches. I think it will succeed although it will take ages, for he is fearfully shy, and I am likewise afflicted. He wants a girl friend and I want a boy friend, and as I like him (or at least what I know of him) and I *think* he likes me, I think it would be good for both of us if we could be friends. I wonder if we shall. I can see you Janet

177

as you read this, with a broad grin overspreading your face. And my grin is even wider than yours. Mary is going to be very gay, having had three invitations to dances already. I have had one invitation, a dance, to which it is very doubtful I shall go because it is to be given such a long way out of town, and the getting home late would be so difficult.

Please give my love to all your family. How very, *very* kind it was of Aunt Emily [Janet's mother] to send me such a lovely present. Please give her my love, and many wishes for a bright and happy New Year. Please give my love to all the family. I do want to see you all, and I will some day even if I have to sell my soul for the railway fare. Would that I had a bike! Give my love especially to Maggie. I wish I knew her better. I feel as if we two have a tiny bit in common, only don't tell her I said so. And last to you, to whom I send this gift with heaps of love and New Year wishes.

Yours very affectionately

*Helen*


6 January 1896                                          6 Patten Road
                                                  Wandsworth Common

My dearest Janet,

As you will see when you get this letter it is no go. I was so excited when I got your letter, for I was sure they would let me go. But I asked Mother, and she said I was to ask Father, and Father said I could not afford it, and it would not be worth while for such a short time. For I said I would only go 'til Friday so that Mother need not be long without me. What he means by not 'worth while' I don't know. I would rather spend my money on seeing you now even if only for a few hours, than on anything else in the world. And so when I heard my verdict I was so bitterly disappointed that I retired to my room and wept many a briny tear. Are you ashamed of me? If you are small blame to you. They simply can have no idea how much I want to see you, or else they would have let me go. I don't know why it is myself but I feel I must talk to you, and hear you talk or else I shall do something desperate. I talk to Mary, and when I am blazing away and think for once that she is being or trying to be sympathetic, she asks, 'What are you going to wear at Mrs Jones's dance?' So I keep my feelings and thoughts to myself, and I feel as if I cannot contain them any longer. Weeping is not strong enough for how I feel, so if there are any smudges on this letter you will know they are tears. How jolly of Aunt Emily to say she would like to have me, and how jolly of you to write me such nice letters.

I and the Thomas boy are very slowly making our way. He wrote and asked father if I might go out with him on one of his long walks. To my surprise he said I might. So I was in a great state of elation. But to my disappointment Edward never turned up for me. And when he came last night and was asked the reason, he said he had never dreamed I would be allowed to come. But he is going to take me someday this week to some lovely woods he knows. Last night I was in a furious rage because Edward asked me to go to his home this afternoon, and he would show me some flowers and nests he thought I would like to see. So I gladly assented. But that little plan was soon put a stop to, for mother would not let me go by myself, and there was nobody to go with me. Did you ever hear such awful tommy rot in your life? I call it very wrong. Mother says What would Mrs Thomas think? I say if she thought till she was tired, she could not possibly think of any wrong. I feel so cramped in. I want to expand my ideas and views, but how can I? When I appeal to Mary she says like a good obedient girl 'Mother knows best' in which I do not agree with her. I know Mother has been brought up in the narrowest groove, and I have often wondered how it is that her ideas are so broad as they are. So now I have to wait until Lance [Helen's brother, six years younger than herself] can go with me, to play propriety I suppose...Here I am eighteen years old, and in a great state of elation because I am going out with a boy. It is disgusting and immoral and a dis-

grace. Why we may go walks together, and not go to his
house where there is all his family I simply cannot imagine.
It is too deep for me. When I have children I shall bring them
up in a very different way, there will be no Mrs Grundy always
looming in the distance.

I am getting dreadfully teased about Edward. I am very
glad to be able to afford them a little amusement. Poor dears,
if such a little thing amuses them they must be badly off for
entertainment. I am going to ask Edward what his views on
the subject will be. I rather think he will be very broad minded.
He looked awfully amazed when my mother said I could not
go with him to see his books. Enough about my affairs and
such like foolishness.

Yours ever

*Helen*

3 April 1896        6 Patten Road<br>Wandsworth Common

My dear and helpful Friend,

The cup of bitterness has been drunk even to the dregs. All
is over and Father is at rest with Philip. He slept and knew
nothing. No pain, no knowledge of anything. Like a little
child he slept and never woke. It was as we had prayed to
God it should be, He heard us and has granted our prayer.
Mother was not there but sleeping peacefully with me, and
when she was called it was over. Our cousin Charley, so faith-
ful always to us, so brave and true, was with our dear one,
and he heard him sigh gently and then silence.

The dear little mother so brave and strong 'til now became
for a few hours quite delirious, and wanted to go to him, but
it was best not, and after a few hours' terrible agony of mind,
she slept. I have prayed all the time that when the end came
I should have the strength for her. And again God was good,
and she found help and strength in me, though what it cost
me God only knows. She and I were by ourselves, for she

chose me to be with her, and in all this terrible time it was a
ray of joy, that after all she should want me.

On Tuesday we part with all we now have of our dear one.
He is to be near us, in the little Cemetery at Wandsworth I
think. We only have to live one day at a time. The thought
of a future without him is too terrible. The little mother who
is so weak must now be our first care, we must do our best
to fill up in part (for the whole world could not wholly make
up for her loss) the blank that is now left.

Your letter dearest child was indeed good and kind and
helpful. Thank you and thank dear Aunt Emily too. His last
words were quite clear and it is our joy to know they were
to the little mother. The doctor told her to go to bed, and
father heard and opened his eyes and smiled so sweetly at her
and said 'Good night, God bless you' as they always say every
night.

The nurses have both been very good and kind and the
doctor a hero. We all love him dearly and so did father. He
has been this morning and comforted mother like a woman.

Edward wrote him a beautiful letter. [See p.258] He never
heard it, but we did and know if he had heard it he would
have loved it, as I know he loved the sender of it. Edward's
name was always on his lips, and it has made the dear boy
very glad. I will show it to you some day, for I have it. Mother
seemed to think that as the dear father could not have it, I had
the next right.

Mary and Lance did not know till this morning. Poor little
ones! they too are brave. Mrs Warner has taken Lance away
for the day. Everyone is so good, so good.

I have not yet seen his dear face, but it is happy and peaceful.
No trace of suffering. He looks Aunt Flora says ten years
younger, and his face is as noble and heroic to look at as his
life has been. As the doctor says it is not a mere splash in the
ocean, his has been like a ship in full sail, often nearly wrecked
but always brave and so overcoming all. Now he is in the
port which he longed to reach and all is well with him. He
has crossed the bar, and he sees his Pilot face to face, and his

181

look is honest and true and good. I seem to see God stooping to kiss him and saying, 'Well done good and faithful servant, enter into the joy of thy Lord'.

Is all this sense? I know not. I feel dazed and my heart seems to be breaking, but I am trying hard to be brave. I have not cried, I think if I could I would be stronger and more help, but my eyes are dry and burning.

Let not our sorrow sadden your holiday dear child. The sorrow would have been double if he was now suffering as he did a few days ago. He was tired and now rests.

Much love from us all to all, and much much from me to you.

Ever your loving friend

*Helen*

*Written while Helen was working at her first job as nursery governess, away from home.*

24 August 1896                                              Rotherfield

Dear old Janet,

It really was awfully bricky of you to write me such a long yarn, when in the midst of such gaiety and pleasure. I would have written soon had I been able, in fact have had several tries, but only beginnings, this I hope to finish.

You seem to have had a gorgeous time on the yacht, I can imagine it all. You madder than ever, cheekier, rowdier, jollier, much sought after by all, especially the males of the party.

And now you are up in Scotland having a good old spree there, and then to Berwick, and an unspeakably good old spree there too. You are a lucky beggar and no mistake.

And here with me the world jogs on as usual, and I am happy, but deadly homesick. Of course this sad time we have had heaps to do, and the days have seemed hours too short to get everything in. But now the worst is over and we seem to be getting out of the wood a little.

Some time, I hope at the end of the second week I go home for a few days, and I count the hours and rejoice inwardly as each day goes by. It *is* such ages since I saw any of them, and when Mary came two weeks ago, I felt that I could not stand seeing her go off to home and leaving me here. However we had a jolly time, and talked our heads off. You see old girl I have never been away from home before for longer than a month, and it seems so strange not to be all together for the Summer holiday, this is the first time one of us has been away. A few days ago I felt too utterly wretched for anything, it was after Mary had been here, and told me of all the home doings, and how they wanted me to join them all. How Mrs Webb [Helen's employer] stands me at all sometimes I don't know. She *is* so kind, if she were less so, at times when I forget things, it would not make me feel so bad. Do you know the agony of trying hard, really hard to do your best, racking your brain to think if you have left anything undone, and are satisfied and pleased to think there is nothing, then when it is too late it suddenly flashes on you, you ought to have done so and so at such a time, and you are reproved and all your trying is useless, and life seems hardly worth living. . . . Today I feel sure I have done all I ought to, at any rate my time has all been fully occupied till now 8.0 p.m., and when I go to bed and lie and think and wonder if in truth today has been as good as I think, I shall remember that Mrs Webb told me to do something, and I have not done it.

I had an awfully exciting letter the other day from Edward. You must know he and father had often talked of a book Edward was to write, father would preface it, and it was all to be lovely. So quite on his own account Edward sent I think twelve or more perhaps of his published papers to Blackwood's to see if he would publish them in book form, under the title 'The Sweet o' the Year' (Tennyson). For a long time he heard nothing, and of course expected his mss. back every day. What was his joy when the other day Blackwood wrote to say he would like to have the book, if his enquiries about its saleableness proved satisfactory. He also asked E. if he would send him his (E's) diary of fields and woods which he keeps to look at with a view to publishing it. Isn't it lovely? Edward is now busy copying out the diary, and we hope great things. I think it is splendid at nineteen to get your first attempt accepted by the first publisher addressed. Don't you? and even asked for more! He is going to inscribe it to the dear father's memory, the next to *me*! He will not get any money for the first. I hope Blackwood is honest. Mr Webb says he is a first class publisher, one of the best, so I suppose it is all right. Only I know as a set they are rather money grubbing and do not mind at times deviating a little from the quite honest.

I hear at times amusing bits about him. Mary generally in a post script puts something about him – P.S. By the bye Edward gets handsomer every day, we are all in love with him. or P.S. Irene and I are in love with Edward, and say you will be an idiot if you do not marry him! We should if we could!! etc. He is very fond of them too, and goes home a good deal, in fact I hear more home news from him than I do from my people, who are fearfully lax about writing. They say I get fatter, horrors! so as I can go out so little for exercise I draw the water up from the well, which is eighty feet deep to the water, and the bucket holds two ordinary buckets full of water. So it is hard work, and Mr Hugget laughs at me. I churn too which is even harder work. I am teased by the farm people about Edward, who get no end seemingly of fun out of us, and I enjoy it as well, and it is good preparation for my holiday, for at home I know what they expect.

This letter seems one long grumble. You see the 'Grief stricken grumbler' stage is not yet in its decline. How jolly it would be now to have you here to tease and laugh my 'blues' away!

Your old chum

*Helen*

*After 1896 there are no letters from Helen until 1899, by which time Janet had married Harry Hooton. Janet was a witness at Edward's*

*and Helen's marriage after which Edward went back to Oxford and
Helen stayed on with Janet and Harry for some months before joining
the Thomas family at Battersea where her child would be born.*

29 December 1899                         61 Shelgate Road
                                          Battersea Rise, S.W.

My dear Janet,
    I would have written to you long ago to thank you for the
charming head flannel you sent me, but I did not know your
Broadstairs address. I hope you are not very offended with
me for delaying so long. Thank you ever so much for the
flannel and your good wishes.
    When are you coming here again? I hope you are not putting
off your visit until the great occasion, which is now not a
fortnight off. [Philip Merfyn Ashcroft Thomas was born on
15 January 1900.]
    Mother told me she had seen you at Ramsgate, and you
both looked very well and jolly. What ages it is since I've seen
Harry, however he's simply got to come when *my* society
will not be the only attraction.
    We were of course very happy at Christmas time. Edward
worked all day and I went to Church and played with the little
boys and every now and then ran up to Edwy to make sure
he was there all right.
    Mrs Dapple sent me a most lovely cot cover in blue and
white, made of course by herself. I was so surprised and
delighted Mater [Edward's mother] gave me, or rather the
babe a huge cozy white shawl so that I think what with the
head flannel and shawl and coverlet my babe did very well
for Christmas presents. I am beginning to feel most awfully
excited about it. I think of it all day, at least when I am not
thinking of Edwy, and at night I nurse Edwy's arm and pre-
tend it's a baby. And when I kiss Edwy's hand which is the
baby's face, he thinks it is because I love him. Isn't he a stupid
old thing to think I care twopence for him. As if I should kiss
his hand! Oh dear me I am quite too silly for anything. I shall

185

utterly demoralize poor solemn Dr Biggs. The babe and I will
simply laugh and make fun of him all day.

Please give our love to Harry and to yourself.

Your loving old pal

*Helen*

*Merfyn is now four years old and Bronwen getting on for two.*

29 June 1904                                                    Elses Farm
                                                    The Weald, Sevenoaks

Dear old Janet,

A few mornings ago, after dreaming of you all night I woke
up with that lyric of Rossetti's and your tune for it, running
in my head. And as I dressed and murmured the song 'I have
been here before' all sorts of memories came crowding into
my mind; hours spent with you, and incidents in my life in
which you shared. And I remembered our wildness and
enthusiasm, and our hopes and desires which we talked over
so often. And I was glad that my dreams had led me to such
pleasant places. Do those days seem good to you now I won-
der, or does it seem foolishness that you and I, who are so far
apart now, should have planned together these present days;
should have talked of our lovers before I at least had one, or
dared to hope for one; and our children when it seemed a
light, pleasant thing to be mothers. And so it is pleasant, it is
the most glorious thing in the world, but Oh the pain, and
the care, and the responsibility. We did not think of that! how
could we when we had no conception of any of those things.
We did not know that in all life's sweetest, most desirable
emotions, pain is inseparably mingled, nor would Love, or
motherhood, or wifehood be so precious were the pain not
there. When are we going to meet again, you and I, the little,
wild, loved impulsive Janet, and I the fearful, and shy and
unconfident Helen.

Here we have an ideal house, with large, light rooms, and

big country kitchen, and the loveliest country all around. We spend our time in the hay fields now, and both my babies are as brown as berries and as well as possible. Baby walks now, tho' she is a little timid. The farm yard is a Paradise for Merfyn. Edwy too likes it, and I hope all will be well here. He is looking forward to seeing Harry, who will tell you all about it afterwards. I wish you could come soon. Oh I do so wish it.

I am busier than ever, and indeed when at the end of the day I consider all I have done, I wonder how I managed it; and there is always something left undone.

I can't write letters nowadays, but I had to write this, tho' it's you who owe me a letter. Still I know just how it is about letters, so don't bother. Harry will tell me how you are, and all about the babies. Do you know I am going grey as fast as I can; at thirtyfive I shall be as grey as a badger.

Goodnight old friend. Come and see us some day. Surely we did not say all in those far away days. Now we have real lovers, real children, to talk about. Goodnight Janet.

Your old chum

*Helen*

9 January 1908                      Berryfield Cottage
                                    Ashford, Petersfield

My Dear Janet,

It was nice to have a letter from you, for letters now are such a boon. I read them over and over again for company's sake, and get out of the shortest, dullest sort of letter an amount of pleasure and satisfaction that would astonish the writer. People – especially Mary, Irene and Mater – have been very good to me in this way; and there's one thing to be said about writing letters to me, I always answer them, for my one delight in my lonely evenings is pretending I am talking to this one or that, and I can pretend best with my pen in my hand. Of course my best letters are from Edwy, and never have I had such cheerful healthy sounding letters from him, no never

187

since I have known him. It's simply glorious the good he seems to be getting, not only from the air, and the sea and the beautiful country, so wide and free, but also from the dear people who are being so kind to him; the people so different from humdrum me, and the number of them, and their light-heartedness, and their unconstraint. And not only because the sea is what it is, and the air, and the people, but because the whole is different in every detail from life here; and I think a downright change like that is good for everyone, especially for Edwy. I wish sometimes that I might go and renew my youth in that gay kindly family; but at present I am filled with a deep content, a glad thankfulness that all is so well with my dear old boy. Every day he surprises us – I and the children laugh at his strange doings: dancing, playing whist, having Molly and Chub in to tea and getting on splendidly. My only fear now is that lack of funds will prevent his staying there till he's done the book [*The Life of Richard Jefferies*]. We are very hard pressed at present, and of course it is an expense but I daresay he'll manage it somehow. He seems so hopeful about his book too, and the writing of a book is generally accompanied with groans of despair, fits of depression, fits of anger. Let us hope the book will not suffer, but I'm sure it won't. Do you think I feel a bit jealous of the Aldis's, the Webbs, the cottage, the sea, the air, the everything that has so soon worked wonders with him? Well I do a little. I would have liked after all this while of vain striving to have felt that I had had a finger in the pie. He is my whole life, my love in whose existence I exist and yet I can do so little, so very little for him. I know that a lot of the spirit in me is gone, and I had been a far better, wiser, more helpful wife if I had not let him mould me as he liked. One can love too well. But I don't know why I drift like this, it's foolish and useless. And just now my heart is filled with a great hope that this change may be the turning point, and that with a body so strong and healthy he may return with at last the confession of happiness. To see him happy that is what I want, and he has said it was impossible. Not that I believed him, but the thing was to find the key to the door of the empty chamber where happiness ought to live. And I believe it has been found; and if he gets health, the door will be kept always open now. And it's you I'm grateful to dear old friend; you know a little but you can't know all it would mean to me and the children and Edwy and our whole life if he were well and content and happy.

Well! I've never thanked you for your surprise Christmas parcel. The coffee was most acceptable, and the children loved their things, especially the indoor fireworks; we have delighted quite a lot of children with those; and the last three are to be shown to a few children who are coming for Merfyn's eighth birthday. Fancy having a boy of eight!

They are both splendidly well, in spite of the cold. It's freezing hard again tonight.

Now I must get to some sheets I am making. Lots of love to you and Harry, and Joan and Pat from

*Helen*

P.S. Oh I'm having a lovely green Liberty frock for Edwy's homecoming. I mean of course Liberty stuff and design, but made here. I bought it out of some money I had sent me at Christmas, and I *shall* be a bobby dazzler I can tell you.

[Early Summer 1910]                                Wick Green,
                                                  Petersfield

My dear old Janet

I'll not begin to apologize or anything, because I feel I'm too great a sinner to expect any kind of forgiveness. All I'll say is that I loved your last letter, and fully meant to write a long one in reply, then Harry's coming seemed to do instead, but however your mild reproach in Edwy's note today has goaded my conscience, and I literally snatch a minute from my overcrowded day, to put down the letter I've had in my head ages ago for you.

I think it's grand the way you are working, and I do admire you. In fact I'm full of envy, for capableness of any kind, especially that which can grasp a crisis and be of use to others, *does* appeal to me. But I do hope and hope that you and Harry between you, will decide that life here in England on a small income (and I'm sure with all Harry's enterprise and practicalness and both your brains combined – the income would not be a small one, any way not so small as we have lived and been happy on for ten years) is worth over and over again riches in Brazil, cut off from all ties; especially for Harry who is such a very home loving creature. With all your combined qualities what a jolly, healthy joyous life you could lead – you writing and teaching, Harry poultry keeping, gardening and all kinds of allied industries. I personally cannot understand the point of view of anyone who thinks that such a life, such a splendid life for one's children could be bettered. I do hope and hope you will decide not to go, and let Harry work out his own salvation and yours too in a life full of so many possibilities of happiness and health and interest. I feel awfully deeply about all this, because I love you both so much and tho' it's no business of mine, I can't help saying what I feel, or a bit of it anyway.

Well, as to ourselves we are flourishing. We've never been rich or even well off, so we can look forward quite calmly to an income just enough and no more. Our children are having a quite perfect childhood, going to what we think is the best school [Bedales] preparing in every way we know of for a good man and womanhood. We are all very well indeed in our hill top house with its beautiful view over the vale to the great restful downs. Every day in my heart a great wave of thankfulness comes for all this life holds for me. And now especially, with my babe knocking every day to tell me he's all right and longing for me as I for him; and my breasts full already of milk for him, as if to tempt him out of his hiding place. I still teach at school, and so earn the children's fees, and do my five miles every day, and twice a week ten miles and a half of that up and up and up a great hill. Then in the holidays I am to have two Anglo Indian boys here who will pay me well, and so things go on, a hard pull sometimes, and then a time of rest, but always life, life, life. You know I've had a queer sort of life in a way, full of dark shadows, too dark many of them for speech, but on looking back the brightness is so bright that my life has been like a field of gold I see, and where little clouds freck the gold, the brightness at the edge is brighter than anywhere. The children are splendid. Such sweet strange creatures, so different, each expressing a quite opposite point of view. Bless them, how they will rejoice when they hear of what is to be theirs in the summer. Edwy is well too, he grows stronger each year, and does better and better work. It's a good thing I'm so simple a sort of creature, when his nature is so complex and difficult. What times we've had! What rapture, what despair, and always our love absolutely undisturbed, like a great beautiful placid bird, spreading its wings over us.

I'm *so* busy, for of course I'm away from eight o'clock when we start for school, till 11:30 or 12 when I return. Then there's lots waiting for me to do, and just now of course *piles* of sewing. However I'm getting on, and shall soon have my baby things finished. Then I have to make things for myself – nightgowns, a dressing gown, all kinds of things, and Bronwen too has to have a lot of things for next term. I never have a minute. Everybody says how well I look, and I'm just bubbling with health, and happiness. This baby is a great beautiful present Edwy and I are making to each other, he ought to be very extra lovely, he starts from so much of beauty and happiness and calm after storm.

Well, well, here I go jabbering on, and friends are coming for the weekend, and I've heaps to do. So farewell dear old girl. Love to you all, and to the Webbs when you see them.

Ever your old pal

*Helen*

# TO EDWARD, IN WALES

[September 1910]                                        Wick Green

Dearest one,

We were all up early today for breakfast at 7. It was so very misty that I was half afraid the weather had changed, and that we should get fine rain, but now at 9 o'clock the sun is coming through and I think it's going to be hotter than ever. Bronwen, Merfyn and Edith went off in good time, and I have just watched the train steam across the valley. Bronwen was very excited and pleased to be going, and coo-eed joyously to me at my bedroom window. Merfyn and Edith are driving up with Fox who is going to take me a little drive for a last treat for Nurse, who I have just paid, and wished I could have given her more, she had been so particularly good. However of course I quite see we can't, so don't think I'm feeling anything about it. I'm very sorry you are again poorer than you thought. How is it you get your accounts so wrong, and always on the bad side.

I'm thinking of you today with Gwili and so is Merfyn. He *has* so wished he was with you – Wales is a real love and a strong feeling with him, and we have been trying to sing Welsh songs together. I wish he could learn the language. How nice if we had a Welsh speaking servant, a pretty smiling Welsh girl with a beautiful figure and complexion and large white teeth. Oh but where would poor old Helen be then, always beside such a fair Eluned or Megan!

Your parcel came at dinner yesterday, and as I had had a lovely letter by the morning post, I did not open the parcel thinking it only soiled clothes. So late at night when I opened it, your letter was a lovely surprise. I'm glad you and Arthur [Arthur Ransome] managed at any rate to part friends. I was half afraid something might happen, and think you must have had yourself under good control to avoid a quarrel with one so absolutely antipathetic (is that the word?). It was a lovely letter just as I was going to bed, tired rather after a busy day;

192

with that description of your slow walk and feeling so content dear. *Nothing* makes me happier than to know of such moods with you, and if only it could be oftener that life is so restful and careless for you, how good it would be!

Yesterday we took our tea to the slope of Wheatham, and enjoyed the soft misty afternoon, tho' the midges tormented us dreadfully. The children had the cart, and were letting it run with them in it down the slope by its own weight. They had one or two tumbles, but there was great laughter over it. Merfyn, Baby, Peggy [Digby] and I are going again some day soon. It's as far afield as we can go down the lanes, for they are so rough that we cannot take the perambulator, but have to carry Baby, who is too heavy for me to carry far.

Weeding is very difficult now, the ground is so hard and dry, and a little rain would do good, tho' these days of sun and peace are delicious.

By the way that piano of Miss Wells is very cheap, for it's a good one. Could we beg, borrow or steal the money. It *would* be lovely to have it, and it's such a chance of a really good piano.

Merfyn and I will feel very strange tomorrow when he and I and Myfanwy are alone, I think we shall like it; for he is most devoted to his little sister, and loves to be where she is, and is delighted when he can hold her for a minute or when she smiles at him. Her smiles are fascinating now, and she *almost* laughs. We get soft little coos sometimes and she tries hard to express her content and health in sounds. Everybody is amazed at her intelligence and size and general forwardness. She is three months old as far as everything except dates. She will be four weeks on Tuesday.

I had a nice letter from Mrs Little. I'll send it. You see William Davies keeps her well posted up in our news. Isn't it funny about the one unreadable chapter. How proud he is of it, and I expect it's very *very* mild, tho' no doubt there are many unreadable chapters in his life; but his sense of propriety is so delicate, and his reserve so deep rooted that I don't think the public will get from him anything both quite true and quite unreadable.

Well dearest I long for you home again, and yet while the lovely weather lasts I want you to have all of it to spend in that perfect happiness, and I'm afraid at home you cannot get it quite so well. I want you to get full of it and then perhaps you would keep it always. So don't hurry back dearest, *do not*, but come back when you feel home is best for you, not till then.

Farewell sweetheart. Merfyn sends kisses and Myfanwy will give you hers when you come back – a baby's kisses are too soft and tender and sweet. Her open mouth groping on my cheek gives me I can't say what pleasure, it is almost a pain of happiness to feel her oneness with me, her absolute dependance on me, and her knowledge that it is well for her that she has me. Farewell dear heart. Ever and wholly I am yours

*Helen*

Love to all at Waun Wen.


## TO EDWARD, IN WALES WRITING *GEORGE BORROW*

10 November 1911                                        Wick Green

Dearest one,

The children and I have just got back. I have been to Miss Simeon's where our reading developed into a furious argument between Miss Simeon and Miss Townsend on the new aspect of the suffrage question that the government have dropped this thunderbolt in the form of a manhood suffrage bill. Then I called for the children and we walked home together, in the very dark and cold night.

It's been bitterly cold all day, very raw and cycling my hands and feet got numbed.

It's the violinists' concert tomorrow, and of course I'm not going. I can't afford ten shillings, and so arranged for some children to come to tea. Then to my great disappointment I heard that none but strictly Bedales people were to be allowed to hear them at Bedales on the Sunday – not even Mrs Fish, Mrs Badley's great friend. So of course I knew I could not go. But today I met Mr Powell who told me that Mrs Russell had especially invited me, and that I alone of outsiders am to go at her special request. She of course is the promoter of the whole affair. Isn't it nice of her, so I shall hear the music after all, and I do so love it.

I did not tell you did I that Mrs Scott has asked me to go next Thursday morning to see the drawing classes. She says she considers both the children very good, and Bronwen exceptionally so, particularly in her observation of small details of plants, twigs etc. So I am going. Mrs Scott asked me to thank you for your letter.

I saw Merfyn boxing the other night and he seemed to be doing very well. Mr Scott said he was a long time getting into it, but he's very pleased with him now. And tonight Merfyn tells me, he knocked his opponent into smithereens. They are both very well, and happy, and just as keen on school, and not too tired when they come home.

I had a letter from Sarah Ann today thanking me for some things I sent her. Her mother has been very poorly, but is rather better. She sends her love to you.

I also heard from Mrs Unsworth. They have let their house for the Winter, and are going to Spain and Algiers and she wants me to go and see her. The other day at breakfast Maud was in here, and she saw Mrs Lupton come up from the wood in her nightdress and overcoat. She said, 'There *are* some funny folks about, if the old people could rise from their graves, *wouldn't* they see some comic cuts?'

The other day we were talking of designs for stamps for Merfyn's 'island' and then got on to talk of the typical animals of the country apropos stamps. I said the English stamp ought to have a dog on it, Merfyn said the Welsh a sheep, and Bronwen said, 'And the Americans a Teddy Bear', which I thought quite smart.

The MacTaggarts are quite nice people. He is a typical Scot, *very* Scotch – tall, grim looking, not much humour. She is short and plump and half German, plenty of humour, and quite clever I should think. They've heaps of money, he's a retired Burma rice merchant, and for the first time have they and their children really settled altogether in a home of their own. I liked them both.

At meals I've been reading Pepys Diary which I like most awfully. Is it complete here, or expurgated? I only have meal times to read at, I sew on all the evenings I'm not writing to you, and I'm gradually working through my pile of mending and making. So a diary just suits that sort of time. Wells' book I liked, but feel it dissects too much all the time. It is very interesting and the character of the girl (Miss Pember Reeves I suppose) is very fascinating. But the book is not nearly so good as *Tono Bungay*.

I do hope you are sleeping better, and that you are cheerfuller. I don't like the thought of your being alone so entirely, but of that I suppose you are the best judge. But I can't help thinking it would be best if you could when you wanted to drop in on a congenial friend.

By the way I should like to see if it comes your way that poem of Masefield's reviewed by Wuff today. His novel *Multitude and Solitude* felt awfully unreal and wishy washy after Wells. I simply could not read it. Cobbett, or Pepys or Wells, real people talking about real living and real life, that's what I like in books. *The Story of my Heart* too because it is so full of life and experience. But most modern novels sicken me with their unreality. Masefield's poem may be good I thought, the Wuff review is enough to damn it for evermore.

Well, I wonder if you are right about my being unable to be strictly economical. You are quite right about the twelve children and £2000 a year. But I can't cotton on to the red faced husband with an embryonic paunch. My idea of a husband is tall, thinnish, handsome (sometimes ever so handsome) fair, and tho' not red, certainly not pale. But the best of him is his smile, and with twelve children and £2000 a year he'd often be smiling. Oh I do love him when he smiles, it sets everything right, and if everything does not want setting to rights, it makes me ten years younger and more in love with him than ever, which is saying a good deal I can tell you. I'll forgo the dozen children and the £2000 a year, but I must have you and only you; just you with us happy and smiling and laughing. I could not be happy with red faced paunchlet, I hate the sight of him. I'd not touch him with a barge pole.

Don't work too hard at the Borrow. What is Mr Wilkins and how comes he to have Conrad, Meredith etc. in his shelves?

Have you seen any pretty Welsh girls yet?

I wish you could bring a nice little cockle donkey back with you. *Do.*

Do write to Bronwen. She's expecting a letter by every post. It's my letter day tomorrow. I hope there'll be some people in it. Churches and pilgrims and old farm houses are all very fine, in fact I like them when you've been there to warm them a bit, but best I love children and animals and people and girls and boys, and I like you among them better than all alone among mouldering things.

Baby is lovely, only she's got a large dark bruise on her cheek where she bumped into a corner. She says 'dada' when she sees the picture of a man, so she does not forget yet what a 'Dada' is.

Well it's bed time now, and I suppose I must go. So goodnight. How late do you sit up? You write to me early in the day I suppose, for I get your letters the following day by the first or second post.

When you think of me what is in your mind. How am I to you. I often wonder if I should know myself if I could look at myself through your eyes and mind. Goodnight sweet heart. It's a still night, but Oh it's far away from you. Farewell. If you ever smile when you think of me well that's lovely, but do you? Answer *all* these questions.

Goodnight. You're pretending to be too deep in your book to look at me. Goodnight. Ever and wholly I am yours.

*Helen*

# TO EDWARD

Dearest One,

Only a few lines hoping this finds you as it leaves me at present, very well thank you!

There is no news except that there are only four days to your homecoming. And that when you get this there'll only be three, unless you count Tuesday itself as 31 days. It will seem a month of wet Sundays from getting up time till starting off to meet you time. The children and I may meet you, that is if I can find time, I daresay I'll stroll down to the station, but if I am not there, I daresay I shall have gone to the Mc-Taggarts' for tea, so in case I am otherwise engaged I've told Maud to make tea for you, though if you like to wait supper till 7.30 or 8 I'll be sure to be home then. The McTaggarts are so very nice, and have asked me to go, and as *nothing* is happening on Tuesday after all the gaieties of the term I thought it would be a good opportunity.

I cannot answer your two last loving lovely letters, it's no good trying. I did not get *too* wet and cold in the hailstorm, but I'm very grateful all the same for the warmth and cheeryness of the sun after it. You see it's intoxicating me somehow. I'll be as mad as ten hatters by Tuesday if this sort of thing goes on.

I'll air your clothes for you, and get out the sweater and the old mac. (There's some wedding cake for you which I did not send on.) I've put the notebooks in your letter chest, and locked it. I paid the bills and have got receipts. Baring wants £8 all at a fell swoop, but it was a glorious debauch of bill paying and receipts reaping.

The children go to Bedales with the School to see *A Midsummer Night's Dream*. They won't be out till 9 o'clock, and of course I shall be there to meet them. I'll keep their books hidden.

I'm so glad old Borrow is done and that we are a yard or so

further than you thought from the workhouse. I'm not sorry you have left Llaugharne. Those singing, running, pale girls with creamery voices who pass the windows of hard-working, handsome young married men fifty times a day, don't do it for nothing I'll be bound. Oh no. You're better at home with your old woman, who once ran and who once passed your windows as often as she could, and sang too when she'd a mind to, but who was never pale nor creamery (not that I think much of either quality in young girls), but who kissed you before you kissed her (was it yesterday?). Cream or no cream girls are pretty much the same all the world over, and I'd not give a snap of the finger for one of them passing your windows while you are bending over your Borrow (forsooth). Sit there with one eye perhaps on your book, but the other wanton eye looking for cream and roses and what not while the hussies pass before you that you may the more rove after them. Even so the hailstones may have got into my heart, but if they did the warmth and foolishness they found there soon changed them into magic wine 'which maketh glad the heart of man'. Well, don't expect me at Petersfield will you. Oh, but do expect Myfanwy who I daresay will go by herself *on her own two legs.*

For yesterday at the Bedfords' she walked from Molly Bedford to me with a delicious little chuckle of delight and pride, and then again a step or two.

Not a single line or word more till Tuesday. I'm so excited about my tea party at the McTaggarts'. It will be jolly won't it? Give my love to Mother, and tell Julian I'm sorry he can't come, and kiss your father for me, because I must let out somehow and that seems to me quite a good way. Good luck in town, and the best of luck at home, and a *sensible* wife, not the scatter brain creature I half expect you've got. Anyway such as she is she's yours,

*Helen*

# TO JANET HOOTON

6 August 1913
Yew Tree Cottage<br>Steep

My dear Janet,

Thanks for the tea. Here's 7/- for it and its postage.

We are in our cottage now, and we love it. It's awfully cosy and pretty and I love doing all the work. I expect you along with everybody else wondered what sort of job I should make of it, and shook your heads over it. Well, I felt that and I am just determined that it shall not fail through fault of mine. I keep it beautifully clean and tidy and have great joy and pride in it. It is I who am making a home for Edward, the only time I've had it all in my own hands, and I believe it's going to be the happiest home we've ever had. I know I shall do my best, and my dear old boy is trying too. Yes! Isn't he handsome but he's more than that. I've never met a man who could come anywhere near him in looks or in character either. If only he had a little more native hope and joyousness, so that all this bitter discouragement and anxiety had not driven him to despair. But I don't give up hope, I feel he *must* come out all right. He's tried hard during these last two years to kill my love for him but it's just the same as it always was, it's my great treasure, the thing that keeps me going, that is my life, that and the children. In my heart I have memories so splendid that I am rich in happiness tho' I spend so very many days of utter misery. Sometimes I think he does not love me any more, and my soul goes into a panic of terror, and then out of the darkness comes some wonderful gleam that gives me new hope, new life, new being and I start again. And now in this cottage it's all going to be easier. Even Edward's mother so doubtful at first often is hopeful now after seeing it and seeing that I'm not as bad as she thought. The fact is that nobody in this world but my sister Mary knows me at all. I'm too simple and primitive in many things and too sensitive and morbid in other ways, and everyone even Edward makes the greatest mistakes about me. I'm like my mother a little, but more like Father, but it absolutely surprises me how people mistake my motives and my reasons and my point of view. I'm grateful for the bit of Mother in me, or else I had been crushed absolutely flat by now. I couldn't have gone on, had I not her wonderful power of recovery, and did I not love people *all* people so much that I would not hurt them if I could help it by showing how hurt I was. I often and often feel utterly lonely, and I *am* very lonely, for there is not one soul I know except Mary who really cares for me, and who tries to understand me, or thinks it worth the bother. I have lots of good friends here, but they just know my social side (for I have a terrific social instinct like my mother) but I'm still lonely, and often cry and cry in my solitude.

Oh well, life's not the easiest thing in the world is it? Goodnight.

Ever your pal,

*Helen*


TO ELEANOR FARJEON

Friday night [October 1914]                                   Steep

Dearest Eleanor,

One consequence of your not telling me this joyful news [Herbert Farjeon's marriage to Joan Thornycroft] is that I am worrying you with these affairs, which had I known I would not for the world have burdened you with. So there! Isn't it just splendid. I feel it so deeply, I don't quite know why; at least I do, there are so many reasons. I wrote very impulsively to Bertie, and have had a sweet note back which has made me so happy. I was not sure that he would believe my gladness could be sincere seeing I am so far away, outside, beyond him and his world. But I think he did feel it. Anyway I had to say it, and it was kind of him to acknowledge my nervous little word.

Now dear about all you have done for me. The parcel has not arrived yet, but will tomorrow I expect, then I must set to work and dress the doll, for which thanks, as thanks for all.

About the watch which is really Edward's concern. He's disappointed you've got one so cheap, and asks you if you could get another better one, spending all the 15/- and going up to £1 or 25/- not more. Edward has 5/- of Bronwen's, and 5/- he wants to put himself and get her a good watch. I'm *so* sorry about it. It was my fault, for I thought a cheap one would be good enough for her. But he hates the idea of anything cheap. Selfridges will I'm sure change it, but I wish I had not to trouble you about it. The same kind only better is what he wants.

Now as to blouses. I think the pattern charming. It's just what I like, and I'm in love with it. But my dear it's too lovely and dainty and unwashable to work in, and I'll just make it into a tunic as you suggest for afternoons, and to wear with the new skirt I'm going to make, to go with the new coat. Edward likes it too, *very* much. But you see there's still the morning blouses to consider, so you must not be hurt or foolish, but just let me buy either this woollen crepe, or the cotton blouse stuff you mentioned before. For I *must* have morning blouses, and I should have to buy stuff, and I can't let this tunic idea go, it pleases Edward so. So there you are. So be a good child and tell me how much it is and please let me buy it, for I can't send it back, and I shan't have my working blouses either.

About the coat, you are an angel to take such trouble, but I can't make up my mind. I yearn for the 18/11d. of course, but I really don't know what to do, for it's no good spending 12/11d. and then it's going loose and bad shaped and making me look sixty instead of fifty, and awful at that. I pore over illustrations and can't persuade myself that the 'serviceable' coat at 12/11d. is anything like as good, or will do at all when on the next page I see the 'smart' coat for 18/11d. However, ever and ever so many thanks for your dear help.

Tomorrow, tomorrow, tomorrow. My love and my heart

is with you all. Having known the greatest joy that was ever known, after such a beautiful growing into love as ever was, my whole soul goes out to them.

Good night now.

Ever my love is yours

*Helen*

I return the P.O. 7/6 and Edward says any extra you spend up to 10/- will you spend and he'll repay you by cheque having no cash just now. Edward likes the woollen crepe *very* much, but it's too lovely for working in, so please let me buy the cotton from you. *Please*. The doll is perfect.

## TO JANET HOOTON

4 April 1917                                      High Beech
                                              nr. Loughton

My dear Janet,

How I should love to accept your invitation but just now it's quite impossible and I'm most dreadfully disappointed. Irene is here now and will be for another week, then Margaret Valon is coming and then I have the little John Freemans coming. So you see I'm fixed here. And anyway it's not easy for me to leave home. I've got no nice Mrs Rodd to look after things while I'm away – I don't know a soul here – and tho' I have left Bronwen for a few days to mother Merfyn and see him off at 6.45 (he has to have breakfast at 6.15 and he and I get up at 5.30) still I don't like doing it and it's never been more than a day or two at a time. So you see my dear how it is. Sometimes I long to get away for a real rest and change and I'll have to make some arrangements sometime for a little holiday, but my visitors make it impossible now. Also I expect Bronwen will be away most of her holidays.

Ever so many thanks all the same. Myfanwy and I would have *loved* it. I'm getting on all right tho' this terrible winter will stand out in my memory as a sort of nightmare. The intense cold and the long dark days in this strange place, and then on January 11th that terrible parting, not knowing when we should see each other again; knowing nothing but that for each of us it was so terrible that I did not know one could live through such agony. But knowing so well our love for each other and the deep down happiness that nothing can disturb *has* made life possible, and tho' in those first few lonely weeks I just existed from day to day doing my work and trying to keep fear from my heart, at last something more is possible, and our love for each other which has seen us through so many dark times and over rough places is making life possible now, real life I mean with happiness and laughter and hope.

I hear very often from Edward, splendid letters full of his work and his life and also of that absolute assurance that all is so well between us that that is all that really matters come what may. And I write long cheery letters to him, all about our little doings and interests, and the children and the country, and for both of us the post is the event of the day.

I think he is just wonderful, doing his soldier's work as well as ever he can, and yet still the poet too delighting in what beauty there is there, and *he* finds beauty where no one else would find it and it's good for his soul and he needs it. He gets little time for depression, and so do I. That awful fear is always clutching at my heart, but I put it away time after time, and keep at my work and think of his homecoming. The real thing that matters is eternal, but Oh tho' my soul is perfectly content, my poor old body does want him. My eyes and ears and hands long for him, and nearly every night I dream he has come and we are together once again. But I can wait easily enough if only my beloved will come to me at last. If I *knew* he would come how easy would be this interval! Oh Janet how lucky you and Mary and all the other women I know are who have got their men safe and sound, I can't imagine what the war means to them. And yet I know how we do feel it all those fine young lives and all the terror and horror and vileness of it. And then too our pockets. We just scramble along somehow, I just making ends meet and wondering how

I can do it next month when things are still dearer and what I can cut out next of our already so very simple menu and general expenditure. Isn't it difficult? But nothing matters to me I don't care how I have to work and manage and scrimp and scrape in fact I'm glad I have to do it, I'm glad I, like my dear man, have material troubles as well as those others, and if at the end he comes back to me safe and sound and we can start life again how worth while it will all have been.

And it will be a new start for him you know. The army at least provides a small income, not enough but something anyway. When he's out of it we shall have nothing and he will have again to make a place for himself and all the old struggle over again.

Well surely the end is in sight.

Thank you dear for thinking of me and Myfanwy. Give me another chance sometime. I get *so* tired for I do everything here, washing and all and never have a bit of help, and I'm not the quite untirable horse I used to be. Still, I'm game for a good bit more.

My dear love to Harry and the children and your dear old self from

*Helen*


[April 1917]                                         13, Rusham Road
                                                          Balham

My dear Janet and Harry,

Before you see it in the newspapers I want to tell you that Edwy was killed on Easter Monday. You knew and loved him and he loved you both. I am trying to hold steadfastly to life and the realisation of the great peace that is in my soul and his too.

Mater and I are trying to comfort each other.

With love

*Helen*

205

14 May 1917                                          c/o Mrs Locke Ellis
                                          Selsfield House, East Grinstead

My dear old Janet,

It's only quite lately that I've felt able to write to any of the numerous friends who have written to me and helped me through these terrible days that so nearly were utter despair.

Here is country that he knew and loved and among friends in whose lives he had made an unfillable place a great peace has come to me. His great strong tender arms have lifted my soul out of despair, and he and I are one again, our love unchanged and eternal. Sometimes the pain comes back, terrible, soul rending, but it is as if he took my hand in his dear one and gave me fresh courage to live again the life he would have me live, happy and carefree with the children. I try to remember how rich I am in his love and his spirit and in all those wonderful years, and so forget that I am poor in not having his voice and touch and help. I *am* rich. What a man is mine, above all other men. How little he guessed dear boy what a place he had in the very hearts of his friends. He exacted all or nothing, and those who knew him loved him with a love surpassing anything I have ever known of. All kinds – men and women, great and small, rich and poor, clever and simple, they loved him as very few men are loved. And now because of their love for him it is poured on me. I am enfolded by it, Oh it is wonderful. I send you a copy of the letter his commanding officer wrote to me. It is above all letters precious to me in its simple sincerity and the characteristic picture it gives of my beloved. The very last letter I had from him was written the day before death came, and it was bubbling with happiness and eagerness and love. My God how rich I am in such love. 'He has awakened from the dream of life' and someday like the prince in the story he will kiss me to waking and we shall be together again as we never conceived, closer closer than ever we have been, one in body and soul, one in essence.

Janet dear I can't undertake the children. A great weakness came to my body, it failed me as it never had before, and I don't feel able yet to face my own little affairs and cannot think of taking on more than I have. Thank you for thinking of it, later perhaps I could but not yet.

I shall be in town before long, and will come and see you and old Hallow. May I? I want to keep in touch with all that he loved and that loved him, people and places and things, and you are our old old friends.

I'll write no more now dear. Goodnight to you both my two dear friends. Pray for me for indeed sometimes my courage goes and the way seems too far and lonely. Only sometimes because I get tired and full of pain, really he is so near me we speak to each other and I have but to put out my hand and he takes it. He is my all, my life, all all to me.

*Helen*

## TO ROBERT FROST

2 March [1917]                               High Beech
Late at night.

Dear Robert,

What a bit of luck to get your letter at all. I thought all the mails had gone down in the Laconic, but evidently not. I'm *so* excited and happy about your splendid news, and I've already written to the dear man and told him, and to John Freeman to find out about those 'oughts'. I feel sure it will be all right. I'm not at all sure that Edward Eastaway will consent to be Edward Thomas, but I will add my 'insists' to yours and hope for the best. Also I like the idea of your preface and feel sure he will too. It's all very good news and you sound as pleased as you knew we would be.

By now you will have heard from him. He's at Arras and expecting a hot time presently. I don't suppose I can tell you much about him may I. He's at present at head quarters as adjutant to a ruddy Colonel whose one subject is horse racing and jockeys and such and with whom our man gets on so well that he's longing to be back at his battery. He's afraid the Colonel has taken a fancy to him and will keep him. It will probably mean promotion, but Edward wants the real thing and won't be happy till he gets it. What is one to do with such a poet. In a pause in the shooting he turns his wonderful field glasses on to a hovering kestrel and sees him descend and pounce and bring up a mouse. Twice he saw that and says 'I suppose the mice are travelling now' *what* a soldier. Oh he's just fine, full of satisfaction in his work, and his letters free from care and responsibility but keen to have a share in the great strafe when it begins where he is.

At first after we'd said 'Goodbye' and we knew what suffering was, and what we meant to each other, I did not live really, but just somehow or other did my work, but with my ears strained all the time for his step or his coo-ee in case he came back. But tho' one can only wait and hope and not let panic take a hold of one, his happy letters and the knowledge that all is so well between us, are making life life again, and the Spring helps too and the feeling that the end is near – *must* come soon, and that that end will be – if it is at all – a beginning again for us with such knowledge of each other as nothing can ever obliterate, *nothing can ever*, that is what we know and what makes life possible now.

I must tell you that last evening we were talking of people of ourselves of friends and of his work and all he'd like done. And he said 'Outside you and the children and my mother, Robert Frost comes next.' And I know he loves you.

I send you this photograph. Merfyn took it. People don't like it because they say he is too much a soldier here, and not at his best. But I send it thinking that you know him so well you'll be able to read into it, if he is not there for you. Me [a photograph] too I'll send for Lesley.

We are all well and Merfyn has attested (?) and will join up when he is 18. Bronwen is happy and careless and so useful and willing. Baba is well and growing fast, and clever and disconcerting often with her shrewd observation and her totting up of character. And I'm just the same, and mixed with

all the terrible anxiety and terror in me, a great calm nothing
can unruffle. I'll leave this letter open for details to be added
about the book.

Edward will be 39 tomorrow, March 3rd, and we are hoping
our parcels of apples and cake and sweets and such like luxuries
will get to him on the day. Our letters take a week to reach
him. Yours not much longer I expect.

*Two weeks later*
I've kept and kept this letter and just have not had the oppor-
tunity to add to it. You've heard by now I expect from Edward
and perhaps from Mr [          ] I suppose too. Eastaway will
not be Thomas and that's flat he says, but all about the 'rights'
you'll have heard from others. Edward's letters are still full
of interest and life and satisfaction in his work. He's back at
his battery now in the thick of it as he wanted to be, firing
400 rounds a day from his gun, and listening to the men talk-
ing, and getting on well with his fellow officers. He's had
little time for depression and home sickness. He says 'I cannot
think of ever being home again, and dare not think of never
being there again' and in a letter to Merfyn he says 'I want to
have six months of it, and then I want to be at home. I wish
I *knew* I was coming back'. Oh if only I knew that too!

Have you seen the 'Annual'? I've only had it in my hands
a minute, because I sent it at once for his mother to see, and
she has not returned it yet. So I've not read your poems in it
or anyone's. I think Edward's are wonderfully good. I love
'Aspens' particularly.

You have W.W. Gibson over there I hear. Have you met
him yet? I hope he's not being the success he expected to be.
De la Mare I hear talks of nothing but America and is keen
on going out again. He made a lot of money I think and got
a lot of adulation too I think. I suppose Gibson might make
some money, but I can't imagine anyone giving him adulation
– there's something so very small and mean about the man.
Davies I hear is mad with rage that de la Mare and Gibson
have been out and getting rich before he's had his 'go' at the

Americans, and is planning to go and read his poems at 500 dollars a time. So you'll get the whole brood of English poets out there before long. All the ones not helping in the war that is, tho' Gibson has written several 'moving' poems from the trenches damn him.

Well, it's about time I sent this off. So'll say goodnight. I hope one day when this cursed war is over we'll see you all again over here. Poor England, but isn't she fine eh? But oh so tired and weary and sick, but never hopeless, never losing courage and faith. Underneath all her rottenness of greed and hypocrisy she is splendid still, and I think that scum that threatened and still tries to cover her will be skimmed off her by this war, tho' now the best are all away. But some will come back, one must, and he will he says.

Goodnight. My love and the children's to you all.

*Helen Thomas*

This letter was returned by the Censor ages after I posted it. I have had to take out the photographs.

But today I have just received the news of Edward's death. He was killed on Easter Monday by a shell. You will perhaps feel from what I have said that all is well with me. For a moment indeed one loses sight and feeling. With him too all was well and is. You love him, and some day I hope we may meet and talk of him for he is very great and splendid.

*H.*

# FOUR

## *A Remembered Harvest*

# WELSH RELATIVES

Not long after we were married, Edward took me to Wales to visit relations of his father's. The family I remember most vividly all worked in the tin-plating works in South Wales and lived in one of the quite new and very ugly villages on sites that a few years before had been wild mountain country, and still retained traces of beauty which one came upon unexpectedly. A stream flowed down from the mountain still uncontaminated in its upper reaches, though lower down chemicals and refuse degraded it into a sewer; wild bits of mountain with curlew calling and horizon unmarred by industry. The people too were countrymen though they worked in factories, and whenever they could went tickling trout or rabbiting, or just for love of the solitude and beauty walked out to picnic or explore. They still had their clear eyes and skin and glowed with health. They were not touched by the new ways and were in those days a most happy, independent, closely knit people.

The house in which we stayed was a grim-looking detached house on the edge of the village. It had been built by its owner and here he had brought his bride back from the country, to work in the factory, and here they had reared a large family of sons and daughters.

The ground floor of the house was divided into one spacious kitchen, a small parlour and a large scullery which also served as a bathroom. Here was the huge copper, always full of hot water, and the great tin bath, and here the men of the house, coming in at all sorts of odd times from their shifts, took their baths before having their meal. The door of the scullery stood open and lively talk went to and fro between the man bathing and the rest of the family in the kitchen.

I never got to know the relationships of all the people who

213

thronged in this kitchen. But I knew they were sons and daughters and their wives and husbands, who did not live with their parents but who foregathered there and came under the rule of Mrs Hughes.

She was a very fat shapeless woman who had never been outside this village since her marriage. She was the head and centre of the family, even for the married sons and daughters. She had been handsome and her hair was still jet black and her eyes bright. Her face was unlined and her complexion clear and unblemished and her strong teeth which she often showed – for laughter was natural to her – were even and white, though when I showed her my tooth-brush she roared with laughter, as she had never seen one before. In spite of her great bulk she was never idle. If she was not tackling a huge family washing-day, she was baking a batch of large crusty sweet-smelling loaves, or cutting thick rashers from the delicious home-cured bacon which was their chief food. Everything in this kitchen was on a large scale. The long heavy table scrubbed white, the giant-sized oval frying pan always on the hob, the enormous enamel teapot, its contents black and boiling, for food and drink were always ready for the men coming off shifts. A white cloth would be spread over the table and plates full of home grown food, meat and vegetables, would be put round; and to the noise of laughter and talk would be added the clatter of knives and forks and the clink of cups and saucers, for always tea accompanied every meal.

These meals used to terrify me because one was expected to eat so much. First of all the meat and vegetables, and before one had half got through that, a thick wedge of apple tart would be put alongside, and after that waiting to be eaten a plate of cake or slices of bread and home-produced honey. I looked along a line of piled up plates of food which it would offend not to eat, and my courage often gave out.

After dinner and all washed up, we would still sit round the table, or the men would, while Mrs Hughes carried in a basket full of white sheets and shirts and aprons which she damped down and folded in piles ready for ironing. Several irons were propped against the bars of the range now half-way up the chimney with glowing coals. This fire was never allowed to go out except when the chimney needed to be swept. The married daughters or sons' wives would call in for an after-dinner gossip. The same dark-haired and bright-eyed girls all with wonderful skins and gleaming teeth, and all with a tiny child at their skirts and an infant carried in the large flannel shawls wrapped round to make a kind of sling and then over the mother's shoulder and round her back, thus leaving her hands free and the baby safe and comfortable.

I sat entranced listening to their musical Welsh voices speaking their mother tongue, for some of these people could speak very little or no English. London was to them a fabulous place where the Queen lived, and they would ask me all sorts of questions about life there. 'And do you know Mr Rhys of London?' As it happened, I did! I remember their incredulous surprise when I told them there were no fairs in London, and in high falsetto notes one of the girls cried, 'Then where do you buy your flannel?'

It was summer and some of the babies would be brought in little short shifts scarcely covering their dimpled limbs. I remember Mrs Hughes addressing one of her infant grand-children who had struggled from his mother's lap on to the kitchen floor under the table where he lay on his back playing with his toes. 'For shame our Thomas Traherne Thomas for showing your nakedness to the London lady.'

While we women were talking, one or two men, all black from their work, would come in, and Mrs Hughes would get up to fill the bath for them and get the frying pan replenished, and one of the sons would stoop down and pick up his son from the floor and toss him in the air and speak some endearing Welsh baby talk to him.

Everything in the house shone with cleanliness and polish. The linen could not have been whiter, the brass candlesticks – six pairs of them in graduated sizes on the mantelpiece – could not have been more shining, and the brightly coloured jugs hanging from the dresser could not have been more gay.

215

Mr Hughes was a tall spare man passionately interested in politics and hardly less so in his garden and his pig. His orchard was his particular pride and he got his appletrees from the very best nurseries. He was very proud of Edward and of his writing and liked to talk of the literary people Edward – whom he called Edwy – knew. I was Mrs Edwy. Edward had a lovely speaking and singing voice; though he could not speak Welsh he knew many of the Welsh folk songs and if he would sing one of them the pride and happiness in him were wonderful to see. If I shyly uttered some simple Welsh phrase, they would clap their hands with delight at hearing their language so badly pronounced.

We never sat in the parlour, which was hardly ever used except for ceremonial occasions such as a wedding or a funeral. Here the family Bible and family portrait album were kept, and the best black clothes for use on Sunday. The parlour housed a set of Chippendale chairs and other lovely pieces of furniture handed down from generation to generation, highly polished, unused and incongruous-looking among the gaudy pictures, wool mats and rag hearth rug, and fireplace filled with crinkled coloured paper. In front of the lace curtains were pots of geraniums, and a huge maidenhair fern stood on the Bible. Here the books Edward had written were kept with other family treasures. And indeed the room represented the family shrine, sacred and cold and stuffy.

But the kitchen was warm and homely and brimming with activity. I never saw or heard among all the young people who gathered there any disharmony. It seemed to be an idyllic existence of people still untouched and unexploited, simple and warm, grouped in families of hardworking happy affectionate people whose pleasure and skill in music was their passion. In that ugly village street there would, more often than not, be a band of men returning from their work, singing in perfect harmony one from among their fine heritage of hymns and folksongs.

# W.H. DAVIES

When Edward was looking over a batch of minor poets for review, he came across a small paper-covered volume called *The Soul's Destroyer* by W.H. Davies – a name then entirely unknown to him. The book, which was privately printed and issued from an address in the East End of London, contained a single long poem, and my husband was surprised and delighted to find that he was reading the work of a genius. He communicated his discovery to his friend Edward Garnett and together they went to see W.H. Davies at 'The Farmhouse' – a Common Lodging-house. This meeting and the enthusiastic review Edward had written of the poem, established a friendship between himself and Davies which resulted in his coming to stay with us at our real farmhouse in Kent.

Davies was a short, stocky, dark man, rather Jewish-looking but with a strong Welsh accent. He soon made himself at home with us and we all grew to love him for his keen appreciation of family life, his unaffected happy nature and his lively talk. Merfyn and Bronwen were very fond of him and he of them. His wooden leg intrigued them greatly, and on one occasion when we were walking with him down a lane and he called the children to the side to avoid being run over by a farm wagon, Bronwen said to him, 'It would not matter if it ran over you, would it Sweet William, because you are made of wood!'

This wooden leg got broken and Davies was anxious to obtain another, but had a morbid dread of any of the villagers knowing about it, or indeed about any of his business. So under Davies' guidance Edward made a sketch of an appliance which he asked the village wheelwright to make, without of course telling him its purpose. He made it perfectly to Edward's design and when the bill came in it was for: 'Curiosity Cricket

217

Bat 5s. 0d.', the joke of which Davies enjoyed as much as we did.

In the evenings, over a pipe and a pint of beer, he told us of his life: of how he could never settle to a job as a young man; of running away to sea on a cattle boat to America where the plight of the wretched animals greatly distressed him, for Davies had none of the attributes one might associate with a tramp. He was not tough or callous or rough and his manners were gentle and sensitive, especially to children and animals, and in dress and personal cleanliness he was fastidious. I never heard him swear or use a gross word. His narrative went on evening after evening and Edward said, 'Davies, you should write this', and though Davies had never thought of writing prose, he set about the task eagerly, asking Edward's advice now and then.

When the book was finished it was all that Edward had anticipated, and a publisher was sought; but since Davies was an unknown author, his book was returned several times, until one publisher said he would take it if Davies could get some well-known writer to write a preface. This proved difficult, but at last George Bernard Shaw was approached and agreed to undertake it. Shaw suggested the title, but the whole inspiration of the book and the help given to Davies over it was Edward's. *Autobiography of a Super Tramp* was an immediate success.

Edward rented a little cottage about a mile from our farm-house for 2/6d. a week and used one of the rooms as his study, and he proposed to Davies that he should occupy the rest of the cottage. For this we provided the bare necessities in furni-ture – a bed, bedding, table and chair, pots and pans, and here Davies went, living on the ten shillings a week which his grandfather, the skipper of a coal boat, had left him.

Davies had an intense dislike of anybody's knowing about his domestic arrangements. He hated the idea of drawing attention to himself and raising questions in the minds of his neighbours. For instance, if he had once been into an inn to have a drink, he felt obliged whenever he passed the inn to do

218

the same, however little he wanted a glass of beer, because he felt the landlord would ask himself – Why doesn't he drop in? Is he offended? Doesn't he like the beer? Is he short of money? – so if he did not want a drink he avoided passing the inn, often having to make a long detour.

When we left the farm and Davies, after some time, wanted to give up the cottage, I wrote to him and asked if he no longer needed the furniture and odds and ends we had given him, could a maid of mine, who had married and was very poor, have them? Davies answered that having had no idea of what to do with the things when he left the cottage, he had bit by bit chopped up and burnt the furniture and buried the indestructible pots and pans! So there was nothing left for the young couple.

He moved now into a furnished semi-detached cottage. On the other side of the party wall his landlady lived, and in order to impress her with his suitability as a tenant, his piety and good character, he sang at the top of his voice, to be heard through the wall, a selection of hymns and pious songs which he had been used to sing in the streets when he was saving his little income to pay for the printing of *The Soul's Destroyer*. But whether his lusty rendering of 'Where is my wandering boy tonight?' and 'Cwm Rhondda' had the desired effect, no one will ever know. Davies told us this in all seriousness as a good diplomatic move.

He was now making a little money by his poetry, which Edward never lost a chance of praising. When we left Kent for Petersfield, Davies went to London. There he was rather taken up by high society and became very much aware of himself as a poet. Poets, he observed, often wore velvet jackets, so he bought one and wore it constantly. He had a flat over a grocer's shop in Great Russell Street which was furnished by him as he felt befitted a poet. He had heard that literary people burnt peat on their fires, and he felt it incumbent upon himself to do the same. He asked Edward's advice about this and where he could store the peat in his tiny flat, and Edward suggested teasingly that he should burn his books and stack

219

the slabs of peat on their edges in the bookshelves. However, Davies ordered the peat and then was in an agony lest it should arrive when he was out and give rise to unwanted speculations from the shopkeeper below. So he stayed in day after day. At last the peat arrived, and having nowhere else to put it he arranged the slabs as a sort of hearthrug in front of the fireplace; having settled that to his satisfaction, he was free to go out once more. What was his dismay when returning home one day he found a crowd outside the house, people running up and down his staircase and smoke pouring from the windows. A spark had set his peat alight, the firemen had entered his room and were busy dowsing it with water: the whole street was interested and excited. This intrusion into his privacy was the nightmare occurrence which Davies dreaded above all others, and that was the end of the peat.

I went to see Davies in his flat several times, and once he apologized for a picture which was hanging on his wall. As I am very short-sighted I had not noticed it, but he explained to me that it was a picture which he himself thought very improper. It had been given him by the artist, Austin Spare, and though Davies considered it quite unsuitable, he felt he must hang it on his wall in case the artist called and asked, 'Where's my picture?' So if Davies was expecting a lady visitor or a conventional friend, he would take the picture down and stand it with its face to the wall; poor Davies was in a constant state of trepidation about the picture, which was always going in or out of grace.

In this room the bust by Epstein was a prominent feature. Davies told me that when sitting to Epstein and watching him repeatedly adding lumps of clay to the nose – which Davies already felt was much too big – he got very nervous and begged the sculptor to desist.

For all his naivety, Davies was no simpleton. He was a Welshman through and through, and was shrewd in his sizing up of people's attitudes to him. His pose of what was due to or from a poet was never paraded before his intimate friends. Nor was he taken in by flattery, and when rich and fashionable

people invited him to their houses and showed him off at their
dinner parties, he well knew that such things were not a tribute
to his genius but that these people only amused themselves at
his expense by putting the tramp-cum-poet in an alien setting.
Davies became as bored with them as they with him after a
time.

To our children he was always Sweet William, generous,
gentle and good-humoured, and he remained our dear and
delightful friend until Edward left for France. Davies com-
memorated this friendship in a moving poem to Edward's
memory.

# ELEANOR FARJEON

*This memoir was written at Eleanor's death in 1965. A few months later, in August of that year, Merfyn died suddenly, soon after his retirement; and in the same month Arthur Valon died in his nineties – the husband of Helen's beloved sister Mary who had died many years before, in the late 1920s.*

For more than fifty years – only ended just now – Eleanor was a part of our family. In later years of course as our lives took on different shapes, her part in our family became less active, less intimate; but she never ceased to be the one who rejoiced with us on happy occasions or on whose sympathy and comfort we relied in sadness. And this is how it came about.

Edward had been staying with Clifford Bax and a party of young people among whom were Rupert Brooke and Bertie Farjeon and his sister Eleanor. In his letter he told me of this original and clever girl. He obviously liked her very much, and it had been arranged that she was to stay with us at Steep for a few days.

We lived then in a small workman's cottage, and the day before Eleanor was to arrive I spent in cleaning and polishing and cooking. I was a bit apprehensive about our guest, for I thought I should not come up to her expectations of what Edward's wife should be. But on the day she was to arrive I put the finishing touches to the house – a bowl of violets in her bedroom – laid the table for tea with homemade bread and cakes, and set out to meet her. Edward was at work in his study some way up in the beech woods.

I knew her as soon as I saw her walking with quick steps and an eager expression on her face. Her skin and hair and eyes were dark. The hair was black and done in a careless bun

222

from which curling strands escaped. She looked very gipsyish in her bright cotton dress and thick walking shoes with a large rucksack on her back.

'You are Eleanor!' I said and 'You are Helen!' she replied, and from that moment all shyness and diffidence fell from me and I felt utterly easy with this girl – for though thirty years old she had the complete unselfconsciousness and eager enquiring manner of a much younger woman. She talked of Edward and I of the children, and soon we were at the cottage. She loved the tiny house and flung her arms round my neck in her impulsive way, with which I was to become so familiar, to show how happy she was to be there.

Soon the children came in and Bronwen and Myfanwy found that she was the perfect companion for a child. She could draw and cut out all sorts of things in paper, she could sing and play a variety of games and best of all could tell enchanting stories. No wonder they admired her. She loved them and never grew impatient of their constant demands.

For Edward and me she was just as perfect a guest. Her witty, vivacious talk and her eager appreciation of our simple ways made her the easiest person to entertain. Indeed the entertainment came rather from her than her hosts. For her abounding vitality and quick intelligence made her a match for Edward's talk, and I could see how they stimulated each other and how her wit delighted Edward and banished for a time his deep-seated melancholy.

Eleanor had a strange upbringing. She was the only girl in a family of four, all brilliant in their way. Her father – whose Jewish blood showed itself in Eleanor's features – was a Victorian novelist and her mother was an American, the daughter of a famous actor, Joseph Jefferson. Being a delicate child, Eleanor had received no conventional education and had never been to school. She often laughed at her lack of knowledge of history and geography and arithmetic, but her father's library had been her school and from this she had educated herself. She had read deeply and from a very early age was encouraged to write. Her eldest brother Harry, a tutor at the Royal Academy

223

of Music, had instituted himself as the dictator of the Farjeon children. His rule had been of the kindest, but was unquestionable. And Eleanor at the time we met her had only just escaped from Harry's dictatorship and for the first time in her life was tasting the excitement of freedom. No wonder this world of men and women and the natural beauty of the earth intoxicated her sensitive imagination. She was another Miranda experiencing the brave new world. No wonder that her emotions were as uncontrolled and innocent as a child's, no wonder that she fell in love with Edward. This I very soon discovered, for at the sound of his 'Coo-ee' calling across the fields as he came down the hill from his study, her whole being would become alert, her eyes shining and her expression assuming an expectancy most tender and deeply moving. I could not feel any jealousy of the girl's love for Edward. For one thing jealousy is not a part of my nature, and for another I realized the innocence of this inexperienced girl's emotion. She gave no thought to anything but the present and the rapture of being near the first man she had met whose mind kindled hers and whose affectionate manner fed her own unsatisfied heart, and who was moreover a man of great physical beauty with an elusive charm which made him beloved among a large circle of friends. Edward was aware of Eleanor's devotion, but with the most sensitive tact kept it at a light-hearted level which she happily accepted. This strange bond brought Eleanor and me very close and created in me a kind of motherly protectiveness, for I could see into what difficulties such an untried and impulsive nature might lead her.

For us three all was well. She proved to be a marvellous walker, though her quick step and her forward-leaning body seemed unsuited to the long tramps we took over rough ways. But she never tired and her interest in all that she saw – the flowers of whose names she was quite ignorant, the beech woods which were a feature of that countryside, the extensive views right away to the South Downs and the sea – filled her with a genuine wonder and ecstasy. Her comments on it all were fresh and came from a heart and mind uncontaminated by convention or insincerity.

Bronwen – then aged about ten – was shocked at Eleanor's ignorance of country things which she had learnt unconsciously. She set out to teach her the names of flowers and leaves, and set her examination papers to test what she had learned. And Eleanor was as eager to learn as to please the child and tried her best to win high marks from her earnest teacher.

Her stay with us for these few days was the first of many such times, and she became familiar with our ways and grew to know the strange and difficult nature of the man to whom she gave her first love. In later years, when the war had come and Edward became a soldier and a poet, she was a great help to him in typing his poems, written on odd pieces of paper, at odd moments in camp. During his three months in France which ended in his death, Eleanor sent him many letters and parcels of food and things for his comfort, and when he was killed she came to me and we comforted each other in our despair.

My life was in a sense over, but Eleanor's entered a new phase. She had become a writer of great promise and had an enormous circle of friends, many connected with the stage, through her brother Bertie. Her emotional life too was to be enriched and satisfied. I lived in the country and she in London and we saw little of each other, but the bond between us lasted till the end of her life and now that she has gone, the last link with Edward's and my friends has gone and I alone am left.

# 4 AUGUST 1914 – ROBERT FROST

We were to spend a long summer holiday with Robert Frost and his family. They had taken a furnished cottage in a remote hamlet in Herefordshire near Ledbury, and we had taken rooms in a farmhouse across fields nearby. Edward and Merfyn were already there, having cycled from Steep, and I was to follow with our two girls, our dog Rags, and a Russian Bedales boy, Peter Mrosovski, who spent his holidays with us. So on 4 August 1914, quite undeterred by the news in the morning papers that war between England and Germany had been declared, we set out on the long and complicated journey from Petersfield to Ledbury.

I forget if there was any unusual crowd of passengers on Petersfield station, but as we proceeded on our journey it was obvious from the crowds in the stations we stopped at that people were in a state of excitement. Families on holiday were hurrying home, reservists were being called up and soldiers recalled from leave, and everywhere the stations were thronged with trunks, kitbags and other luggage and with restless and anxious people. However, very much later than our scheduled time we reached Oxford. Here we were told to leave the train which, in the ordinary way, would have gone on to complete our journey. The station was in a state of chaos. It was now late in the day and I asked the station master when I could expect a train to Ledbury. He said he could not tell me, and advised me to stay the night in Oxford when I told him I had three children with me. But even if I had been able to afford such a thing, all available accommodation was filled, I was told by a man who had helped me with the luggage.

So we waited and waited, after sending Edward a telegram. At last a train came in and the station master told me it was at least going in the direction of Ledbury, so I and the children

226

got in hopefully. After a slow journey with many stops between stations, we arrived in Malvern at midnight and here we were told the train would go no further. So out we all bundled, the children tired and frightened. I again found the station master and asked if a train would be going to Ledbury. He answered, 'Not tonight.' I asked him if I and the children could sleep in the waiting room, but he was quite firm in his refusal. I asked him what he would suggest I do, but he had no ideas at all. All he knew was that I must leave the station. However, a kind and intelligent porter heard my story and said he had a friend who owned a cab and he thought he would be willing to drive us to our remote farm beyond Ledbury. The cab eventually came and our considerable luggage and the children were packed in and off we went. The country was entirely unknown to me, and I had not the least idea, as we drove off uphill in the darkness, how far away we were from our destination or in what direction it lay.

But I shall never forget that drive over the Malvern Hills which a huge full harvest moon lighted up like a stage set. Even in my distress and weariness I was entranced by the beauty of the scene and the silence and mystery of the deserted countryside, either in deepest shadow or brilliant moonlight.

Once over the Malvern Hills the country changed and became very wooded and gently undulating, and still the moon most dramatically lighted it for us. And before long we were in the lovely little town of Ledbury, silent and empty and sleeping. In the market square our driver stopped to ask a solitary policeman the way to the farm. He came over to the cab and shone his lantern on to the sleeping children and me.

'Who are you and why are you travelling at this time of night?' he asked suspiciously. So I described our journey from Petersfield and told him that I was joining my husband at the farm. He wanted to know who everyone was individually and when he came to Peter the Russian boy his suspicions grew to a certainty that we were up to no good. The fact that our friend Robert Frost, whom I had mentioned thinking his name would be known, was also a foreigner, did not help. However, after taking down all I had told him in his notebook, with some agonizing delays over the spelling of Mrosovski, he let us go, after giving the driver directions to the farm, which he told us was about three miles further on.

The driver went slowly along the last mile so as not to miss the house in that sparsely inhabited country and before we reached it I saw in the bright moonlight – Edward standing at the gate. So all was well. We had arrived.

In the morning we were able to take stock of our surroundings and found everything very much to our satisfaction. The farmhouse stood among large orchards in which were grown the choicest of dessert plums, each hanging in its own muslin bag to protect it from wasps, birds and insects. These plums had to be without blemish and of perfect shape. When they had reached perfection, they were packed for Covent Garden, each in its own cotton-wool-lined compartment. The outside of the farmhouse was hung with delicious fruit which we were allowed to pick – greengages and large golden or purple juicy plums.

We met the Frosts. Robert and Elinor and their four children – three girls and a boy. They had rented a very scantily furnished cottage standing in the middle of a field about a quarter of a mile from our farm.

Robert was a thickset man, not as tall as Edward, with a shock of grey hair. His face was tanned and weatherbeaten and his features powerful. His eyes, shaded by bushy grey eyebrows, were blue and clear. It was a striking and pleasing face, rugged and lined. He was dressed in an open-necked shirt and loose earth-stained trousers held up by a wide belt. His arms and chest were bare and very brown. His hands were hard and gnarled. He spoke with a slight American accent. Elinor Frost – in comparison with her husband – is only a vague memory to me. She had a rather nebulous personality and had none of the physical strength or activity of her husband. Housekeeping to her was a very haphazard affair and I remember that when dinner time approached in the middle of the day, she would take a bucket of potatoes into the field and sit on the grass to peel them – without water to my astonishment – and that, as far as I could see, was often the only preparation for a meal.

It was at once obvious that Robert and Edward were very congenial to each other. They were always together and when not exploring the country, they sat in the shade of a tree smoking and talking endlessly of literature and poetry in particular. When it was wet we all assembled in the Frosts' cottage; and as there were only two chairs in the living room we sat on the floor with our backs against the wall, talking or singing folk songs in which of course the children joined. I say 'against the wall' but actually the walls were stacked up with ramparts of shredded wheat packets, tins of rather cheap sugary biscuits and boxes of highly-scented soap – the Frosts' idea of preparing for a possible siege.

The poet Wilfrid Gibson lived a mile or two away and Edward and Robert often visited him. But sometimes Mrs Gibson would not invite them in as her husband was in the throes of some long poem and must not be disturbed. This evoked in Edward and Robert an attitude of faintly contemptuous ridicule. Behind this lay a little honest jealousy, for Gibson was at this time a very successful poet whose work was eagerly accepted by the American magazines and highly paid, whereas Robert hitherto had had hardly any sort of recognition in America. On the whole however the relationship between the poets was friendly enough, and Wilfrid wrote a charming poem, 'The Golden Room', commemorating this time of their association.

We had not been there many days when the village policeman called on us and told us that several anonymous letters had been received at his headquarters, suggesting that there were spies among us. Evidently, we thought, the result of our midnight interview with the policeman at Ledbury, or of the villagers' suspicion of us as strangers who sat up very late at night in the Frosts' isolated cottage, and whose unconventional ways they could not understand. The policeman was, he said, convinced that the suspicions were false, but he said it was his duty to follow up any complaints from the public and to make enquiries. Edward of course took the affair as a joke, but not Robert. He was very angry and said, 'If that policeman comes nosing about here again I shall shoot him.' In the end Edward managed to calm him and we heard no more of it.

I remember another remark of Robert's which also surprised and distressed me. In the course of talk the Negro question was raised, and Robert said, 'If my wife and I were in a gathering and a Negro came in, I should immediately take Elinor out.' I cannot remember if the subject was pursued or if it was at once dropped.

I never became close to Robert as Edward was. To Edward he was an inspiration, and he and Robert could hardly have been more devoted. They had been drawn together by Edward's recognition of Robert's genius, when Robert had failed to make any mark in America. Edward's reviews of his early volumes of poetry published in England laid the foundation for Robert's success here and later in his own country. And Robert in his turn encouraged Edward – who had not then written any poetry – to think of himself as a potential poet, and thus in the last two years of his life to give Edward his deepest intellectual satisfaction and pleasure.

The month soon passed and we returned to Steep. The war had come and all our lives were to be changed. Robert and his family returned to America where he found himself famous, and Edward enlisted in the Artists' Rifles and began to write poetry. But there was no enthusiastic reviewer to praise his poems. No publisher would take them and only a few of his intimate friends thought well of them. He never saw a poem of his in print under his own name, just two or three under the pseudonym 'Edward Eastaway', which he himself had, with a wry smile, included in anthologies he was commissioned to edit.

# D.H. LAWRENCE'S VISIT

I have forgotten what I had expected D.H. Lawrence to look like, but I remember being very surprised and startled by the thinness and the pallor and the red beard accentuating both. He came, brought by a friend of mine, to spend a weekend at my cottage in Kent. I admired his work; indeed his coming was to me a great event, and I was excited and a little nervous in anticipation of entertaining the man who I felt might be the prophet who would save the world. For the war which was but lately over, and had taken my husband, had also destroyed all my old romanticism. I felt the world had taken a wrong turn, and Lawrence's books had made me hope that he was to be its saviour.

The first sight of him was a disappointment. He looked so delicate, and lacked a sort of rough earthiness which I had expected. As I became familiar with him, I forgot the look of ill-health and was aware only of the clear burning of his eyes, and the intensity of his being; and he became for me the master as I had imagined, and I became his disciple.

I forget what we talked of, but I remember his outburst of anger, his voice rising to a high shriek, when in the course of a discussion about the trend of scientific discovery, my friend suggested that some day life might be generated in a test-tube. And I know the response in myself to all Lawrence poured out in a passion of hatred and ridicule on such a blasphemous idea. His laugh of derision was high and piercing, and there was something sinister in it: there was a hint of cruelty in it too. I heard this unpleasant tinge of cruelty again when he was most amusingly mimicking a psychoanalyst treating a patient. Lawrence sat in a chair, back to back with an empty chair in which the patient was supposed to be sitting, and in the role of doctor he asked intimate questions, and in the role of patient answered them, and enjoyed poking witty and biting fun at the treatment, which was becoming a popular subject for journalists. I know he prejudiced me for ever against psychoanalysis and made me feel the artificiality of it and the danger.

I remember his saying, in a more serious moment, that to become a journalist was to sell your soul to the devil.

The part of his visit I remember with most pleasure is the time we spent in the garden. I had made it all myself from a waste piece of ground, and it was beginning to grow up and acquire the mature look that cottage gardens in the country have. The cottage and the garden are one, and already my herbaceous border with its polyanthus and violas and clumps of delphiniums with great lavender bushes at the corner, and the apple tree on the lawn, looked as if they had always had the black and white walls of my Tudor cottage for a background. I also had a vegetable plot and a tiny orchard and a few fruit bushes. It was all on a very small scale, for even the surrounding hedge of maple and beech and hawthorn I had planted myself from seedlings brought from the woods.

I lost my shyness in pointing out to Lawrence enthusiastically what I had done and asking his advice about things to do. He was full of suggestions and entered into everything with the greatest zest. He told me to put groups of winter aconites under my flowering bushes, and to let a clematis montana ramp over a shelter I had made for Myfanwy to play in when it was wet, and he seemed to be as pleased as I was that a white bryony had sown itself in my hedge, and that a seedling of gorse was growing strongly in a corner. He borrowed some gloves from me and showed me how to prune the gooseberry bushes, teaching me with the most minute care what to do and why, so that I have never forgotten. In all this there was something intensely lovable about him – his deep interest in it all: not merely the polite interest of the visitor, but the real interest of a man who loved the earth, and to whom a plant or a flower or a tree was a living thing needing wisdom and skill, care and love.

## D.H. Lawrence's Visit

We spent a long time pottering about in the garden, and though it is no longer mine, the hedge and the gooseberry bushes and the aconites are still there. The place is sanctified for me because once he was there and left his spirit there.

Myfanwy soon found out that he was the man for her, and brought into the sitting room one of her favourite books of Edward's for him to show her. It was a volume of photographic reproductions of Goya's pictures, and for an hour she sat on his lap, as he with the same absorption and interest that he had given to the garden, showed her the pictures, explaining them and pointing out to her the details that children love, while she settled herself against his arm. The pictures of war and bull-fights he would not let her look at. 'I don't like those pictures,' he said, and turned to others. The child was spellbound as she looked at the book, sometimes turning her solemn face up to his to look at the man who was making the pictures more fascinating than they had ever been. He did not tease or cuddle her, as so many would have done; his interest and the child's were for the time identical. There was no condescension, no pretence; the child knew it, and believed in him.

When I had put the child to bed I prepared the supper. I laid the table, then quickly began dishing up, tidied my hair, took off my apron, and sat down to serve my guests in my afternoon dress. Lawrence praised the food, and we talked of cooking in various countries, for he was a good cook and showed knowledge and appreciation of food. Then he told me that however simple the food was – and as he and his wife had been very poor, it often was very simple – his wife always changed her dress for the evening, and treated the meal with a little ceremony, which he liked; and he said he wished I had done that, for it was satisfying to see a woman make the best of herself. I felt abashed and was sorry I had not changed, as I had a very pretty dress, which afterwards I put on; this pleased Lawrence. We talked of clothes, and he told me that he liked to see well-dressed women. He hated to see a woman patting her hair, or re-touching her face, or adjusting anything. He liked her to come from her room looking her best, confident and poised. He told me that he had made a peach-coloured satin dress for Frieda out of one given her by a rich friend, and remarked, 'Unpicking a Poiret gown is like unpicking Rheims cathedral.'

During a talk about moral conduct apropos something which I forget now, I said, 'But how am I to know what is right?' And he said, 'Follow the first spontaneous impulse of your heart, and it will be right. The reasoned conclusion is almost certain to be wrong.'

The next morning, Myfanwy, armed with the Goya book, asked if she could go in to his bedroom and with his permission climbed under the eiderdown beside him; and when I took in tea, there they were, she in the crook of his arm, and he, now looking rather like Don Quixote, showing her the pictures all over again.

Bronwen was still at school and though hitherto she had been a most sweet-tempered child, easy to bring up and amenable to our simple way of living – for I was poor – at the age of sixteen or seventeen she wrote that she would not return to school. She became self-willed and intractable and I was at my wit's end how to treat her. She must of necessity be trained to earn her living but she refused to consider any career that I suggested. I spoke to Lawrence of my difficulties and asked if he could help me as he had over the pruning. He asked if she was good at anything at school, and I told him that her art teacher had commended her drawing. 'What is she interested in?' he asked then, and I answered, 'Clothes and young men.' 'Well,' he said, 'why not combine her talent for drawing and her interest in clothes and send her to learn dress design?' This seemed an excellent idea which I soon took steps to put into practice, and after a time Bronwen went to an art school. But it was no good and she left at the end of the first term with a very poor report. Young men had got the better of Art! However, she married very early and her charm and sweetness returned and all was well. But the kindness and interest of Lawrence in helping me and his sympathetic understanding of my difficulty brought back my hero-worship of

234

which he was fully and kindly aware.

On our last evening, the friend who had brought Lawrence said, 'Our hostess is the maternal type, don't you think?' But Lawrence replied, 'That she is, no doubt; but much more is she the disciple.' I felt very self-conscious at being the subject of this frank conversation, spoken as if I were not there. At that time, when I was still trembling with despair after Edward's death, I took it all meekly; but later, when I was calmer, I asked myself rather indignantly, 'By what knowledge and authority did these vain men assess me so easily and put me in my category?' They are both dead now and I am an old woman.

Lawrence wrote to me a warm and gracious letter of thanks and said, 'I have talked too much, but you tempted me by your capacity for listening.'

I only saw Lawrence once after that for a few minutes, and when the other day I read in his recently published letters one mentioning his visit to me, I felt a deep pleasure in reading the words written to a friend of his: 'I have met Helen Thomas. I like her.'

# W.H. HUDSON

*'A personality most dear to me' wrote my father of W.H. Hudson. The two men, Hudson aged 65, my father 28, met in 1906, introduced by Edward Garnett at one of the informal Tuesday luncheons at the Mont Blanc in Gerrard Street. There also came W.H. Davies, Belloc, de la Mare and others, occasionally Joseph Conrad, and my father looked forward to seeing Hudson either in Gerrard Street or at his home in Westbourne Park, on his fairly regular visits to London from Hampshire.*

*My mother's only meeting with Hudson, so soon before his death, made a tremendous impression upon her. Although the set of first editions which the frail old man said would come to her did not materialize, this generous intention and his thought for Edward's family, but more than anything his deep love of Edward, were a source of comfort to her in those desolate years. – M.T.*

A friend recently sent me a reproduction of a fine portrait of W.H. Hudson by William Rothenstein, and as I looked at it there flooded into my mind the memory of the only time I met him. A meeting I could never forget.

He had been a dear friend of Edward's – I could not say a close friend because Hudson's nature was aloof and solitary like the eagle whom he so much resembled. He and Edward had very much in common. They shared an intimate knowledge of nature and a love of the ways of wild creatures. They both admired the men whose work was on the land and whose hands were skilled in the crafts of the countryside, and who had acquired through centuries of contact with the earth a knowledge and a wisdom which Edward and Hudson liked to evoke from them when they met in the village pub over a mug of beer or scrumpy. Another interest they had in common was a great knowledge of English literature in which both were deeply versed. Hudson, in his great book *A Shepherd's Life* and Edward in his *South Country* have recorded the words and doings of English countrymen – a race now almost vanished, swept away by the machine, greatly to the impoverishment of life.

It was in 1922, five years after the death of Edward, when I was at Oxford doing some work, that a message reached me – I cannot remember through whom – that Hudson would like to see me the following day in the luncheon room at Whiteleys. I was a bit flustered with the thought of meeting this great man for Edward had told me that he did not suffer fools gladly and could be very crusty, and I was feeling aware of my own intellectual inadequacy and quailed to think how I should acquit myself as he would expect Edward's wife to do.

I remember that the only hat I had with me at Oxford had a pheasant's feather in it, and this I pulled out, for though I knew he, like Edward, regarded the pheasant as an interloper in English woodlands and the *raison d'être* of the gamekeeper with his gallows of enemies to pheasants, I thought Hudson might well regard the wearing of any part of a wild creature as reprehensible.

At the entrance to the restaurant I gazed about in my short-sighted way, but could not see him among all the people there, until a waitress pointed out to me, sitting alone at a table in a quiet corner, the man I was looking for.

'Mr Hudson, I am Edward's wife.' After silently taking both my hands and gazing into my face with his hawklike eyes, he sat down. Mr Hudson was a tall man, spare and loose-limbed. His hands reminded me of Edward's strong, large working hands, the skin bronzed from exposure to all weathers, cared for but not manicured. His handclasp was as I liked, firm and friendly. His hair was abundant and grizzled as was his short-cut beard and moustache. His face was lined and bony with hollow cheeks and high cheek bones, but the eyes were startling in their darkness and yet brilliancy. They were deep-set and looked only, it seemed, at far distant things. They were eyes that I thought could flash with anger, but on nothing petty would they focus. They and the nose gave his face a fierce wild look as of some great bird. But the lids drooped over the eyes and I thought he looked weary and terribly sad. His gaze rested on me sometimes and the eyes became less bright, less piercing, tender and protecting.

When I had composed myself and Mr Hudson had ordered our simple meal, he began to talk. His voice was very quiet and at first he tried to reassure my obvious shyness by asking me questions about the manner of Edward's death in France. I then lost all self-consciousness in telling him of a most strange and dramatic occurrence when quite by accident I had met a man who had been in Edward's battery and had been present at his death. I could see by the expression on Hudson's face that he was deeply moved and he stretched his hand across the little table and said as his eyes filled with tears, 'Mrs Thomas, I loved your husband as I would have loved a son. I loved him for himself and I admired him as a writer. There was no one like him.'

'I remember,' I told Mr Hudson, 'that you were one of the very few of his friends whose opinion Edward valued, who encouraged him with praise of his poetry.'

'Yes,' he said, 'I thought highly of the few poems he showed me. I knew at once that he had found his true medium. But that does not mean that I did not think him a remarkably fine prose writer.'

Then the talk turned to deeply personal things. He asked about the children and about my means. He said 'I have a complete set of my first editions for you and these you shall have. They will be valuable.' I thanked him. Then he said 'You know I am ill. I can't talk any longer, it is good that we have met.' We parted in the noisy London street. He went his way, I mine. Two days later he died.

238

# IVOR GURNEY

I think it was about 1932 that I had a letter from a woman whose name was strange to me. She was Marion Scott, but as I did not move in musical circles I did not know that she was distinguished in that world. The subject of her letter was strange to me for the same reason. I was therefore filled with surprise and pity when she told me that she was the champion and friend of a young musical genius named Ivor Gurney. This young man had lost his reason in the war and was in a lunatic asylum. He passionately loved my husband's work and was deeply interested in anything to do with him. Indeed Edward Thomas's name – for Ivor Gurney had never met him though they had been near each other at the front in France – evoked in him what one can only call love. She wrote saying that if I could face the ordeal of visiting him, she felt such indirect contact with Edward would mean more to him than we could imagine. So it was arranged that I should go. I met Miss Scott at Victoria Station and I had my hands full of flowers.

On the journey to Dartford she told me about him, how he came of a very humble Gloucestershire family, how he had always been highly sensitive and eccentric and that those fit to judge thought him a musical genius. How his mind – always on the borderline – had quite given way at the front and how he had tried more than once to take his own life.

We arrived at Dartford Asylum which looked like – as indeed it was – a prison. A warder let us in after unlocking a door, and doors were opened and locked behind us as we were ushered into the building. We were walking along a bare corridor when we were met by a tall gaunt dishevelled man clad in pyjamas and dressing gown, to whom Miss Scott introduced me. He gazed with an intense stare into my face and took me silently by the hand. Then I gave him the flowers which he took with the same deeply moving intensity and silence. He then said, 'You are Helen, Edward's wife and Edward is dead.' And I said, 'Yes, let us talk of him.'

So we went into a little cell-like bedroom where the only furniture was a bed and a chair. The window was high and barred and the walls bare and drab. He put the flowers on the bed for there was no vessel to put them in; there was nothing in the room that could in any way be used to do damage with – no pottery or jars or pictures whose broken edge could be used as a weapon.

He remarked on my pretty hat, for it was summer and I had purposely put on my brightest clothes. The gay colours gave him great pleasure. I sat by him on the bed and we talked of Edward and of himself, but I cannot now remember the conversation. But I do remember that though his talk was generally quite sane and lucid, he said suddenly, 'It was wireless that killed Edward,' and this idea of the danger of wireless and his fear of it constantly occurred in his talk. 'They are getting at me through wireless.' We spoke of country that he knew and which Edward knew too and he evidently identified Edward with the English countryside, especially that of Gloucestershire.

I learned from the warder that Ivor Gurney refused to go into the grounds of the asylum. It was not his idea of the country at all – the fields, woods, water-meadows and footpaths he loved so well – and he would have nothing to do with that travesty of something sacred to him.

Before we left he took us into a large room in which was a piano and on this he played to us and to the tragic circle of men who sat on hard benches built into the walls of the room. Hopeless and aimless faces gazed vacantly and restless hands fumbled or hung down lifelessly. They gave no sign or sound that they heard the music. The room was quite bare and there was not one beautiful thing for the patients to look at.

We left and I promised to come again.

Ivor Gurney longed more than anything else to go back to his native Gloucestershire, but this was not allowed for fear he should again try to take his own life. I said, 'But surely it would be more humane to let him go there even if it meant no more than one hour of happiness before he killed himself.' But the authorities could not look at it in that way.

The next time I went with Miss Scott I took with me Edward's own well-used ordnance maps of Gloucestershire where he had often walked. This proved to have been a sort of inspiration for Ivor Gurney at once spread them out on his bed and he and I spent the whole time I was there tracing with our fingers the lanes and byways and villages of which Ivor Gurney knew every step and over which Edward had also walked. He spent that hour in revisiting his home, in spotting a village or a track, a hill or a wood and seeing it all in his mind's eye, with flowers and trees, stiles and hedges, a mental vision sharper and more actual for his heightened intensity. He trod, in a way we who were sane could not emulate, the lanes and fields he knew and loved so well, his guide being his finger tracing the way on the map. It was most deeply moving, and I knew that I had hit on an idea that gave him more pleasure than anything else I could have thought of. For he had Edward as companion in this strange perambulation and he was utterly happy, without being over-excited.

This way of using my visits was repeated several times and I became for a while not a visitor from the outside world of war and wireless, but the element which brought Edward back to life for him and the country where they two could wander together.

# A REMEMBERED HARVEST

*I have chosen this piece to finish Mother's memories, not because it happens to be the last she wrote, but because it evokes her eager spirit and her love of the earth and of those who work on it and are part of it. – M.T.*

Sixty years ago we lived for three full years on a farm, Elses Farm, in the Weald of Kent, and looking back over my long life I choose this period as the happiest – the one during which my knowledge of and intimacy with the English country and farming way of life were immensely deepened. So much so that for ever after, even though I had to be alone, in no other element could my spirit and body be satisfied.

There, in that plain but dignified mellowed red brick farmhouse standing vigilant in its own fields, I became familiar with the rhythm of the seasons and the activities which inevitably went with each. It was chiefly a dairy farm and was farmed by our landlord, Mr Killick, who only let us the spacious farm house as he preferred living above his dairy shop in Sevenoaks. We became identified with the great variety of work which went on without haste or noise, done by men who understood and whose fathers had understood the tough Kentish clay and made it fruitful.

The hop garden was on the southern border of the farm, beyond the great oaks of Blooming Meadow in which the house stood, and it was a pleasant walk, just as far as the children, who were babies, could manage. Over the meadow by the hedge, through the gap by the pond, and there you were.

I had watched from the early time of the year the cultivation of the hops, involving a variety of skills, from the ploughing with horses between the 'hills' – the perennial hop plants of

242

which nothing could be seen in winter but the slightly rounded mounds stretching away in symmetrical rows – to the delicate 'twiddling' of the bines when the shoots appeared and had to be trained to the strings which had already been stretched criss-cross from pole to pole. The strings made an intricate design, seeming to envelop the garden in a glowing mist.

But it is the great festival of the year on our farm that I want to recall, for it had a pagan quality, age-old and primitive, which especially appealed to me. The strings, by this time late in August, were covered with the harsh hop bines and their golden pungent fruit hanging in bountiful garlands among the dark leaves. This was the time for the harvesting of the hops – more like flowers than fruit, with petals overlapping. Under the green arches, canvas troughs slung on rough wooden frames were placed in rows some feet apart, but close enough for the pickers to chat and exchange jokes and gossip with each other.

The picking on our farm was done by village women and children: the garden was not large enough for the need of 'east-enders', who emigrated in their thousands to other parts of Kent from Lambeth and Whitechapel to spend six weeks on the Kent clay to replenish their marvellous vitality. For us the only men to give zest to the bawdy jokes which the atmosphere of this harvest evoked, even in the most chapel-minded women, were the tally-men, perhaps six to this small garden. These men had much to do. It was their job to cut, with the razor-edged sickle-shaped knife at the end of a long pole, the bines from the strings and drape these armfuls of hop-laden tendrils over the bar of wood raised above the trough so that the pickers could loosen the tangle and rob its fruit, dropping each hop separately – never in bunches – into the bin.

I was there with my maid, Daisy Turner, and my two children: Bronwen only a baby carried by one of us, and Merfyn, a sturdy boy of four. When the ceremony began (hop-picking had its strict etiquette and procedure) each trough had already been garlanded by its share of bines and beside each waited the women and their families. Until the tally-man blew his horn not a hop might be picked, and in those faraway days law and order entered into every department of life. Especially, I think, was this so in those activities closely related to the earth. Even in the wild prodigality of nature there is a rhythm and order with which the countryman is instinct. So that the heady smell of the hops and the freedom from indoor chores evoked in the women an element of licentiousness and all went as merrily as a marriage bell during those golden revels.

The horn having sounded we fell to our picking and this was done by experienced women, who from babyhood had been trained in this skill, with delicate neatness and swiftness. The hops that fell into the bin had to be clean of any leaf and of each other. It took me a long time to learn how to do this. The hop fruit is a cone of petals, and the skilled picker will manage to detach one from its bunch whole and compact without, as I often did, scattering the fruit in a flurry of petals into the bin. Children sat on little stools or piles of coats with a box or bucket or perhaps a hat between their chubby knees. Their mothers would throw them bunches of hops to pick and when their buckets were full they would proudly add the contents to the mounting mass in the bin.

The tally-man would come round and cry, 'Pick up yer 'ops! Pick up yer 'ops!' Especially with inexperienced pickers and children some hops were dropped on the ground, and each had to be retrieved, for there must be no waste and no untidiness in this harvest. With him the women would bandy words, and always there was a hilarious and pretended enmity between them and this master of ceremonials, and though Daisy would laugh uproariously at some of the bawdiness, it was so new to me I did not understand it at all, but I knew by the quality of the laughter and the look in the eyes of the jokers that the ribaldry was of the dark earth of which I, town-bred and innocent, knew nothing.

At noon the horn would sound and we must finish picking the bine we had in hand, for to begin a new one was forbidden. Now the tally-man came with his bushel-basket to measure the hops each picker had in her trough, and with a lovely gesture the women plunged their bare arms deep into their cargo and with a sort of flutter of the hands and fingers raised the heavy load to let the air and space into their packing, so that the precious fruit would go lightly into the tally-man's measure and pile up to the bushel mark more quickly. With what keen eyes they watched his measure, for pay was by the bushel. I think the pay for my pick entered in the tally-man's book was sixpence.

Now with our appetites whetted by the heady hop-impregnated air we sat around our bins for lunch. This consisted of the traditional bottles of cold tea and slabs of baked bread-pudding full of fruit and brown sugar, sticky and extremely satisfying. We sat on the hard clay, enjoying the food and laughing and talking. The children got restive when they had eaten their fill and played hide-and-seek in the still untouched bowers, and the suckled babies were changed and put back in their prams. The women's rough and golden-stained hands were for a moment idle. Looking away down the avenue of green leaves I could glimpse brightly coloured groups of women and children in attitudes of repose and presently a silence would fall under that fruit-laden darkness of leaves and the children would curl up by their mothers and sleep, and the women, unused to idleness, would nod. The tally-men lay flat out on their backs with heads resting on their upraised hands, and there would be no sound but the murmur of insects and distant lowing of cattle.

Such a scene, such a quality of living enriched my spirit for ever.

But the horn blew and quickly each got to her task and the bins were filled and measured again and again until the sun lowered behind the hill and we picked our last hop at the command of the horn.

The tally-men now turned to their last job of moving the long rows of troughs into unravished aisles. Each woman noted her new position for tomorrow, and straggling home with children whimpering with tiredness, she faced the evening's work, cross with the heat, but happy and satisfied having earned perhaps ten shillings. After a fortnight's picking each received her money upon which she depended for the children's winter boots and perhaps a new jacket for her man and for those necessary things the ordinary wages could not stretch to.

'Good night, Mrs Turner.' 'Good night, our Nell.' 'Good night, Mrs Killick.' 'It looks set for fine.'

# FIVE

## *Myfanwy's Childhood Memories*

# ANOTHER GIRL

On 26 December 1909 Edward Thomas wrote to his friend Jesse Berridge: 'Both children were at Bedales last term as Helen was teaching there, but I don't know if Bronwen will manage the longer walk next term especially as Helen may be unable to teach – she is going to have another baby in the summer.'

On 15 March 1910 he mentions to Jesse: 'Helen is very well indeed and has been teaching at school again this term.'

And on 26 August 1910: 'I am sorry I did not write. Helen addressed a lot of postcards to send out after the event and did not do one for you and so I forgot too. It was 9 days ago now, another girl I am glad to say, and Helen and she have done very well from the start though the birth itself was a laborious one.'

And later in December of that year: 'Helen is nearly as well as ever now – not quite. The baby is Helen Elizabeth Myfanwy. I must tell you how to say Myfanwy, tho quite easy if you are not frightened by the look of it. She is very well and bright.'

After being in labour for two weary days and nights, as the sun rose on a hazy August morning Helen Thomas was at last safely delivered of a ten-pound daughter. Mother and child were exhausted, bruised and torn by the long struggle of parting. Helen had expected a boy, but Edward wanted a second daughter; after much thought and consulting the *Mabinogion*, pondering on Olwen, discarding Blodwen as being too much like Bronwen, their second child's name, he chose Myfanwy, Helen, after his wife, and Elizabeth, his mother's second name; her first name, Mary, had been given to Bronwen.

At the age of thirty-one Edward Thomas was an established writer of essays, of books on the English country and of biographies, and also a literary critic of some reputation. In 1909 with his wife Helen and their two children, Merfyn born in 1900 and Bronwen in 1902, he moved in late autumn to the house where I was born the following summer. Three years earlier they had moved from Kent to Berryfield Cottage, a mile or so from the village of Steep, near Petersfield, Hampshire, in order that the two children could go daily to Bedales, a co-educational boarding school founded early in the century. The school had high ideals in art and literature, and in general living, expressed in its motto, 'Work of each for weal of all'. Lessons and other activities in the open air were encouraged. Merfyn and Bronwen's contemporaries included John Rothenstein, who later became Director of the Tate Gallery; Ramsay MacDonald's son Malcolm; Konni Zilliacus, MP; John Wyndham, creator of *The Triffids*; Edward Barnsley, furniture maker; Julia Strachey; and many others who were to become distinguished in art and politics. There was no religious instruction. Helen helped in the preparatory school, Dunhurst.

The new house, built for Edward and Helen by Geoffrey Lupton, stood high above Berryfield, which lay at the foot of the steep downland called the Shoulder of Mutton. The house had no name then but stood with two or three others in Cockshott Lane in the parish of Froxfield; Edward headed his letters either 'Week Green' or, more often, 'Wick Green'. The terraced garden sloped down towards the great hanger of yew, beech, ash and wild cherry, often hidden in mist; and after a rainstorm plumes of smoke-like vapour would suddenly rise from the layers of trees. It was a large house, built sturdily from oak timbers and seasoned red brick. The floor of the long living-room was made from planks taken from a barn threshing-floor, three or four inches thick and polished to a soft pewter colour by the flails which had beaten out the grain from hundreds of harvests, and from the sliding movements of the ash-wood shovels used to fill the sacks with corn. Most of the windows looked on to a wide brick terrace which ran along the garden side of the house; a curved niche in the kitchen wall near the oven made a sunny, warm place for Helen to sit making baby clothes with minute tucks, lace edgings, and tiny buttonholes. Surrounded by the soothing scent of lavender, bergamot, sage, rue and southernwood, and the dreamy hum of Lupton's bees ravishing the flowers. In the distance lay Berryfield and the village of Steep, and beyond, the great ridge of the South Downs. Edward did his writing in Geoffrey Lupton's Bee House, half of which was adapted for use as a study.

Merfyn was delighted with the new baby, Bronwen a little scornful: 'You think yourself so proper now you've got that baby.'

The Michaelmas term at the school had begun by the time the monthly nurse had left; Helen, still a little weak from the long labour, was advised by the doctor to go for occasional airings in an open Victoria carriage.

Bronwen and Merfyn went daily to the junior school, walking and running down the steep Old Stoner Hill, using the path Edward was to recall in the spring of 1915:

> Running along a bank, a parapet
> That saves from the precipitous wood below
> The level road, there is a path. It serves
> Children for looking down the long smooth steep,
> Between the legs of beech and yew, to where
> A fallen tree checks the sight: while men and women
> Content themselves with the road and what they see
> Over the bank, and what the children tell.
> The path, winding like silver, trickles on,
> Bordered and even invaded by thinnest moss
> That tries to cover roots and crumbling chalk
> With gold, olive, and emerald, but in vain.
> The children wear it. They have flattened the bank
> On top, and silvered it between the moss
> With the current of their feet, year after year.
> But the road is houseless, and leads not to school.
> To see a child is rare there, and the eye
> Has but the road, the wood that overhangs

251

And underyawns it, and the path that looks
As if it led on to some legendary
Or fancied place where men have wished to go
And stay; till, sudden, it ends where the wood ends.

My earliest memory of my father is of sitting astride his foot, with him holding my hands and waving his leg up and down, higher and higher, until that delicious gasping moment when he let go my hands and I flew through the air into his arms.

> This is the way the farmer rides,
> Hobble-de-hoy, hobble-de-hoy;
> This is the way the lady rides,
> Nimminy-nim, nimminy-nim;
> This is the way the gentleman rides,
> Trit-trot, trit-trot;
> And this is the way the huntsman rides,
> A-gallop, a-gallop, a-gallop
> And TUMBLES into the ditch!

My mother's face and person, particularly the touch of her strong, firm hands, I knew well: my attachment to her filled my being. She had held me close so often since my birth, near enough for me to see and absorb her presence with my dull-sighted eyes. Everything more than a yard or two from me must have been hazy and indistinct, and I needed to be near those I loved and depended upon. It was a particular pleasure to be on my father's knee, wrapped in a blanket after being bathed, while he sang in Welsh, or my favourite 'Oh father, father, come build me a boat', or the sea shanties he had learned from Marston, one of the crew from Shackleton's Polar expedition – because then I could see his face clearly, admire his curling hair, and catch a glimpse of his gold tooth. This, I thought, must be his 'sweet tooth' which Mother and Bronwen teased him about.

In the early morning I enjoyed the warm, close world of the blanket fronds on the fold of bedclothes in my parents'

bed, while they dressed and sipped early morning tea. Some-
times I was given a saucer of milk with a dash of tea for a
treat, and when I had sipped it, I would watch the procession
of tiny shapes close to my eyes, made by the upstanding wool
which moved when I gently blew and changed their outlines.

Later, when I had come to know the room and its furniture
and pictures intimately, I was fascinated by the portrait of
Shelley, with his delicate, rather girlish features and long curl-
ing hair. Death was a mysterious subject, towards which I
sometimes tried to steer the talk, while blowing gently on the
procession of tiny figures on my horizon.

'Wouldn't it be lovely if we could see all the dead people in
the churchyard.'

'I don't think it would at all.'

'Why?'

'I'm rather tired of this talk about dead people.'

'Do you know any?'

Impatiently, 'No.'

'Oh you *do* – you know Shelley and Rags.' Rags was the
sheep-dog which had been a beloved companion. He and I
had often been found curled up asleep together, with me suck-
ing the silky tip of his ear.

Bronwen was a contented, self-contained little girl, cheek-
ing her father if he seemed stern, happy to wander the lanes
picking wild-flowers and learning their names from him, or
sitting on the terrace making tiny dolls'-clothes for her cupie
doll. Once she left her sewing in the garden while she came
indoors for lunch; afterwards, several of the tiny garments
were missing. She hunted among the lavender bushes where
the wind might have blown them. Months later she found a
robin's nest in the toolshed, carefully lined with the missing
clothes. Only occasionally did Bronwen have black moods;
during one she growled in her deep voice: 'I hate Mummy, I
hate Daddy, I hate Edith, I hate Merfyn, I hate Rags and I
hate the baby.' I remember our gentle cousin Margaret saying
in a shocked voice, 'Fancy hating *Rags*!'

With her corn-coloured hair, large brown eyes and russet

cheeks, Bronwen was a great favourite with visitors to the house. Ralph Hodgson, who gave her a splendid bull-terrier called Dinah, had her on his knee one day and was flirting with her. My father, puritanical in many ways, expostulated: 'She *is* only eight, Hodgson.' 'That's nothing to what I'd do if she were eighteen!' he replied with a great roar of laughter. Dinah was a much-loved creature and was gentle and biddable with the family, but extremely fierce to tradesmen; they refused to call on her account so my father had to find another home for her. Ralph Hodgson was deeply hurt and for a long time avoided coming to the house.

Mother would take me out in a wooden push-chair called a mail-cart, along the lanes or down the long hill to Steep. Sometimes we were given a ride in Mrs Dennet's pony trap, from which she delivered pats of dewy butter wrapped in a fresh cabbage leaf, and brown eggs from a large basket. Often we would picnic on the Shoulder of Mutton among the juniper bushes and yew-trees, while Bronwen picked bunches of harebells, milkwort and sheeps-bit scabious. If my father were with us he would swing me up on his shoulders, one stubby leg either side of his neck, and grasping my ankles while I clenched my fists in his curly hair, he would gallop down the slope, I catching my breath with joyous fear as the wind rushed by my ears. The picnic knife for cutting the fruit-cake, of which my father was so fond, was cleaned by digging the blade into the springy turf, apple-cores were hidden in bushes and wrapping papers put back into the haversack.

The exciting terror of bounding down the Mutton on my father's shoulders was quite different from the fear I felt when I clambered up the stairs, looking for my mother who was resting; Edith would bundle me in her arms, telling me that Mother had 'gone for a soldier'.

While we lived at Wick Green, I don't remember many people outside the immediate family. But I vividly recall a visit with Mother to an elderly childless couple who also lived in Cockshott Lane. The husband, a timid, quiet man, had the unusual Christian name of Amphlet. At lunch I found a long

hair in my custard – the first time this had happened – and I
felt my gorge rise and to Mother's consternation and our host-
ess's irritation, I could eat no more and had to try and look
anywhere but at the disgusting plate before me. At tea, the
gingerbread was burnt, so not only did the ginger burn my
tongue, but the black charred sides were dry and bitter and I
could scarcely swallow my first mouthful; although it was
forbidden, I had to take a gulp of milk to wash it down. I
could eat no more. 'It *is* rather hot, my dear,' ventured Amphlet,
and I felt grateful for this comment in an otherwise disapprov-
ing atmosphere.

The strange hazy world of short-sight which I lived in for
my first four years made me extra-dependent upon my mother,
and I felt insecure when she was out of the house. My peering
eyes and left-handedness made me clumsy; I dropped cups
when helping to lay the tea-things, I bumped into furniture
and tripped over steps. My father would say I had two left
hands, and called me 'scrammy-handed'. My short-sightedness
was first noticed on the day when he called us into the garden
to see a hoopoe sitting on the fence with its crest spread. My
screwed-up eyes and tears of frustration at being unable to
share the excitement made my parents realise that all I could
see was a fuzzy blob. So I was taken to an oculist in Portsmouth;
small wire-rimmed spectacles soon opened up a new world
for me. But although I have worn glasses all my life and with
their help can see perfectly well, I am clumsy and still have
two left hands. And I have never seen a hoopoe.

Edward must have had some pleasant times up at Wick Green,
with Geoffrey Lupton in his workshop, though there is no
mention in any of his letters of the considerable number of
hours he must have spent there learning to be a passably skilful
carpenter. He made himself a circular-topped three-legged
writing table; when working late on it he used a candle with
a polished reflector which burned very slowly and gave a soft
light. He made a large blanket-chest with big handmade nails
down the sides, a three-legged stool – perhaps for me. It was

apt to tip over and is now made steady with a circle of plywood screwed to the legs. And, choicest of all, a hand-wrought – perhaps by *his* hands – iron-banded oak deed-box. All are still in constant use. How he must have enjoyed working with good sharp tools, choosing his wood from the neatly stacked piles in Lupton's store – sawing, chiselling, chamfering, hammering and finally polishing with wax from Lupton's own bees. He made book-shelves, too, which he kept in the Bee House for his reference books and review copies; and in this study he stuck on the walls various posters which amused him – one for an indigestion mixture had printed in bold type at the top,

*SPRING IS COMING!*
BRINGING DEBILITY

But the house where I was born – indeed, mine was the first birth it had known – was one in which my parents were never at ease. The mists, the wind and the flinty earth of the garden depressed my father's restless spirit, and at last the family moved down into the village of Steep to one of six semi-detached workmen's cottages.

The poem 'Wind and Mist' was written on 1 April 1915, not long after we had moved from the house down to the small cottage. In it the poet has a long conversation with a stranger who is admiring the house:

'...Doubtless the house was not to blame,
But the eye watching from those windows saw,
Many a day, day after day, mist – mist
Like chaos surging back – and felt itself
Alone in all the world, marooned alone.
We lived in clouds, on a cliff's edge almost
(You see), and if clouds went, the visible earth
Lay too far off beneath and like a cloud.
I did not know it was the earth I loved
Until I tried to live there in the clouds
And the earth turned to cloud.'

256

'You had a garden
Of flint and clay, too.' 'True; that was real enough.
The flint was the one crop that never failed.
The clay first broke my heart, and then my back;
And the back heals not. There were other things
Real, too. In that room at the gable a child
Was born while the wind chilled a summer dawn:
Never looked grey mind on a greyer one
Than when the child's cry broke above the groans.'
'I hope they were both spared.' 'They were. Oh yes.
But flint and clay and childbirth were too real
For this cloud castle. I had forgot the wind.
Pray do not let me get on to the wind.
You would not understand about the wind...'

# FAMILY

The family circle – grandparents, aunts, uncles and cousins – was an important part of our lives, even though a long time often passed between visits to and from them.

I never met mother's parents, James Ashcroft Noble and Esther. Grandfather Noble died in 1896, a gentle man, much loved by both Helen and Edward. Edward had been greatly helped by Grandfather Noble and dedicated his first published book, *The Woodland Life*, to him. Edward wrote this letter to him on the eve of publication, but sadly Mr Noble died a few hours before the postman arrived, on Good Friday, 3 April 1896. Edward was then aged eighteen years and one month.

Postmarked *Wandsworth S.W. 3 p.m.*
*Ap 2 96*

61 Shelgate Road
Battersea Rise

My dear Mr Noble,

It is not the happiness – can it be the inexperience or lightness? – of youth, which makes a storm, calm though it be, a dream. Though I *am light* the thought troubles me.

Could this letter reach you able and ready to read it, I would try and tell you what I have been thinking; though I once told you I cried because I was incapable of thought.

But though the present seems a dream, I can look back on our friendship and its bright reality and truth as indeed no dream; unless that, too, is one of those fairy touches that we feel in sleep.

This is no time for thanks, but perhaps now and then you have recollected our gone letters and talks; then you will feel that your good influence and help has sometimes drawn me from the enwrapping pleasure of scenes which

before held me alone with them. At Swindon in the stillness
of birdsong when I tried to meditate, I wandered back to
the time when with your surpassing kindness and insight
you made ways clear which before had been dark or fearful
with doubt. I can not say more plainly what I mean, but at
any time a word would recall how you helped me in my
passes of life. You who have lived a life will know, as none
who do not know me can know, what you have been to
me. You have brought light where there was uncertainty;
you have shown me what I knew not; perhaps in part you
have made me know myself, understood before by you.

I cannot say goodbye. I cannot hope; I can almost wish
that it, that all, will pass in dream. If only my silly simple
words could swing a breath of pureness and health like the
violets I might rest.

In life, your affectionate and grateful friend

EDWY THOMAS

Helen wrote to Janet Hooton on 6 January 1907:

*Berryfield Cottage*

My dear Janet,

I've just had a letter from Irene, saying that Mother died
on Friday afternoon. I expect you knew she had been ill for
three weeks, with what was thought to be ulcerated stomach.
I saw her for the day last Monday, and tho very weak and
fragile, she was mending the doctor said, after a dangerous
two days. On Friday she seemed better than ever, when
some complication in the throat occurred, and she died with
only poor little Mary with her, I believe, Irene scouring the
neighbourhood for a doctor.

It's all very sudden and terrible. Mother was so well and
jolly when she helped me move here, and death seemed so
very far away. I am not going to the funeral. It is 2.30 on
Monday. So now we've got neither Mother nor Father,
and there's a dreadful gap made. I don't know what Lance
will do. I thought I'd let you know, as Irene might not think

259

of writing in all the hurry and bewilderment that death
causes. I can't realize it at all. Mother and death seemed so
impossible, her life brimmed over so.

Ever yours

Helen

Bronwen remembered Grandmamma Noble, small and trim,
who died three years before I was born.


Mother's two sisters – her favourite younger sister Mary
Geraldine, and her rather formidable elder one, Irene – had
both married. Uncle Lance, the youngest of the family, we
did not meet for many years: Aunt Mary had married a hand-
some young consulting engineer, one of a big family of jolly
brothers and sisters; Uncle Arthur Valon was full of fun and
popular with his nephews and nieces. Their daughter Margaret,
born between Merfyn and Bronwen, was my specially beloved
cousin who often came to stay with us, sometimes with her
mother. Unlike Bronwen, she adored little children and en-
joyed playing with me, pushing me in the small mail-cart and
telling me stories.

Aunt Irene had married Hugh McArthur, a delightful man.
He had two interesting maiden sisters, each of whom did wel-
fare work, one among the desperately poor cotton operatives
of Manchester. The McArthurs visited us less frequently.
Aunt Irene had no children of her own and took no interest
in us; moreover she disapproved of Edward's and Helen's
marriage. The McArthurs lived in a flat in Grosvenor Road
which overlooked the Thames. They were tremendous cyclists,
and they walked a great deal too. Uncle Hugh was tall and
angular, with a long face and drooping moustache. He usually
wore a Norfolk jacket and knickerbockers, and thick knitted
stockings with fancy turnover tops, carefully re-heeled and
darned by his wife. He was kind and gentle, but we were
never very easy with Aunt Irene, who seemed stern and dis-
approving.

As children we travelled a great deal with one or both of our

260

parents. I wish I could remember going by train with my
father to visit Granny and Gappa Thomas in their tall, dark,
basemented house in Balham, to Aunt Mary's at Duke's Avenue
in Chiswick, or to the de la Mare family. Bronwen went to
Wales several times with her father and vividly remembered
the ferry at Laugharne, and the ferryman who carried passen-
gers one by one on his back through the shallows to the shore.
Edward's friend, Thomas Seccombe, went with them on one
occasion. He was a very tall, large man, who had to have a
bicycle specially built to carry his big frame. Bronwen never
forgot his clambering on to the back of the ferryman, who
was already carrying the enormous bicycle.

Like the rest of us, Bronwen was a little in awe of Gappa,
and remembered especially being taken by him to a service at
the Positivist Chapel off Lambs Conduit Street, Bloomsbury,
and being patted on the head by large, bearded gentlemen in
frock coats.

Gappa always wanted to know how we were getting on
with our reading and school work. He would take us for long
walks on Wandsworth Common, asking questions and talking
hard. But as he was so tall one only caught a word here and
there and was too nervous to keep saying 'What did you say?'
so one answered yes or no indiscriminately, which didn't
always fit what he was saying. He would walk at his usual
brisk pace, and grasped firmly by the hand we would trot
beside him, our short legs aching more and more. However
even with him Bronwen sometimes went her own way. Once
when he was staying with us at Berryfield he asked Bronwen
to walk to church with him. 'No,' she said, 'I'm going dung-
ing.' And away she went down the lane, carrying bucket and
shovel for the droppings of the tradesmen's horses, so good
for the garden.

Granny, on the other hand, was soft-voiced and gentle. She
wore long skirts with mysterious hidden pockets, and always
a wide, black, stuff belt into which was tucked her little gold
and blue-enamelled half-hunter watch on a long gold chain.
This watch was a source of delight and wonder to me: Granny

would slip it from her belt, hold it out, and invite me to blow: magically the lid would fly open. When she had time, Granny would roll Bronwen's or my hair into tight papers before we went to bed. The unaccustomed knobbiness of our heads was happily endured for the glory of ringlets when Granny unrolled the curl-papers in the morning, brushing each lock round her finger. At the house in Balham there was a fierce Welsh cook named Emma, who lived most of the time in the basement and wore a very long, white, starched apron.

I first met my father's five handsome brothers on their occasional visits to Granny's house. Like their father, they were tall and dark, whereas Edward, the eldest, was fair and blue-eyed like his mother. They all had deep, soft, attractive speaking voices. Uncle Ernest was the quietest of the brothers. He was tall and loose-limbed with a swinging walk which Mother always said was just like Edward's way of walking. Ernest was an artist and earned his living by designing posters and advertisements for an agency. In those days this kind of work was seldom signed, but to us the pretty girls on his posters for the Underground were as recognizable as Barribal's fluffy young ladies. He spoke in a mocking way, seldom smiling, and when he was amused he looked slightly sardonic, with a sideways smile. Ernest had married Florrie Witts, a tall, rather angular but attractive cockney girl who had served in a tobacco shop. They had a son, Dick, to whom I was devoted. He was a little younger than I. Like his mother he had an eager vitality, and was always full of excitement and plans. For instance, when we went to the seaside he said he would throw off his clothes and jump off the last groyne – without even testing how cold it was. He knew, he said, exactly how to cope with a charging bull, too: one should just stand still until the animal was within a few feet and then calmly step aside so that the bull got his horns caught in the hedge – then one simply strolled away.

After the war I stayed occasionally with Auntie Florrie and Uncle Ernest in their small flat in Sheen. Uncle Ernest made a painting of me reading Dick's *Playbox Annual*, my spectacles crooked where I had knocked them.

Auntie Florrie had a sister, Venie, small, quiet, and palely pretty. She wore a high surgical boot and walked with a painful heavy movement, and played the piano in a cinema. Their father had been a tram-driver; widowed early, he had brought up the two girls himself, very strictly. Florrie, the headstrong tomboy, had once had his belt across her back; she had saved up weekly pennies to buy some silver bangles which she jingled on her wrist at the tea-table. 'Where did you get that rubbish?' he asked. 'Saved up and bought 'em,' said Florrie. 'Take them off,' ordered her father. At first Florrie pretended she couldn't get them off, but seeing the game was up, she slid them off her wrist. Her father took the bangles, twisted them into a silver knot and put them on the fire; then he gave her a cut with his belt and sent her to bed. Florrie was often sent to bed for being late, for tearing her clothes or for wearing out good boot-leather playing hop-scotch. Venie never married, but lived in a bed-sitting room with Tiddles, her large ginger and white cat, quietly dying of consumption.

Florrie was easily upset and inclined to nag at Dick and Uncle Ernest. I don't think she had much happiness with her silent, sardonic husband. He would often get up halfway through a meal and without a word take his cap and stick and swing out of the flat, leaving her warm-hearted cockney spirit frustrated. Her cockney lore fascinated us. For instance, she would say that if one ate a boiled egg without salt one would get worms; and speaking of a mean person: 'He threw his money about like a man with no arms.' Although he didn't have much to throw about I think perhaps Uncle Ernest was one of these; Florrie received only a very small share. She always carried her marriage lines tucked into the top of her corsets.

Uncle Ernest's portrait of Edward, dated 1905 and now in the National Portrait Gallery, is not, Mother always insisted, a good likeness.

I don't remember seeing Uncle Oscar at Granny's house;

his connections with the theatre and a lady called Blanche Tomlin may possibly have kept him away from his stern father. Throughout their childhood the six boys had been discouraged from bringing their friends to the house. Oscar's work was to do with motor tyres. He was handsome and well-groomed, and had great charm. Later he often came to Otford for the weekend and was a kindly audience for my dancing. When we lived at Otford we were on a party telephone line, with five other subscribers – Sevenoaks 325Y4 – and when the bell rang four times it was for us. Uncle Oscar would answer the telephone and putting on a comic voice would say, 'This is the sewage works – what's your trouble?' which I thought hilariously wicked. Bronwen was a great favourite of his and he often took her to the theatre; he had a passion for *Peter Pan* which he had seen thirty-four times. He drank a fair amount of whisky and was always genial and affectionate. His invariable farewell seemed to me as a little girl the most romantic in the world – 'And may the roses blossom in your heart, 'til I come to gather them again.'

Uncle Dorie – short for Theodore – must have been Gappa's pride and joy. He too had worked his way up through the Civil Service, in public transport. He was married to Auntie Gertrude, a handsome, stately lady, and they lived in a large house at Forest Gate with their two boys, Ivor and Philip. Uncle Dorie played the piano well and would regularly practise for half an hour when he got back from the office in the evening. He lived an orderly life regulated by the clock. Ivor, tall and fair and extremely handsome, was two or three years older than I, and kind and gentle. I was frightened of his dark and stocky brother, Philip. In the garden he would tease me with worms, threatening to put them in my mouth.

In the 1930s Uncle Dorie was made Traffic Manager of the London Passenger Transport Board, and miraculously overnight on every bus and tram in London there appeared the words THEODORE EASTAWAY THOMAS – TRAFFIC MANAGER, painted in small white letters.

At that time one saw everywhere in London beautiful posters

advertising the Underground, all designed by famous artists.
One of these, by Richard Nevinson – son of H.W. Nevinson
who had been such a friend to Edward at the beginning of his
writing career – illustrated the poem 'Thaw':

> Over the land freckled with snow half-thawed
> The speculating rooks at their nests cawed
> And saw from elm-tops, delicate as flower of grass,
> What we below could not see, Winter pass.

These lines of Edward's were printed below an oil-painting
of treetops and rooks. Just before the Second World War I
wrote to Uncle Dorie and asked if it would be possible to buy
the original painting. I didn't hear from him immediately and
I felt I had been tactless and brash to ask. But soon the picture,
beautifully framed, arrived at my cottage door, a wonderful
present for me.

By this time Uncle Dorie had married again. Aunt Elsie
was homely and even-tempered, managing without fuss to
have Uncle's meals punctual to the minute, and fitting in with
his minutely-ordered time-table. In 1939 he was responsible
for the transport arrangements made for the evacuation of
London children, and later received a knighthood. He spent
a happy retirement at Eastbourne, going for his constitutional
along the front at precisely the same time every day and return-
ing punctually.

Uncle Reggie, dark and handsome, with curly hair, was
my favourite. He could play and sing at the piano, and like
Oscar was connected with the stage – concert parties and music
hall. I only saw him once or twice at Granny's house, looking
very fine in his uniform. I remember Auntie Madge being
mentioned now and again, but I don't know whether she
belonged to Oscar or Reggie. He learned map-reading from
his brother Edward at Hare Hall camp, but did not go to
France. My last memory of Uncle Reggie is of sitting beside
him in the chilly, rather fusty, front room at Granny's house,
on a stool by the piano, its ornamental fretwork backed with
faded green silk, either side of which were the moveable candle-

holders. I remember being entranced by his singing sentimental ballads, with tears in his eyes, and being puzzled at the chorus of the one which ended, '... across the faun', wondering what fauns had to do with the ocean that separated Uncle Reggie from his sweetheart. Long afterwards, I realized the word was 'foam'. Uncle Reggie died in the influenza epidemic in 1919 before he was demobilized.

Uncle Julian, the youngest of the brothers, all his life devoted to Edward and his memory, was tall and delicate. He and his wife Auntie Maud came to Granny's house more frequently than any of the brothers, apart from Edward. I remember them well because they brought their two little children, Cicely, a toddler, and Edward, crawling. I adored babies when I could nurse them on my lap. David and Elizabeth Ceinwen followed later.

Uncle Julian's four children and I are now all that remain of that generation of the Thomas family.

Mary, mother's youngest sister, with her prosperous, hardworking husband lived in Chiswick and kept a living-in maid, Amy Gunner. Their only child Margaret, whom I called Margon, was gentle and quiet and had two long plaits: the hair on the crown of her head was wavy, with little curling tendrils over her ears and in the nape of her neck between the plaits. Margon came to stay with us at Steep, and our family stayed with hers in their comfortable spacious house, with a telephone and a gramophone – things I had never seen before. Auntie Mary was firm, but very warm-hearted and hospitable. As I was not yet at school I was perhaps the niece they knew best, for if mother went to stay at Chiswick, then I went with her.

Later on Bronwen was to live with them for a time when with Margaret she attended Norland Place School and had exercises for her round shoulders.

I looked forward to staying with Aunt Mary – it was only there that I could bear to be separated from Mother – for we went shopping in Chiswick High Road, sometimes riding on trams where I collected the exotic purple, magenta and emerald tram tickets, so much more exciting than the wishy-washy coloured bus tickets. We always called in at a dairy for cream cheese and I would be given a glass of milk and cream, a great treat; Aunt Mary would say, 'Why, you've got a white moustache,' and fish out of her pocket a clean hankie smelling of Trefoil scent to wipe my mouth. The big draper's shop was a special magical pleasure for it had a cash railway. When the shop assistant screwed the bill and the money into the little cylinder, put it on the wire with a neat twist and pulled the brass handle, so that the cylinder whizzed out of sight along the wire close to the ceiling – how in the world did it return a moment later with exactly the right change? Oh happy shop-lady, who measured yards of ribbon with its underlining of white paper exactly the same width as the ribbon, on the brass measure let into the polished wood counter, and had charge of the cash railway. Sometimes instead of a farthing change one was given a pink paper neatly stuck with several rows of dressmaker's pins.

At Aunt Mary's house I was allowed to turn the handle of the knife-cleaner – a tall object rather like a penny-in-the-slot machine, with slots of different sizes for large and small knives. I have no idea what happened inside this kind of mangle, but the steel knives came out bright and shining. I was allowed to stay in the kitchen and talk to Amy while she washed up, and I sang sad songs to her, like 'Sweet William'. I have never heard it since; it was one of the songs my parents sang by the fire after my bath, and a special favourite:

> O Father, Father, come build me a boat
> That on the ocean I may float
> And every flagship I chance to meet
> I will enquire for my William sweet –
>
> For a maid, a maid, I shall never be
> Till apples grow on an orange tree.
>
> I had not gone more than half an hour
> When I espied a man-o'-war

O Captain, Captain, come tell me true
Is my sweet William on board of you?

    For a maid...

O no fine lady, he is not here,
That he is drowned most breaks my fear
The other night when the wind blew high
'Twas then you lost your sweet sailor-boy

    For a maid...

I'll sit me down and I'll write a song
I'll write it neat and I'll write it long
At every line I will drop a tear
At ev'ry verse I'll set 'My Willie dear'

    For a maid, a maid, I shall never be
    Till apples grow on an orange tree.

I loved, too, 'Little Sir William', who was stabbed with his
school penknife on Easter Day and left to drown in the Boyne
Water; 'All round my hat I will wear a green willow', and
'Where have you been all the day, Randal my son?' – Randal
who had eaten his sweetheart's proffered snake-pie. Some-
times Amy read to me out of *Helen's Babies*, but I really only
wanted the same bit again and again – where the child wants
the back of the watch opened to 'see the wheels go round'.
Amy preferred the sad and pious *Jessica's First Prayer*, which
was in penny novelette form, with paper covers and steel en-
gravings of the unreformed Jessica covering with her bare foot
the sixpence dropped by the whiskered, top-hatted gentleman.
    Another treat at Chiswick was to be shown my Uncle
Arthur's masonic regalia – royal blue satin studded with
gleaming gems and enamelled emblems. In his satin apron
and chain of office I imagined him looking like a splendid Red
Indian brave. Much of the glamour went from these fantasies
when I learned that the ornaments were worn over a dinner
jacket. Still, there was always the delicious secrecy, for except

for the legendary lady hiding in the grandfather clock, no woman would ever get a glimpse of Masonic ceremonies. But one day I might perhaps go with my uncle to the Ladies' Night banquet, when every guest found a costly present beside her plate – a feather fan, a silver powder compact, or even a tiny bedside clock from Aspreys. Each year Auntie Mary had a new evening dress made specially for Ladies' Night, of magenta, purple or royal blue satin, with milanese silk stockings and satin slippers dyed to match the dress.

It was soon after the outbreak of war in 1914 that the first gramophone I ever saw was played to me at my aunt's house as a great treat. The enchantment of imagining those tiny ladies and gentlemen singing and dancing inside the box! I would peer up through the wooden louvres when the two doors were opened and fancy I caught the swirl of a frilly petticoat or the glint of a white evening shirt-front. I did not, however, fancy the idea of a tiny German, dressed in grey uniform and coal-scuttle helmet – as in the newspaper cartoons – saying over and over again, 'Voz you dere? Voz you dere?' on a comic record called 'The German on the telephone'. Would he one day squeeze through the louvres and confront me? The picture of the plump white 'His Master's Voice' dog, head cocked, listening and looking down the big cone-shaped horn, whose portrait was on all the records, convinced me that he *saw* what was only just hidden from me – the tiny people on minute gilt chairs resting until required to dance 'Valse Triste'.

Still another joy at Chiswick was my uncle's pianola. Sometimes when he came home from his office in Victoria Street he would choose one of the many rolls of mysteriously patterned paper, fix it in a recess on the front of the piano between the two candle-holders, and pedal away to turn the cylinder; the keys would move as it played a Chopin Nocturne or Mazurka.

If I visited my aunt in term-time I might be lucky enough to be taken to Miss Bear's School of Deportment where my cousin Margaret was a pupil. The girls were dressed in azure-blue short skirts, with woollen stockings to match, white silk shirt blouses, blue ties and white gym shoes. I was told not to stare at Princess Mary, who was also a pupil, as she was shy and didn't like to be noticed. I thought her most beautiful, with neatly arranged flaxen curls held in place at the back of her head by a flat blue velvet bow. These elegant girls played ball to music, swung Swedish clubs in breathtaking patterns, 'And – one, two, swing', or walked round the hall with books on their heads or even a white ball. After each exercise, when the teacher, dressed like the girls in blue and white with a pretty diamond fob watch pinned to her busty blouse, called 'Rest!' the Princess would hurry to the chair beside her governess, who spread a lacey Shetland shawl over her shoulders until the next exercise.

Our relatives all lived in London then, and for our visits to them we wore 'best' clothes all the time!

# STEEP

A month or so before my third birthday the family moved to a small cottage in Steep. Although it must have meant leaving some of the larger furniture at Wick Green, Mother enjoyed her first experience of living in a village. I can imagine her using to the full her great gift for arranging, and making the cottage cosy and pretty, and planting the garden with flowers. Edward, meanwhile, having taken cuttings from the Old Man plant (also called Lad's Love) which grew by the Bee House study and which Gordon Bottomley had first given him, and from other favourite plants, dug and cultivated the vegetable patch, chopped firewood and filled the coal-scuttle. When all was shipshape and Bristol fashion he would go up to his study and write. Later on Mother and I would go a little way to meet him returning, listening for his distant *coo-ee* and answering it until we could see him striding towards us.

Our neighbours in the pair of cottages were Mr and Mrs Dodd and their boy Tommy, who was about my age. If he got half a chance, Tommy would dive his grubby fist into the salt jar and stuff handfuls of salt into his mouth; for this he got a slap from his mother who warned him that his blood would dry up. In spite of my short sight, or perhaps because of it, I must have been observant, and also rather unnaturally fastidious. I remember our own and our neighbours' privies particularly. They were, of course, earth-closets. Ours was always fresh and wholesome, with a box of sifted earth which my father dealt with in the early morning. But next door to us ashes were used instead of earth, and these gave off a fusty, sour smell; instead of crêpey paper in a roll, a copy of Bradshaw's railway timetable hung on a string. The paper was stiff and shiny, though it was fun tearing off the pages.

In the evenings, after tea, when we sat round the kitchen

271

fire with Mother preparing to wash me in the zinc bath in front of the range, my father smoking his clay-pipe would perhaps need to clean one which had become brown and bitter. He would blow up the fire, put some sticks on and when they were glowing embers put the stained pipe right into the red glow, leave it awhile, then draw it out with the tongs, cool it on the hearth and it would again be as white as chalk. The sealing-wax tip he always put on would of course have melted away, so he would light a spill at the fire – Bronwen was a great spill-maker – take a stick of red sealing-wax and make a new mouth-piece on the renewed pipe. This was to avoid the clay sticking to the lips and perhaps pulling off the delicate skin.

Once he let Tommy and me play soap bubbles with two of his bigger clays. But Tommy got over-excited and ran down the path, stumbled, and the pipe-stem lodged in the roof of his mouth. Ever since then it has been imprinted on my memory and if I see a child running with anything in its mouth, I cannot help my fear; and I shrilly threaten the offender with Tommy's fate.

Another time Tommy and I had been bouncing in our muddy shoes on Mother's big bed with its white honeycomb counterpane, when my father appeared, picked us up, one under each arm, carried us downstairs and spanked us.

Merfyn and Bronwen now had a much shorter walk to Bedales; only five minutes instead of two miles or so. Edward was once questioning Merfyn about his school work and got the usual reply after the enquiry, 'What did you do today?' 'Oh, nothing much.' He persisted and said, 'Does Mr Scott take you out on Nature walks?' 'Sometimes.' 'What do you do on these walks?' 'Oh, nothing much.' 'But you must do something. Doesn't Mr Scott talk to you at all?' 'Yes, sometimes.' 'Doesn't he tell you about the plants, trees, birds and so on that you see? What does he say?' 'Oh, he says "Keep up, boys!"' which made Edward laugh, as it so much expressed not only the master's lack of interest in taking reluctant small boys for a walk, but the boys' complete boredom.

272

To help with the housekeeping, children from Bedales, whose parents were abroad, sometimes spent the holidays with us. Peter Mrosowski was one of these. Up to the time he came to Bedales he had spent most of his childhood in a Jesuit monastery and knew nothing of family life. He was Merfyn's age, dark, fierce and handsome. He and Merfyn fought now and then and my father had to separate them. Peter was travelling with us on the day war broke out in 1914, a nightmare journey which Mother never forgot. We were to join my father at a farmhouse near to the Robert Frosts in Herefordshire. Years later, when we met Peter again as a prosperous business man with several beautiful daughters, he always remembered Mother's rock-cakes and our homely cottage with affection. When she died, he stood in church, a tall, handsome, elderly man, his cheeks wet with tears.

On winter days at Steep, when Mother was busy teaching her foreign ladies, I spent many happy hours upstairs in the chilly bedroom, dressing up a small ladder-back chair and talking to it. Mother was occasionally given parcels of scarcely worn girls' clothes by a well-to-do lady who lived in the village. But alas on the whole they were far too grand for me to wear or even for Mother to alter to more suitable garments. It was these clothes perhaps that first gave me a longing for lacey, flouncy frills, so unsuitable for my tall, angular shape, which has never been outgrown – and neither has the longing. But I delighted to hang a whole change of clothes on the uprights of the chair – my elegant and biddable playmate – chemise, liberty bodice, flannel petticoat, tucked and herringboned, next the white cotton one frilled with lace at hem and neck, and lastly the frothy party frock, all broderie anglaise frills, tied with its wide satin sash around the middle of the chairback. I was content to admire them hanging so gracefully on the shoulders of the chair and not to be wearing these fancy things myself.

We had plenty of visitors: apart from my cousin Margaret, who was best of all, Eleanor Farjeon was the one I looked forward to most. For Eleanor and I kept up a constant exchange of letters. I think Eleanor chose the names: she was Cocky Peacock and I was Polly Parrot. I always wished I had been the handsome peacock, with delicate crest like a princess's crown. Her letters were mostly in pictures, which I had to read myself, and mine were mostly written in my left-handed 'looking-glass writing' which Mother spelt out for me. Mother gave me daily lessons from an old-fashioned little blue book called *Reading without Tears*. I was learning to read fast, but I could not spell and write words yet. I remember Eleanor writing to tell me that she was bringing me a birthday present and I was to guess what it was; the drawing was of a box on rough wooden wheels, with a piece of string to pull it along. I was terribly disappointed that she should think such a babyish pull-cart was a suitable toy for me and I almost dreaded her coming. But when she did come it was a beautiful dolls' pram, which I took everywhere, except of course on long walks with my father, when I needed a free hand to hold his. Eleanor was full of fun, telling stories, singing and dancing. She could draw beautifully, too. I would describe the dress I wanted the princess in the story to wear and there she would be, appearing on paper from Eleanor's pencil.

Often Eleanor would walk over to Steep with her brothers, Bertie and Joe, and their friends. One summer day Mother was expecting them all. After spending a hot morning in the kitchen baking bread, scones, gingerbread and rock cakes, she laid tea in the cool sitting-room. I see it in my mind's eye: freshly baked goodies on plates covered with clean tea towels, a saucer of Mrs Dennet's deep yellow butter sprigged with parsley, a jar of homemade damson jam and another of Lupton's honey. The tea service was of white earthenware edged with a wreath of flowers and leaves in red, blue and green. The arrival of so many laughing ladies and gentlemen with walking sticks and rucksacks made me shy and silent. As we sat down to tea, while mother poured out I watched the sugar bowl and milk jug, suddenly noticing an unusual addition to the tea tray. There was a slight lull and I said, 'Aren't we swanky today; we've got a slop basin.' This made them all

*Steep*

laugh, and I didn't dare look up again.

The poem my father wrote for me was so true! When I had learned to read it I was sorrowful for many years for I thought he could not have loved me: there were so many chinks in my armour – straight hair, spectacles and 'Wanting a thousand little things, that time without contentment brings'. There was always something I longed for and when it was mine, the expected happiness never quite followed. There was, for instance, the hat with cherries that I wanted so very much. 'They're not *real* cherries, you know.' 'Yes, I *know*.' I wheedled and made promises and at last the hat was bought. When the elastic under my chin – always too tight at first – had been loosened, I was entranced to hear and feel the red and purple cherries bobbing on the stiff straw brim. After admiring my reflection in shop windows, skipping along to make the cherries bounce, not looking where I was going and nearly bumping into people, there was a quiet time on my own when I had to be sure about those great glossy cherries. I could see that the leaves were not real but made of stiff waxy cloth. But the cherries themselves, such succulent perfection! I pressed my fingernail through the skin of a red cherry; it split quite easily and out bulged its white cotton-wool stuffing. That one certainly wasn't the real thing, but this purple one, surely – and soon the cherries all round the hat lay disembowelled in a desolation of grubby cotton-wool and I sobbed inconsolably over my lost finery, which somehow I had expected would magically turn back to its former glossy glory.

On the other hand, I was a sharp, rather precocious child. My beloved Aunt Mary often reminded me of the time when the wind was taken completely out of her sails.

We had had a Russian lady staying with us, to whom Mother was giving English lessons. I had named a new kitten Teeka which, I declared, was Russian for 'dear little Pussy'. Auntie Mary came to visit us and when I showed her the kitten, she asked very knowingly what its name was.

'Teeka,' I replied. 'It's a Russian name.'

275

'Yes,' said my aunt proudly, 'and *I* know what it means.'

'Well, what then?' said I, crestfallen.

'It is Russian for "dear little pussy".'

'Oh no it isn't. It means "just to make her look pretty",' I answered smugly.

My father must have been there at the time as he mentions Teeka in a letter to his friend John Freeman.

I had as a small girl an aversion to anything male, apart from my immediate family and friends. All my toys were called by girls' names and I would have nothing to do with a fluffy toy dog which had the name Toby on its collar.

On 16 November 1915, Edward wrote to Robert Frost:

> Now I am going to trim a hedge and have tea with Bronwen while Helen fetches Baba from a dancing class. Baba said the other day 'The only thing I should like to be *in the way of men* is a Scottie with a kilt.' I asked what she would like to be 'in the way of women' and she said '*a widow*'.

I was proud of my father in his uniform and enjoyed watching him polish the brass buttons on his tunic, using a button-stick to keep the polish off the khaki. In May 1916 he wrote to Robert:

> As I was walking home with Helen and Baba last week, Baba asked whether Mrs ——'s baby was a boy or a girl? 'A boy.' 'Everyone has boys.' But, I said, boys were wanted to replace the dead. 'You don't think I haven't heard that before, my lad, do you?' she said to me. She is acquisitive and not generous, but she gets her own way without annoying much. I have some new songs for her from camp, and rather more for you.

I have recently been reading for the first time my father's letters to Robert Frost. For most of my life I have felt that he did not care for me. It gave me a deep shock of pleasure to know that he reported my sayings and doings and that I was just as dear and amusing to him as were Merfyn and Bronwen. Apparently he frequently took me to London for a week or so when he went to do some research in the British Museum library. I remember well a time he was irritable with me. He had a cold bath every morning and I had asked if I too could have one. I remember standing shivering in the zinc bath and filling the sponge with cold water and squeezing it against my chest while leaning forward so that no water touched me, and eventually being yanked out and dried rather roughly, whimpering at my cowardice. My sister's memories and adoration of her father and his delight in the 'Merry one' helped to increase this feeling of being the non-favourite.

I have happy memories too: the happiest were the walks Edward and I took together and I have had a renewed pleasure when reading his poems, which sometimes told of these walks, in, for instance, 'The Cherry Trees'. I had seen their scattered petals and remarked, 'Someone's been married.'

> The cherry trees bend over and are shedding
> On the old road where all that passed are dead,
> Their petals, strewing the grass as for a wedding
> This early May morn when there is none to wed.

On 23 May 1915 Edward wrote to Frost: 'I hope you have a dooryard as neat as ours is, with all the old man and rosemary and lavender strong and the vegetable rows fairly continuous and parallel and the may thick in the hedge.' He had already, in December 1914, written the poem which Mother declared was the one that most evoked his complex nature of self-doubt, musing introspection and honesty. I am proud to remember that I was the villain 'snipping the tips':

> Old Man, or Lad's-love – in the name there's nothing
> To one that knows not Lad's-love, or Old Man,
> The hoar-green feathery herb, almost a tree,
> Growing with rosemary and lavender.
> Even to one that knows it well, the names
> Half decorate, half perplex, the thing it is:
> At least, what that is clings not to the names
> In spite of time. And yet I like the names.

The herb itself I like not, but for certain
I love it, as some day the child will love it
Who plucks a feather from the door-side bush
Whenever she goes in or out of the house.
Often she waits there, snipping the tips and shrivelling
The shreds at last on to the path, perhaps
Thinking, perhaps of nothing, till she sniffs
Her fingers and runs off. The bush is still
But half as tall as she, though it is as old;
So well she clips it. Not a word she says;
And I can only wonder how much hereafter
She will remember, with that bitter scent,
Of garden rows, and ancient damson-trees
Topping a hedge, a bent path to a door,
A low thick bush beside the door, and me
Forbidding her to pick.

         As for myself,
Where first I met the bitter scent is lost.
I, too, often shrivel the grey shreds,
Sniff them and think and sniff again and try
Once more to think what it is I am remembering,
Always in vain. I cannot like the scent,
Yet I would rather give up others more sweet,
With no meaning, than this bitter one.

I have mislaid the key. I sniff the spray
And think of nothing; I see and I hear nothing;
Yet seem, too, to be listening, lying in wait
For what I should, yet never can, remember:
No garden appears, no path, no hoar-green bush
Of Lad's-love, or Old Man, no child beside,
Neither father nor mother, nor any playmate;
Only an avenue, dark, nameless, without end.

That was the second of our Old Man cuttings: the first came
from Gordon Bottomley for the Wick Green garden, the
second was planted at Yew Tree Cottages. Since that time we

have always taken a cutting with us and planted it in the next garden. A bush of Old Man flourishes on Edward's grave at Agny, near Arras in France, and on Mother's grave in Eastbury churchyard. When Lord David Cecil came to Eastbury, on the occasion of the dedication of Laurence Whistler's exquisite church window which celebrates the lives of Helen and Edward, he read this poem beautifully, and later drove home with a cutting of Lad's Love which he tells me flourishes still in his Dorset garden.

The walk with Edward that I remember most vividly is the setting for the poem called 'The Brook'. In the year 1973 Anne Mallinson of the Selborne Bookshop, and John Bowen, instituted the Edward Thomas Birthday Walk, and this takes place on the first Sunday in March. In 1979 the Walk set out from Bramdean Common, near Steep – the scene of 'The Brook'. I half wanted to join in to see if it was as I have remembered so clearly, but on the other hand feared I would not recognize it. In my mind's eye it is high summer and very still and I see the site as though I were a kestrel questing above it. Green slopes of short turf are either side of the stream, where my father sits reading and smoking his clay, perhaps writing in his notebook. Not far from where I am paddling in the swift shallow water is an arched stone bridge. There is a sharp pain in the soles of my bare feet, which look greenish in the stippled water. It is very still and serene as I scramble out of the stream and join my father; he rubs my feet, crinkled and cold. We sit there quietly and the silence is intense and I have that strange certainty and excitement that comes only once or twice in a lifetime, which I share – 'No one's been here before.'

> Seated once by a brook, watching a child
> Chiefly that paddled, I was thus beguiled.
> Mellow the blackbird sang and sharp the thrush
> Not far off in the oak and hazel brush,
> Unseen. There was a scent like honeycomb
> From mugwort dull. And down upon the dome
> Of the stone the cart-horse kicks against so soft

A butterfly alighted. From aloft
He took the heat of the sun, and from below.
On the hot stone he perched contented so,
As if never a cart would pass again
That way; as if I were the last of men
And he the first of insects to have earth
And sun together and to know their worth.
I was divided between him and the gleam,
The motion, and the voices, of the stream,
The waters running frizzled over gravel,
That never vanish and for ever travel.
A grey flycatcher silent on a fence
And I sat as if we had been there since
The horseman and the horse lying beneath
The fir-tree-covered barrow on the heath,
The horseman and the horse with silver shoes,
Galloped the downs last. All that I could lose
I lost. And then the child's voice raised the dead.
'No one's been here before' was what she said
And what I felt, yet never should have found
A word for, while I gathered sight and sound.

How enviable was the crunching sound of my father's heavy walking-shoes on the gritty lanes, as pleasing as the sound of a horse munching hay. How delightful it would be, I thought, when my insignificantly small feet, now making scarcely a sound, would grow large and crunch as his did. 'There'll be a wren's nest in that old wall, see, there's a cranny,' and we'd stop and he would peer in and I'd peer in, but usually could not see what he could see. Then his long gentle finger would touch the eggs I could not reach.

In those two crowded years before my father went to France, we stayed once or twice with Vivian and Dorothy Locke-Ellis in their large and, to us, luxurious house in Sussex. My father liked to work in a stone out-building in their very large garden, and he recalls it in 'The Long Small Room':

## Steep

The long small room that showed willows in the west
Narrowed up to the end the fireplace filled,
Although not wide. I liked it. No one guessed
What need or accident made them so build.

Only the moon, the mouse and the sparrow peeped
In from the ivy round the casement thick.
Of all they say and heard there they shall keep
The tale for the old ivy and older brick.

When I look back I am like moon, sparrow and mouse
That witnessed what they could never understand
Or alter or prevent in the dark house.
One thing remains the same – this my right hand

Crawling crab-like over the clean white page,
Resting awhile each morning on the pillow,
Then once more starting to crawl on towards age.
The hundred last leaves stream upon the willow.

Vivian had a motor which he drove unpredictably, once bumping over the grass verge, to my terror, so that in subsequent rides which were meant to be a great treat, I would beg Dorothy to tell him not to 'go on the grass'. This and watching him eat his breakfast porridge with a trickle of cream running down his chin, which had been badly patched up after a careless shave with a blob of cotton-wool, offended my nervous and fastidious fussiness. Dorothy was beautiful and delicate, and much admired by Bronwen for the elegant chiffon tea-gowns she sometimes wore in the afternoon, while lying on a cushioned chaise-longue in the drawing-room. She cured Bronwen of nail-biting, by painting the stubby bits of finger-nail with her nail varnish, and then comparing the result with her own shapely fingers. I recall my first taste of creamy trifle flavoured with a dash of sherry; and the shame and pain of the doctor's having to lance a boil which prevented me from sitting down.

I remember walking with mother from Selsfield House to the post after a heavy rainstorm, when the road was scattered

281

with elm flowers, red and squiggly, which I could not avoid treading on; I became paralysed with disgust thinking they were drowned red worms and would not move for screaming. Perhaps that was before I was fitted with spectacles and could not see well. Mother was irritated and impatient with me, promising they were not worms, but it was no good.

But a walk with my father from Selsfield was horrifying in an interesting way, for we came across a gamekeeper's vermin pole. But this was not a pole but the branch of a tree, hanging low, with his victims strung up to warn off marauding birds and animals from the pheasant chicks he was rearing. The dangling withered carcases of crows, weasels, jays, an owl and a scarcely recognisable cat, their fur or feathers faded by the rain to earth colour, eyeless and swaying clumsily, filled me with a gruesome fascination. 'Can they feel, do they mind being dead, was that a cat, someone's own cat, are they cold, why are they there, why are they dead?'

In July 1916 Edward wrote to Eleanor: 'At the Ellises I could not help writing these four verses on the theme of some stories I used to tell Baba there.' My pencilled copy of the poem has 'For Baba' at the top.

> There was a weasel lived in the sun
> With all his family,
> Till a keeper shot him with his gun
> And hung him up on a tree,
> Where he swings in the wind and rain,
> In the sun and in the snow,
> Without pleasure, without pain,
> On the dead oak tree bough.
>
> There was a crow who was no sleeper,
> But a thief and a murderer
> Till a very late hour; and this keeper
> Made him one of the things that were,
> To hang and flap in rain and wind,
> In the sun and in the snow.
> There are no more sins to be sinned
> On the dead oak tree bough.

*Steep*

There was a magpie, too,
Had a long tongue and a long tail;
He could both talk and do –
But what did that avail?
He, too, flaps in the wind and rain
Alongside weasel and crow,
Without pleasure, without pain,
On the dead oak tree bough.

And many other beasts
And birds, skin, bone and feather,
Have been taken from their feasts
And hung up there together,
To swing and have endless leisure
In the sun and in the snow,
Without pain, without pleasure,
On the dead oak tree bough.

Now in 1916, it was time to move from the cosiness of
Steep, for Merfyn was to be apprenticed to the drawing-office
of an engineering works at Walthamstow and my father was
to be posted to Hare Hall camp near Romford in Essex as map
instructor. Our new home had been a nurseryman's cottage
right on the edge of Epping Forest, with no near neighbours
and no proper village. Edward wrote to Robert Frost: 'We
like our new home. Except on Saturday and Sunday we see
nothing only aeroplanes and deer in the forest. Baba has no
companions – she goes about telling herself stories. She is a
sensitive selfish little creature. Helen has only her, so I suppose
she must be spoilt. The others are really only at home to sleep
except at weekends.'

He wrote to Eleanor: 'I won't speak of the book to Baba.
But when I asked her what I had given her and promised her
6d if she remembered she said, on reflection, "A kiss," which
in fact is all I did give her; so she earned 6d.'

What shall I give my daughter the younger
More than will keep her from cold and hunger?

283

I shall not give her anything.
If she shared South Weald and Havering,
Their acres, the two brooks running between,
Paine's Brook and Weald Brook,
With pewit, woodpecker, swan, and rook,
She would be no richer than the queen
Who once on a time sat in Havering Bower
Alone, with the shadows, pleasure and power.
She could do no more with Samarcand,
Or the mountains of a mountain land
And its far white house above cottages
Like Venus above the Pleiades.
Her small hands I would not cumber
With so many acres and their lumber,
But leave her Steep and her own world
And her spectacled self with hair uncurled,
Wanting a thousand little things
That time without contentment brings.

# MERFYN AND BRONWEN

I saw very little of my brother and sister until I was in my late teens, when the age gap of eleven years and eight years did not seem so great. On Bronwen's occasional visits to Otford – she and Merfyn both worked in London – I felt immensely proud of my pretty sister. She loved clothes and make-up; she amazed me by powdering her nose before she crossed the village street to go to Top Warrens, the post office, to buy a stamp. She had many admirers and went to all the revues and musical comedies, learned ballroom dancing from Victor Sylvester and went to thés dansants at smart hotels. I was a little in awe of her and she felt, with reason, that Mother spoiled me. We had been so much together since Edward was killed, and I was terrified of losing her. I know that Mother indulged me and I knew I could get my way. Her loneliness and restlessness made her very different from my friends' conventional mothers.

During those early years after my father's death that Mother and I spent almost exclusively together, I think Bronwen and Merfyn and I felt the same; we never mentioned our father, unless Mother spoke of him, perhaps saying 'Do you remember the time when Daddy . . .'. But on evenings by the fire at Forge House I loved to ask Mother what Merfyn and Bron were like when they were little. As though I longed to imagine a complete family, when my father would be a part of everything they did, and then his name would come into Mother's reminiscences quite naturally, without my having to ask about him in particular – which I dreaded in case it distressed her. Merfyn as a very small boy loved to sit on Edward's knee and be told stories or read aloud to, and often his father would read him poems and ballads with words and meaning that Merfyn couldn't understand, but he sat quiet and absorbed,

285

watching his father's face, and when there was a pause while Edward re-lit his pipe, would say, 'Read me about the poetry,' while nursing his tattered rag-doll, Mabel. Mother remembered sitting by the fireside darning, baby Bronwen asleep in her cot, and rejoicing in the happy scene of their first-born on his father's lap, content and alert to the soft grave voice reading a ballad in which the word 'victor' occurred, when Merfyn solemnly announced, 'I know a boy called Victor.'

I have told earlier about nature walks and Mr Scott at Bedales Preparatory School. Like a number of boys in the early days of the motor car Merfyn was fascinated, and studied all the engines and bodywork details in glossy, coloured brochures. Merfyn had an attractive and mature handwriting and had written for a Rolls-Royce brochure, which he pored over under his desk lid, probably during wet afternoons when Mr Scott, not disposed to take out the lagging boys, was making sketches of trees on the blackboard.

Soon after the arrival of the brochure, a splendid and luxurious motor pulled up by the gate of Yew Tree Cottages while Mother was mending socks in the garden. A smart, town-dressed gentleman came up the path and asked mother if Mr P.M.A. Thomas lived there. Mother said yes, rather doubtfully, wondering what he wanted with Merfyn. 'He has shown great interest in our new model,' said the gentleman, 'And I thought he might care to look her over and take her for a trial run' – he indicated the shining black motor by the gate. 'But my son is a schoolboy and he hasn't come home from class yet!' said Mother blushing and astonished, 'I'm sorry, you've had a journey for nothing.' The gentleman turned very red, bade Mother an embarrassed good-afternoon, and hurriedly returning to the car, drove off.

Merfyn returned from America in time for Christmas 1915, having spent most of his time with Russell Scott and his family, rather than with the Frosts. His journey to the States was a muddle, for the fifteen-year-old boy had spent three days in primitive conditions on Ellis Island with a number of doubtful characters who were awaiting unlikely permission to land.

## Merfyn and Bronwen

They were kind to the shy English boy and tried their best to make him feel at ease, among other things teaching him the three-card trick, 'Find the Lady'. I think that must have been where Merfyn learnt the expression 'Snow again, sonny, I don't catch your drift,' which amused his father so much. He loved salty speech, and Merfyn always remembered his favourite story of a cockney father taking his son to the zoo. At the sight of the giraffes the boy said, 'Cor, dad, look at 'is bloody long neck, 'ain't 'ee got a bloody long 'un,' and the father admonishing him, 'Elbert, 'ow often 'ave I told yer not to point.'

In the summer of 1914, while still at Bedales, Merfyn was evidently 'doing' *The Merchant of Venice*, for on the flyleaf of the pleasant little leather-bound 'Temple Shakespeare' edition, is written in his immaculate handwriting:

M. Thomas
19.5.14

P.J. Derkum
C.C. Godfrey
C.B. Franklin
J.R. Alexander
A.H. Alexander
S. George
N.H. Brown
J.T. Bashall

The Indian Team for the T.T. 1914
Result

| 1st | Pullin | (Rudge) |
| 2nd | (Godfrey | (Indian) |
| | (Davies | (Sunbeam) |
| 3rd | Colver | (Matchless) |
| 4th | | (Triumph |

and on the other side:

1. K. Lee-Guiness
2. De Resta
3. A. Lee-Guiness

The Sunbeam Car team for T.T. 1914
Results
K. Lee Guiness

287

Apart from this the book shows very little sign of use.

In 1916 Merfyn went to school for a term or two at Coventry, where Mr Hodson, a friend of our father's, was headmaster. Merfyn began his apprenticeship as a motor engineer in Walthamstow that autumn, at the same time as the family moved to High Beech, so that both Edward in camp near Romford, and Merfyn at Walthamstow, were within reach of us. Merfyn cycled to Walthamstow early each morning, returning weary in the evening after his day's work. It was here that Merfyn could help his father with mathematics needed for map-instruction and artillery calculations. Merfyn must have enjoyed hearing stories of camp life from his father, particularly the sergeant's comment when he saw a man coiling a rope awkwardly from right to left: 'What were you before you took the shilling, Soldier, a snake-charmer?' My brother had the same enjoyment of dry and salty wit and I was reminded of that story, which Merfyn loved to tell, when I read my father's letters to Robert Frost.

Although she had had two severe bouts of pneumonia as a baby, Bronwen was a sturdy little girl, with corn-coloured hair and large dark brown eyes; her sight was as keen as her father's. She was independent and serene, and would wander off by herself, singing in a rather hoarse voice. She would often be found sitting in the middle of Blooming Meadow at Elses Farm in Kent, making a daisy-chain or sorting out the handful of wild-flowers the names of which she now knew and would soon be seeing if her father could name too, absorbed and oblivious of the bulky presence of the inquisitive sweet-breathed cows blowing at her. She adored her father, and he loved her dearly; she was the epitome of a true country child. She could always jolly him out of a moody silence.

In his lovely poem to her, almost as well-known as 'Adlestrop', he tenderly immortalizes her love of wild flowers:

> If I should ever by chance grow rich
> I'll buy Codham, Cockridden, and Childerditch,
> Roses, Pyrgo, and Lapwater,

*Merfyn and Bronwen*

And let them all to my elder daughter.
The rent I shall ask of her will be only
Each year's first violets, white and lonely,
The first primroses and orchises –
She must find them before I do, that is.
But if she finds a blossom on furze
Without rent they shall all for ever be hers,
Whenever I am sufficiently rich:
Codham, Cockridden, and Childerditch,
Rose, Pyrgo and Lapwater, –
I shall give them all to my elder daughter.

Not many people realize the implication of the line 'But if she finds a blossom on furze' and also the line in the poem 'October', 'And gorse that has no time not to be gay'. They have their origins in the country saying, 'When gorse is out of flower then kissing's out of fashion'.

Bronwen was often forthright in her remarks about people's appearance, and Mother had warned her about possibly hurting their feelings. It was absolutely all right to remark on, and be curious about, William Davies's wooden leg – 'It won't matter if Sweet William is run over by an old cart, because he's made of wood', and stamping on his foot to watch him *not* wince. But others might be more sensitive. With this freshly in her mind, she sat on Ralph Hodgson's lap – he was a great favourite of hers and she of his – gazing up into his face and saying in her gruff voice, 'When I was in London I saw a man with *such* a funny nose.'

She made her father laugh often. Auntie Mary would recall his buying Bron a bag of shrimps, which she was clutching in her fist. The damp shrimps started to come through the soggy bag and fall on the pavement, when Bron stamped her foot at them saying, 'You stupid old deaf-dumbers!'

Many of my sister's treasures were lost during the Second World War when her things were put in store. Although none of her father's letters to her survived, a page from her autograph album exists, on which he had drawn in dots the constellation of the Lyre and written beneath it:

> This is the constellation of the Lyre:
> Its music cannot ever tire,
> For it is silent. No man need fear it:
> Unless he wants to, he will never hear it.

During the time when Bronwen was staying with Auntie Mary and going with Margaret to the Norland Place School, whenever Edward was in London he would surprise her by waiting on the steps at the entrance; Bronwen would recall that to see him there, tall and smiling, and being lifted up to be kissed, made her day golden, as though they were the only people in the world.

These tales and memories of my grown-up brother and sister enthralled me and I found it difficult to reconcile them with my brother and his motor-bike and my beautiful sister, dressed so smartly and using powder and lipsalve, and regarding me generally as a spoilt, grubby little girl who played hopscotch with the village children or who hung the shavings from the cabinet-maker's plane under her hat, pretending they were curls. But when she came to Otford at weekends she sometimes took me for walks, picking wild-flowers and teaching me their names, between whiles singing in her rather quavering and slightly off-key voice, 'There's a little grey home in the west', Tosti's 'Goodbye',

> Dearest, the night is ended,
> Waneth the trembling moon
> Hark how the wind arises
> Dawn will be here too soon...

and 'Roses of Picardy'. It was blissful to have her holding my hand and taking notice of me, so when her songs seemed to be over I would remind her of other songs: 'Pale hands I loved' and the cobbler's song from 'Chu Chin Chow'. And one very sad one, which appealed to me deeply, beginning 'She comes in through the window 'cos the door is not allowed, Her eyes are like the starlight and her dress is like a cloud. She holds me very kind and tight and talks about a lamb...', but I could never quite catch the last line and didn't dare to interrupt.

Sometimes when we were alone I would venture to ask her about Daddy and she would tell me what a wonderful person he was. In our wild-flower-picking walks at Eastbury I asked her if she and Merfyn were ever aware of any tension at home when Edward was alive. She said firmly, 'Never!' It was a shock to her when she read in mother's book, *As it was – World Without End*, that there had been unhappiness or disharmony; the children were totally unaware of it.

Bronwen is frequently mentioned in my father's letters to Robert Frost. On 3 November 1915, Edward wrote to Frost:

> Helen, Bronwen and Baba are all collected here (Wandsworth) again at my Mother's. It is a London Sunday, and the loveliest warm bright weather after a cold bright hazy morning that ever was in September. Bronwen and I have just walked 4 or 5 miles of streets and crowds. I stand it better with her but it is pretty bad – all the mean or villa streets that have filled the semi-rural places I knew 25 years ago.

And in October 1916 – just before Bron's fourteenth birthday: 'Bronwen is at my elbow reading *A Girl of the Limberlost*.' He was worried about her round shoulders and she had to do special exercises, but they were never really cured, nor were her weak ankles.

# GONE FOR A SOLDIER

That last Christmas for us as a complete family was spent in the Nurseryman's cottage on the edge of Epping Forest. The snow was deep and the forest trees heavily laden, and Daddy at the last moment was coming home on leave.

The house seemed bulging with secrets and I was forbidden to look in cupboards, boxes, even into Mother's work-basket. My father's sudden homecoming had filled the place with gaiety. It was no longer an effort for Mother to create that wonderful festive feeling which she loved to do. Until the arrival of Edward's telegram the preparations must have been heavy-hearted in spite of her determination that the children should have a happy Christmas. Now it was all different. The cake was iced, the turkey stuffed, the parcels sent us by post hidden away, the cards put up on the mantelpiece, the forest searched for holly.

An almost unbearable suspense and excitement – should I *ever* get to sleep that Christmas Eve? Because if Father Christmas found me awake, there would be an empty stocking. Sleep must have come, for I awoke in the white darkness of the early morning and crept from the cosy warmth to the foot of the bed to feel the glorious bulging stocking hanging there, with a trumpet lolling over the top. Daddy was already downstairs, greatcoat over pyjamas, brewing tea; and when he carried up the tray of steaming cups, Bronwen, Merfyn and I all squeezed into their big bed to open our treasures. Stockings never had the proper presents in them, but exciting little oddments, all done up in crisp tissue paper, a painting book, crayons, bags of sweets, white sugar mice with pink eyes and string tails, a Russian lady of bright painted wood, containing a smaller and she a smaller still until there were five Russian ladies and one tiny Russian baby at the end. Merfyn's stocking had always, and continued to have in all the years that we four spent Christmas together, a mouth organ. Besides the mouth organ was an assortment of B D V cigarettes with their beautiful silk 'cards', shaving soap, a comb for his springy curls, which I so much envied and loved to brush, and to see the curls spring back again. Bronwen's stocking had delicious grown-up things like tiny bottles of scent, emery boards for her nails, sketch pad and Venus pencils, hair ribbons and lacey hankie.

This year Merfyn immediately played 'It's a long way to Tipperary' and 'When Irish eyes are smiling'. I still had a doll's tiny feeding bottle to unwrap, and a grey clockwork mouse which Daddy wound up. Mother and we girls obligingly screamed as it scurried over the floor. Second cups of tea were brought and then we dressed hurriedly and ate a quick break-fast, for there on chairs and stools were our five piles of 'proper' presents in their brown paper or Christmas wrappings. Mother had dressed me a doll and had made several outfits, including a schoolgirl's with gym tunic, white blouse and tie. I hastily admired the tiny trousseau, undid the buttons and fastenings, and dressed the doll in an old baby dress of mine. Wrapping her up in a grubby shawl, I tucked her up in the doll's bed which I found inside another parcel.

In a huge parcel of presents beautifully wrapped in pretty paper and with tinselled ribbon, Eleanor Farjeon had sent Edward a large box of crystallized fruits, for he had an insatiable sweet tooth; but alas, they all – pears, apricots, greengages and cherries – tasted strongly of varnish. Mother had earlier received an unexpected cheque for £20 and had bought Edward a beautiful Jaeger sleeping-bag, with double top; Edward wrote in marking-ink, on the specially provided tape, P.E. THOMAS. Bronwen crouched over the fire, crunching nuts and reading *Girl of the Limberlost*.

While I was helping Mother to lay the tea in the kitchen, with crackers by each plate, there was a sudden quiet in the little parlour and when it was time to call the others to tea, there was a Christmas tree, its coloured candles lit, and deco-rated with the most wonderful things I had ever seen: tinsel and spun glass ornaments glittering in the candle-light, and at the top a beautiful fairy, sparkling and smiling and waving her wand. What a Christmas! Never before had I seen a Christmas tree. Merfyn had dug it up from the forest some days before, and it had been carefully hidden in the wood-shed.

After I had been allowed to blow out the red, green and white stubs of the candles, and the lamp was lit in the sitting-room, the fire made up with wood collected from the forest, the family contentedly reading, crunching nuts or peeling oranges, I'm sure I would have remembered the wonderful proof Merfyn had had of Father Christmas's coming. He had hung up his stocking – it was always one of Mother's old, well-darned ones – in the chimney corner at Elses Farm, leaving an orange as a present: and in the morning, beside the bulging stocking was 'Thank you' in letters cut out in orange peel! Mother read me several poems from *The Golden Staircase*, the fat anthology given to me by my father; and then I sat on his knee while he sang my favourite Welsh song, 'Gweneth gwyn', and romping ones he had sung in camp and which were easy to learn. Now I stood on a chair by the window, the curtains not yet drawn, feeling the magic of Christmas, my father's large, strong hand on my shoulder, looking out into the white, still forest, straining with my short-sighted eyes behind the small spectacles, hoping to see perhaps the deer with antlered heads and pricked ears, and whispering 'Shall we see any? Are they out there? Are they cold and frightened? I wish I could see some, or even just one.' The cosy lamplight, the rising flames of the fire, my father's hand: safe, warm and content. Perhaps he was already thinking of the poem he would write when he was back at camp, and send to me:

> Out in the dark over the snow
> The fallow fawns invisible go
> With the fallow doe;
> And the winds blow
> Fast as the stars are slow.

Stealthily the dark haunts round
And, when a lamp goes, without sound
At a swifter bound
Than the swiftest hound,
Arrives, and all else is drowned;

And I and star and wind and deer,
Are in the dark together, – near,
Yet far, – and fear
Drums on my ear
In that sage company drear.

How weak and little is the light,
All the universe of sight,
Love and delight,
Before the might,
If you love it not, of night.

The first of the only two letters I ever had from my father
must have reached me on the last day of 1916. It was posted
on 30 December.

R.A. MESS
TINTOWN
LYDD

29.xii.16

My dear Myfanwy,
   I am so glad you haven't got that nasty tooth any longer,
and I hope you don't dislike the dentist who took it away.
But you did enjoy your Christmas, didn't you? I know I
did. I mean I enjoyed your Christmas and mine too. When
I got here I found two more presents, a pocket writing case
from Uncle Oscar and a piece of cake from Eleanor.
   Did Mother tell you I wrote a poem about the dark that
evening when you did not want to go into the sitting room
because it was dark? Eleanor perhaps will type it and then
I will send you a copy.
   I am going to be very much alone for a few days, because
the man who sleeps in my room is going home to Scotland.

I think I shall like being alone.

On Monday and Wednesday we are going to shoot with real guns. I don't quite now what I shall have to do. (You see I have spelt 'know' without a k.) But as one of us is away the rest will be uncommonly busy from now onwards. I should not be surprised if we were in France at the end of this month. I do hope peace won't come just yet. I should not know what to do, especially if it came before I had really been a soldier. I wonder if you want peace, and if you can remember when there was no war.

It really is very solitary by this smoky fire with the wind rattling the door, shaking it and making the lock sound as if it were somebody trying to come in but finding the door locked and knowing there was somebody inside who *could* open it.

I think if I had a chair or a table I should write verses just for something to do before bedtime. Perhaps I will try.

Give Mother and Merfyn and Bronwen each a love for me and tell Mother her letter came this afternoon after I posted my second one to her.   Goodbye.

Daddy

Towards the end of January 1917 I stayed with Arthur Ransome's wife, Ivy, and their daughter Tabitha, in their farmhouse near Tisbury. Ivy was strikingly handsome in a gipsy way, which was enhanced by her full skirts, high-laced boots, 'peasant' blouses, hooped ear-rings and bright beads, and most of all perhaps by her elaborately arranged hair, with plaits and loops and ringlets, and a flat curve over her forehead to hide an ugly scar. Tabitha was pale and plump with two long snakey plaits. And like gipsies we drove about in a donkey cart which took us over rough tracks on the downs. Kitty Gurd was her maid-of-all-work. Ivy's mother was staying there too. Arthur Ransome was in Russia. Years after I learned that he was said to have skated over the frozen Volga with Lenin's daughter. Constantly Ivy would sing to the rather languid Tabitha:

What is the matter with Tabitha R?
She's ALL RIGHT.
What is the matter with Tabitha R?
SHE'S all right.
Now her Daddy is far away
Then her Mummy has time to play
What is the matter with Tabitha R?
SHE'S ALL RIGHT!

The tune is very clear in my mind still. Ivy read aloud to us *The Fairchild Family*, a moral story in which the naughty child is burned to death.

One evening Tabitha and I were bouncing on a wide couch and I put out my leg and tripped her over so that she fell, but on the couch. I was in disgrace for this and terrified by all the things Ivy and Kitty Gurd told me might have happened to Tabitha's back had she not fallen on the soft couch. I was put to bed and in my snivelling loneliness could hear the old song drifting up to me from the cosy sitting-room.

Ivy's prim mother said to me one day, 'I'm sure your father sings beautiful folk songs to you, can you remember any to sing to me?' Always willing to show off I rejoiced her with 'Gor blimey O'Riley you *are* looking well' and 'Cover up anything red, sir, cover up anything red, sir, cover up anything red, sir, So I covered up me old Dad's nose' – two of the latest songs from camp which Daddy had sung to us round the fire at Christmas. These were received with tight-lipped disapproval and I was not asked to sing again.

My father, who had had his embarkation leave and was waiting for orders to sail, wrote in his diary on 27 January 1917:

A clear windy frosty dawn, the sun like a bright coin between the knuckles of opposite hills seen from sidelong. A fox. A little office work. Telegram to say Baba was at Ransome's, so I walked over Downs by Chicklade Bottom and the Fonthills to Hatch, and blistered both feet badly. House full of ice and big fires. Sat up with Ivy till 12 and slept till 8. Another fine bright frosty day on the 28th. Wrote to Bronwen, Helen, Ivy, Eleanor. Letters from Bronwen, Helen, Mother, Eleanor. Slept late. Rested my feet, talking to the children or Ivy cooking with Kitty Gurd. Hired a bicycle to save walking. Such a beautiful ride after joining the Mere and Amesbury Road at Fonthill Bishop – hedgeless roads over long sloping downs with woods and sprinkled thorns, carved with old tracks which junipers line – an owl and many rabbits – a clear pale sky and but a faint sunset – a long twilight lasting till 6. We are to move at 6.30 a.m. tomorrow. Horton and Smith and I dined together laughing at imbecile jests and at Smith's own laughing. . . .

At Ivy's house, I sat on his knee in the chimney corner of the big sitting-room, he smoking his clay and singing to me, gently amused to hear about the 'folk songs' I had sung to Ivy's mother. I awoke in the night, safe and content in the crook of his arm. We said goodbye the next morning, and watched him out of sight on the bicycle he had borrowed. He sailed on the 29th, crossing to Le Havre at night.

After saying goodbye to my father, every night for weeks I prayed for his safety on the ship, which seemed to me the most dangerous part of going to war. I imagined huge waves dashing against a small tug-boat, which mounted to the crest and then slithered down. My eyes screwed up tightly could not dispel this terrifying picture. The only other prayer I knew was one which Joan Farjeon, Joe's daughter, had taught me. This prayer was a puzzle but I did not like to ask Mother about it: we were not a praying family. But seeing Joan kneel by her bed enchanted me and I became a regular kneeler. The prayer I learned from her was:

> Gentle Jesus meek and mild
> Look upon a little child
> Pity mice and plicity
> Suffer me to come to Thee
> Four corners to my bed
> Four angels round my head

One to watch and one to pray
And two to bear my soul away.

To pity mice seemed logical and proper, disliked and trapped
as they were, but what in the world was *plicity*? I came across
the prayer many years later and felt a great fool to have pitied
mice. A friend had the same puzzlement over the hymn 'Can
a mother's tender care cease towards the child she bear?' Why
were he-bear's excluded?

The time came for me to go back to High Beech. The dangers
of the sea were over now, and I had no further fear. One saw
funny pictures by Heath Robinson of soldiers at the Front,
and occasionally we saw overhead white bursts of anti-aircraft
fire. But mother's terror and anxiety for my father's safety
were carefully hidden so as not to distress us. She was making
me an emerald green coat with a set of small brass Artists'
Rifle buttons down the front. We walked up to the post every
day, which I dreaded as we had to pass the school playground
which bordered the road. The boys would shout 'Hullo four-
eyes' or 'Gig-lamps, there goes gig-lamps'. I could tell by the
jeering tone of their voices that it was something unpleasant,
but I had to ask Mother what it meant. How I hated my
offending spectacles!

The second and last letter I had from my father came from
France with the FIELD POST OFFICE postmark dated 24 March
1917 and overstamped with the oval red mark saying PASSED
FIELD CENSOR – 4227.

The letter is written in pencil on paper torn from a notebook
and has two sketches.

My dear Baba,
    One day I saw a house or a big barn in the country where
the Germans were, with a little roof over a pump or a well
alongside of it, like this: [sketch].
    But next morning when I looked all I could see was the
little roof like this: [sketch].
    All the trees were gone and the house was gone. Also

299

the Germans have gone and since then I have been right up
there and seen Cockneys and Scotchmen but no Germans.
It is a funny country. Now I expect the French people will
be coming up to that village to see if there are any walls
left of their houses and anything in their gardens.

Now you have come back to your house and found all
the bricks there and perhaps some new things in the garden.
You are going to have Joy, too, aren't you? I wish I could
see you in the forest. There is no forest here and no copses
even very near, and no hedges at all, so that there are not
so many birds, but plenty of chaffinches and larks, no
peacocks, no swans. There are lots of little children about
as old as you are, but without specs, living in the cottages
here.

Now I hear I have to get up early and do a hard day's
work tomorrow, so I must go to bed.

Goodnight, Nos da y chwi.

Daddy

Sometimes I would walk to the corner on my own to sit
on a log and wait for Bronwen walking back from school at
Loughton. I was joined on one occasion by a very respectably
dressed man, who began to chat to me. To forestall any offer-
ing of sweets which I felt might be an embarrassment to both
of us I quickly ventured the information that my father was
a policeman, and felt quite safe. The man walked off after that
and I knew I was in control.

But on that bright April day after Easter, when mother was
sewing and I was awkwardly filling in the pricked dots on a
postcard with coloured wool, embroidering a wild duck to
send to France, I saw the telegraph boy lean his red bicycle
against the fence. Mother stood reading the message with a
face of stone. 'No answer' came like a croak, and the boy rode
away. Mother fetched our coats and we went shivering out
into the sunny April afternoon. I clutched her hand, half-
running to keep up with her quick firm step, glancing continu-
ally up at the graven face that did not turn to meet my look.

There were no children in the playground as we hurried to the post office, no calls which I could not have borne – for although I knew the shouts of 'Four Eyes' were aimed at me, Mother also wore spectacles. I waited, with dry mouth and chilled heart, outside the post office, while wires were sent off to Mother's sisters, to Granny and to Eleanor.

The day after, before arrangements were made for us to go to London to stay with Auntie Mary, I was looking at my favourite picture in a story book, an engraving which Bron had delicately coloured for me. Suddenly I ripped it out, screwed it up and flung it on the fire in a rage of tears – for what couldn't possibly happen to us had happened. My father would never come back. Why had I only prayed for his safety crossing the stormy sea? No answer.

301

# WORDS

By 1923 I was attending the County School at Tonbridge. My relations and, surprisingly, some of my teachers expected me to be 'good at English'. It never occurred to me to question this. But it troubled and embarrassed me, as I knew I was not. At that time my father's poems had been published in roughly two halves, in a thin volume a few months after his death in 1917 and the rest in 1918. A small edition of his *Collected Poems* appeared in 1920. They were then known only to a few readers, so that the following rare personal encounter with the headmistress of my school had a salutary effect on me. I had never possessed a copy of his poems and only knew vaguely those he had sent to me from camp, which Mother had read to me.

I had returned from my term's release taller and thinner than ever and at once felt very behindhand with all the work that had been done in my absence. The Headmistress took us for Scripture; we were doomed to study either the Old Testament prophets and tribal wars, or St Paul's missionary journeys. These journeys involved the dreaded drawing of maps from blackboard sketches with illegible chalked place-names and little dotted lines in different colours to show the routes and towns St Paul had visited on his travels. My maps tended to end up looking like pieces of knitting which a kitten had played with. Once for our homework we had to write an essay on one of the Old Testament lessons. After much sighing and pen-chewing I was relieved to find I had managed to cover, with ample spaces between words, the required minimum of a page and a half, on wars, their causes and effects, all quite incomprehensible to me. A day or two later I was sent for by the Headmistress: with dry mouth and my heart knocking, I tapped on her study door. No response. Hope surged that she wasn't there and I would be forgotten. I tapped again. This time an impatient shrill voice commanded, 'Come in.'

'Ah, M. Thomas.' She swivelled round in her chair to face me, my Scripture notebook in her raw-looking hands. 'What does all this mean?' she asked. I waited some moments with burning face before replying, 'Please, I don't know.'

'I find you have used the words "the people" thirteen times. *What* people?'

'I don't know.'

'Your father has written a fine poem about Words. Do you know it?'

'Not really.'

'Come, either you know it or you do not.' Silence. 'You should read it, get to know it. He has a sensitive feeling for words and their use and meaning; in one line he says, "Use me, you English words" as though he wished them to use him as their faithful vehicle. "A language not to be betrayed" he says elsewhere.'

'Yes, Miss Fayerman.'

'Do you think your father would feel proud of the writing in this essay? What would he have thought of this worthless piece of nonsense?'

'Please, I don't know.'

'You will do it again, this evening, and hand it in to me tomorrow morning.'

'Yes, Miss Fayerman. Thank you,' I said, taking the wretched book from her and walking across the study, feeling as though it were an endless expanse, her large light blue eyes behind her rimless glasses on my faded outgrown tunic and black stockings. I went back to my classroom, burning with shame and resentment, anger and misery, that I had so let my father down. But I did read the poem, and something of my father's pleasure in a language not to be betrayed flooded into my mind and heart. I found that I could now read more critically and enjoy the rich sound of words.

I began to read my father's poetry, and had deep satisfaction when I came across those poems in which some words or actions of mine were woven into the poem, and I felt a small part of its creation. For although I knew *I* was part of my father's own unique creation, I had always rather resented the poem that he had written for me: it perpetuated what I longed to be without – my spectacles, my straight hair, my acquisitiveness. True, he had called my hands small, which was tender; but even so, I felt he had accentuated the chinks in my armour and couldn't therefore have liked me as much as the others – Merfyn his first-born and Bronwen his beloved smiling one, who answered him cheekily and who had had eight more years of knowing him than I had. But I recognized myself in 'Old Man', 'The Cherry Trees', 'The Brook' and I remembered the occasion of our seeing together 'The Gallows', and 'Out in the Dark'. And only recently, in my seventies, with grown-up grandchildren, have I discovered that I am the child in 'Snow'.

> In the gloom of whiteness,
> In the great silence of snow,
> A child was sighing
> And bitterly saying: 'Oh,
> They have killed a white bird up there on her nest,
> The down is fluttering from her breast.'
> And still it fell through that dusky brightness
> On the child crying for the bird of the snow.

The poems, in their grave austerity, did not appeal to me as did the warm and sensuous Odes and sonnets of Keats, or the anguish of Shakespeare's love poems, but I felt that something had become more whole in my being and the poem 'Words' which astonishingly my cold headmistress knew and understood, I read again and again – 'Use me, you English words.'

# APPENDIX

## *Six Letters from Robert Frost to Edward Thomas*

*In early 1915 Robert Frost returned to America; he and Edward Thomas continued their conversations by letter. These six were published in* Poetry Wales *(Vol.22, no.4, 1987) for the first time. They are reprinted here by kind permission of Myfanwy Thomas, the Librarian of University College, Cardiff, and the Estate of Robert Lee Frost. Professor R. George Thomas noted in his introduction to the letters that ET received the last letter in France on 8 March 1917, and replied at once, but there are no further letters from Frost. In his letter of condolence to Helen, Frost wrote:*

There is no regret – nothing I will call regret. Only I can't help wishing he could have saved his life without so wholly losing it and come back from France not too much hurt to enjoy our pride in him. I want to see him to tell him something. I want to tell him, what I think he liked to hear from me, that he was a poet. . . . I had meant to talk endlessly with him still, either here in our mountains as we had said or, as I found my longing was more and more, there at Leddington [sic] where we first talked of war.

26 June 1915                    Franconia N.H., U.S.A.

Dear Edward:
Methinks thou strikest too hard in so small a matter. A tap would have settled my poem ['The Road Not Taken']. I wonder if it was because you were trying too much out of regard for me that you failed to see that the sigh was a mock sigh, hypocritical for the fun of the thing. I don't suppose I was very sorry for anything I ever did except by assumption to see how it would feel. I may have been sorry for having given a certain kind of people a chance at me: I have passionately regretted exposing myself.
Sedgwick has come over bag and baggage. He will print the poem along with two others in his August number. I saw the proof of it a week ago. The line you object to has long

307

since taken a different form. I suppose my little jest in this poem is too much between me and myself. I read it aloud before the Phi Beta Kappa of Tuft's College and while I did my best to make it obvious by my manner that I was fooling, I doubt if I wasn't taken pretty seriously. Mea culpa.

I am doing this in sick bed – so to call the thing I am sleeping in till we know definitely where we are going to live. We came down here (from the Lynches) because our rent up there was running too much money. And yet we have no certainty that this farm is going to be ours and so we don't dare to fetch our furniture from Plymouth. There's a flaw in the owner's title as my guardian sees it. Damn the suspense.

You begin to talk as if you weren't coming to America to farm. We have gone too far into the wilds for you or something. It was inconsiderate of us. But listen: this farm is intended for the lecture camp. We won't make it our winter home for more than a couple of years. It is a picturesque spot and it is in the region where I have to take refuge for two months a year from hay fever. That's all you can say for it. About all it raises is grass and trees. Some time we must have a real fruit farm again further downalong. But this place will always be here for our lecture camp scheme when that shall come to anything. Meanwhile it represents a small investment: the year's interest on it is less than the rent we have been accustomed to pay for our two months stay in the mountains. I think the pine and spruce on the place will increase in value more than fifty dollars a year. I think I told you the farm is to cost £1,000.

You may be right in coming over in your literary capacity. Elinor is afraid the rawness of these back towns will be too much for you. You know I sort of like it. The postmaster asked Lesley yesterday "How's Robert?" He's a nice old nasal organist who thinks God has given him the freedom of your heart and mind. I should say it wasn't fair to assume that you couldn't stand him. He might try to place you if you let him get acquainted. And then if he should decide that you were intellectual (approximately) he would start marvelling to you every time he got a chance on the latest invention he has read in The Scientific American.

He doesn't chew tobacco – he is a good Baptist – but many do here. And shoes aren't shined. It is really the Hell of a country. The postmaster for instance traces his descent from someone named somewhere in 500 A.D.

September would be all right – late in September when people are getting back to town. Bring all your introductions. Some of my new friends will be good to you. Some of them aren't good to me even. That is to say they persist in liking me for the wrong reasons and in otherwise disregarding my wishes. And there's nothing licit to drink here. Other objections as I think of them.

As for the war, damn it! You are surely getting the worst of it. You are *not* through the Dardanelles and we know that you are not. Nothing will save you but Lloyd George and a good deal of him. You must quit slacking.

The Prussian hath said in his heart, "Those fool Chestertons." I say so too. All the follies that England is like to die of are gathered in the books of these brothers. And Belloc with his estimate of two thirds of the Germans dead and the rest buried is nothing to respect.

All our papers are your friends. But they all make hard work of your present predicament. I clip from the *Boston Herald* the most hopeful editorial I have seen lately. The letter I enclose may amuse you.

We all to you all.

Yours ever

R


23 November 1915                    Franconia N.H.

Dear Edward:

I have reached a point this evening where no letter to or from you will take the place of seeing you. I am simply down on the floor kicking and thrashing with resentment against

309

everything as it is. I like nothing, neither being here with you there and so hard to talk to nor being so ineffectual at my years to help myself or anyone else. Now I am going to tell you in cold writing that I tried to place your 'Four-and-twenty Blackbirds' with Holt and failed. I know it was something I didn't say or do to bear down the publishers doubts of the book being too English for the American mother and child. It is not too English. Someone will see it yet and I tried to make the publishers see it by not saying too much and by not saying too little. But if I haven't succeeded in doing anything for you, I haven't succeeded in doing anything for myself. If I seem to have made any headway with the American reading crowd, it is by what was done for me before I left England. You over there brought it about that I was named the other day in the 'Queries' department of a school paper as perhaps the equal of Ella Wheeler Wilcox and James Whitcomb Riley. Don't think I am bitter. You know how little I ask. Only I wish I could have the credit for getting a little of it for myself and perhaps sharing a little of it with someone else. I haven't even dug in on this farm yet. I am still a beggar for the roof over our heads. And you know how it is with us: Elinor is so sick day and night as to affect the judgement of both of us: we can't see anything hopefully though we know from experience that even the worst nine months must somehow come to an end. The devil says "One way or another". And that's what Elinor says too this time. There is really cause for anxiety. We are not now the strength we were.

Is this in the miserable confidential tone they are curing you of by manly discipline? You won't be able to hit it off with the like of me by the time the war is over. You'll be wondering how you ever found pleasure in grovelling with me in self-abasement – walking about the fields of Leddington – in the days that were. Couldn't we run ourselves down then without fear of losing too much favor with each other?

Do you want me to tell you the best thing that has come to me for a long long time, let you take it as you will and act on it as you will from the will to be agreeable or from perversity.

It is the news that the country may not ask of you all that you have shown yourself ready to give. I don't want you to die (I confess I wanted you to face the possibility of death): I want you to live to come over here and begin all the life we had in St Martin's Lane, at Tyler's Green, at White Leaved Dale, and at Balham. We should decide it for you. If you can be more useful living than dying I don't see that you have to go behind that. Don't be run away with by your nonsense.

You know I haven't tried to be troubled by the war. But I believe it is half of what's ailed me ever since August 1914. Lately I have almost despaired of England at times. I've almost been afraid that she might be beaten on land and brought to terms which might prove the end of her in fifty years. We say a disturbance of the balance of power was what caused the war. It shows how little the balance was really disturbed – the fight is so equal and so desperate. I agree with what Pat said to Pat and with what Pat answered. Pat said: "It's a terrible war." And Pat answered "Terrible, but after all it's better than no war at all."

I'll write to you in a better vein than this within a week. Tell Baba our silly President thinks well of widows, too. [See p. 276.] Damn some people that get in my light.

Goodbye Soldier

R

Say something pleasant and characteristic for me to everybody not excluding Miss Farjeon and Maitland Radford.

<br>

15 August 1916          Franconia N.H.

Dear Edward:

First I want to give you an accounting. I got here a year ago last March, didn't I? I have earned by poetry alone in the year and a half about a thousand dollars – it can never happen again – and by lecturing nearly another thousand. It has cost us more than it used to to live – partly on account of the war and partly on account of the ill health of the youngsters. Still

311

one feels that we ought to have something to show for all that swag; and we have: we have this farm bought and nearly paid for. Such is poetry when the right people boom it. I don't say how much longer the boom can last. You can fool some of the people some of the time, but you can't fool all of them all of the time, as Lincoln more or less put it. It may be that the gulfs will wash us down. Nevertheless what we have done we have done (and may He within Himself make it pure, as the poem has it).

I was going to add that nobody can take it away from us. But that's not so absolutely certain. Mrs Nutt [Frost's London publisher] threatens from the right flank. The what-shall-I-call-her has never given me one cent or one word of accounting since she took my first book. The lawyers say she has forfeited all claim on me. She can get nothing out of me. But she can make trouble and expense if she wants to go to expense herself. I tell you that so that you will know the whole story. I may have to put the farm into my wife's name for protection. Some day soon I'll have Lesley make you a copy of the lawyer's advice in this matter.

What's mine is yours. I say that from the heart, dear man. I may be a bad letter writer. I have been spoiled for letter writing by a mob of new friends who don't care what becomes of me so long as they get my autograph once in so often. My whole nature simply leaps at times to cross the ocean to see you for one good talk. It seems as if I couldn't bear it not to follow my inclination. I had a thought of you trying to induct me into clay pipes and all the old days swept back over me. I can never live here any more without longing for there, nor there without longing for here. What kind of predicament do you call that?

But as I said, what's mine is yours. Here are a house and forty odd acres of land you can think of as a home and a refuge when your war is over. We shall be waiting for you.

My interest in the war news has picked up of late. Lloyd George is a great man. I have wanted to do something for your cause if it came my way to. I thought of writing to the papers, but everybody was taking all the space and drowning everybody else out. I did my first material bit the other day when I read to a small audience for 'the wounded in France' – *not* for the Red Cross. A collection of a hundred dollars was taken up. I'm to read twice more within a week for the same cause. I only mention this in self-defense. I believe the money reaches its destination through Edith Wharton our novelist who is living in France.

Dorothy Canfield Fisher one of our good writers whom you should know has gone to France with her husband and two babies to help what she can. Her husband has organized a repair shop for automobile ambulances. She will be into something herself before long. You should hear the standard Bostonian on the subject of the Fryatt case.

Send me more poetry when you have any. I have a long thing about Snow you might care for a little. I wonder if it would be likely to get to you.

It seems to me Merfyn is going the best way. I'm just Yankee enough to be sure of that. I saw yesterday the two friends, Mrs and Miss Tilley, who had him with them in New York before he sailed. They said the loveliest things of him. They are Southerners of the old school and see nothing in anyone who is not first of all 'gentle'. They were evidently pleased with Merfyn for the pleasure he made them believe they gave him.

Do you think you could help me get up an anthology of the homely in poetry to be called The Old Cloak after the poem of that name? Or are you too busy? I should want to claim a place on the title page along with you for my part in having got up the idea (great idea). But you would have to think of most of the material. About time I heard from you again. My love to you as you look in that last tall picture Helen sent.

Always and forever yours

*Robert Frost*

28 September 1916                                    Franconia N.H.

Dear Edward:

I began to think our positions were reversed – you had got well-minded from having plunged into things and I had got soul-sick from having plunged out of them. Your letter shows you can still undertalk me when you like. A little vaccination and a little cold and you are down where it makes me dizzy to look in after you. You are so good at black talk that I believe your record will stand unbroken for years to come. It's as if scmebody should do the hundred yards in five seconds flat.

But look at Lloyd George. You may be down-hearted and I may be with you. But we have to admit that it is just as well to be able to say things and see things as courageously as he is. I say that quite for its face value. Lloyd George is one of the very great men. I wish I could expect my sins to be forgiven me as a Yankee, when I return to England, in the measure of my admiration for him. I'm afraid Englishmen aren't liking Americans very much just now. Should I dare to go back to England at this moment? I often long too. The hardest part of it would be to be treated badly for what is none of my fault personally.

Let's let the Old Cloak hang on the hat-tree till you put off soldier's uniform. Meanwhile I wish you could let me have copies of just the poems you are putting into book form. I am not a person of half the influence I should have thought I would be by this time. Nevertheless I must see what I can do to find you a publisher here and save you your copyright. I failed in a way that was no discredit to you with the 'Four and Twenty Blackbirds'. "Too insular" was the praise our publishers damned it with for American purposes. I can see the way Henry Holt looked at it. And then it might have fared better if I could have thrust it upon him as I did The Listeners [by de la Mare]. That might have helped the matter. I am making a clean breast of all this to give you a chance to refuse to let me see what I can do with the poems. You needn't feel obliged to humour me (as I do you in that spelling). I shan't

314

go to Holt this time; but to someone else who dropped in on me lately for a talk on what was doing in English writing. Never mind who it was for the present. Get up no hopes – as I know you are incapable of getting up any. Only let me try. It's a shame you shouldn't have something on someone's list over here where I find so many who know and like you. One of my professors at the University of Pennsylvania was liking the "perfect texture" of your prose just the other day – thought he had read all you had written. Mosher of Portland seemed to have a large knowledge of you. I'm not saying this to cheer you up, damn you. You know the worth of your bays. And I'm nobody to cheer anyone else when I can't cheer myself of late. And winter's coming on.

I'm going to write you some all-fired stuff every week of my life.

Tell me, if you think of it, what your final opinion of Rupert's work is.

Our love. Always yours

*Robert Frost*

6 November 1916                                     Franconia N.H.

Dear Edward:

Tomorrow we vote – I vote for once; and you mustn't be disappointed if we don't turn Wilson out of office. We probably shall turn him out from a mistaken idea of what we are about. But don't be disappointed if we don't. By comparison with a number of Americans I could name he has been a real friend of the Allies' cause. Roosevelt is the only man we have who could have landed us into war with the Germans. And he would have had to betray us into it. It would have had to be almost betrayal; because though we are very much on your side, we seem to have no general wish to be in the fighting. You will see how it will be with Hughes if he is elected. He will set himself to beat Wilson at his own game. Granting that Wilson has given us a good deal of peace with some honour,

315

Hughes' aim will be to give us more peace with more honour – especially the more honour. He's a confident fool who thinks he sees how it will be easy to do this. He is one of those Sunday School products who is going to be every bit as good as he has brains to be. None of him for me.

And yet you know how I feel about the war. I have stopped asseverating from a sense of fitness. You rather shut me up by enlisting. Talk is almost too cheap when all your friends are facing bullets. I don't believe I ought to enlist (since I am of course an American), but if I can't enlist, at least I refuse to talk sympathy beyond a certain point. I did set myself to wish this country into the war. I made a little noise on the subject, but soon found I wasn't half as good at the noise as some who cared less. (Has Harold Begbie enlisted?) When all the world is facing danger, it's a shame not to be facing danger for any reason, old age, sickness, or any other. Words won't make the shame less. There's no use trying to make out that the shame we suffer makes up for the more heroic things we don't suffer. No more of this for a long time. Are not the magazines chuckfull of it?

I hear from a friend of mine who if he doesn't love the Germans as against the British at least loves the Irish as against them, that De la Mare is to dine or lunch or something with him when he gets to New York. The time named is so near that I guess De la Mare isn't going to make me a port of call or he would have got some word to me before this. Is it that he doesn't know that you and Garnett and he and Abercrombie and one or two others have made me even more distinguished than he is in this country. I'm a little hurt. Of course we are a little out of the way. Masefield wrote that he meant to get out here (uninvited), but his agent rushed him off his feet up to the last moment of his stay and he couldn't make it. Very likely Masefield wanted to see my Dominiques (pronounced Dominick) here.

Is there the least use in beseeching you to come over for a week or two out of my pocket? Could you get leave? I wish it beyond anything. I should think it ought to be possible. We could find you a few lectures. Taking the fast boats you ought not to be gone more than three weeks. Does this sound so very un-military? They ought to consider that you were literary before you were military. I have a play I shall be half afraid of till you tell me how it strikes you. It's the same old one I tried to make you read once before when I first knew you – if you remember – and you sidestepped it. It is called An Assumed Part. I (personally) am in what is known as an 'interesting state'. I may have news for you in my next letter. Oh, by the way, I came across my Gibsonian lines On Being about to Become a Parent just lately. Now don't misunderstand me. There are other offspring than of our bodies.

Farewell and adieu to you with a fa la la la la la la, and don't forget your old shipmate.

*Robert Frost, the Frisco-Digger, Boston Beauty, etc.*

7 December 1916                    Franconia N.H.

Dear Edward:

I have been down sick in bed for a week and a half: that's where I have been and that's why you haven't heard from me. Port wine is what I need now if I am going to shine. But I'm not. I find that the chief thing on my mind is not a personal one, what's going to become of you and me – nothing like that – but a political one – the change in the government in England and the possibilities of great changes in France. What becomes of my hopes of three months ago when the drive on the Somme began? Something has gone wrong. How can we be happy any more – for a while? Lloyd George is the great man and he belongs where he now takes his place. But would he ever have arrived there with Bonar Law and Carson on his right and left, but for some desperate need. Silly fools are full of peace talk over here. It is out of friendliness of a kind to the Allies: they act as if they thought you were waiting for them to say the word to quit. It's none of my business what

317

you do: but neither is it any of theirs. I wrote some lines I've copied on the other side of this about the way I am struck. When I get to writing in this vein you may know I am sick or sad or something.

*Robert*

## Suggested by *Talk of Peace at This Time*

France, France, I know not what is in my heart.
But God forbid that I should be more brave
As watcher from a quiet place apart
Than you are fighting in an open grave.

I will not ask more of you than you ask,
O Bravest, of yourself. But shall I less?
You know the extent of your appointed task,
Whether you still can face its bloodiness.

Not mine to say you shall not think of peace.
Not mine, not mine. I almost know your pain.
But I will not believe that you will cease,
I will not bid you cease, from being slain

And slaying till what might have been distorted
Is saved to be the Truth and Hell is thwarted.     R.F.